SEA KAYAKING ALONG THE MID-ATLANTIC COAST

Coastal Paddling Adventures from
New York to Chesapeake Bay

Tamsin Venn

All photographs by the author unless otherwise noted
Cover Design: Nancy Turkle
Book and Map Design: Carol Bast Tyler

Distributed by The Talman Company, Inc.

Library of Congress Cataloging-in-Publication Data

Venn, Tamsin, 1951—
    Sea Kayaking along the mid-Atlantic coast: coastal paddling adventures from New York to Chesapeake Bay / Tamsin Venn.
        p. cm.
    Includes bibliographical references (p. 196).
    ISBN 1-878239-31-7: $14.95
    1. Sea kayaking—Middle Atlantic States—Atlantic Coast—Guidebooks. 2. Atlantic Coast (Middle Atlantic States)—Guidebooks. I. Title.
    GV788.5.V45 1994
    797.1'224'0974—dc20   94–6935
                                                                    CIP

The paper used in this publication meets the minimum requirements of the American National Standard for Information Sciences—Permanence of Paper for Printed Library Materials, ANSI Z39.48–1984.∞

**Due to changes in conditions,
use of the information in this book
is at the sole risk of the user.**

♳ Printed in the United States of America.

10 9 8 7 6 5 4 3 2 1   94 95 96 97 98 99

To my mother, Doylie Venn

Contents

Acknowledgments...*vi*

Preface: Welcome to the World of Sea Kayaking.........................*vii*

Sea Kayaking: An Overview...*xi*

Explanation of Trip Data...*xxxv*

Chapter 1: New York...1

    Hudson River: Goblin-filled Hudson Highlands.........................8

    Hudson River: Majestic Palisades From Englewood
        to Piermont 17

    Manhattan Circumnavigation: Urban Wilderness 23

    Long Island

        Oyster Bay: Paddling Under Sagamore Hill 34

        Fire Island: Wild Beach 39

        Robins Island Circumnavigation: Jewel of
            the Peconics 44

        Moriches Bay: Atlantic Ocean Has Its Way 47

        Circumnavigation of Shelter Island: Ospreys
            and Clear Water 51

        Sag Harbor to Barcelona Neck: Marsh and High Dunes......57

Chapter 2: The New Jersey Shore 60

    Around Sandy Hook: History and Shifting Sand 64

    Brigantine's Wildlife Refuge: Egrets and Casinos 70

    Dennis Creek to Reed's Beach: Marsh That
        Time Forgot 75

Chapter 3: Delaware Bay...79

    Cape Henlopen: Porpoises and Wild Surf............................83

Chapter 4: Chesapeake Bay...88

    Maryland's Eastern Shore

        Wye Island Circumnavigation: A Paddle into History 101

Tilghman Island to Poplar Islands: The Last
    of the Skipjacks 106
James Islands: Eroding into Memory 110
Hooper Islands: Remote Peninsula 113
Deal Island: Forgotten Fishing Villages 117
Circumnavigation of Smith Island: Communities
    of Hardy Watermen 121
Pocomoke River: Intimate Woodlands Near the Bay 129

Maryland's Atlantic Shore
Assateague National Seashore: Wild Beach
    and Protected Bay...133

Virginia's Eastern Shore
Circumnavigation of Cedar Island: Last of the
    Wild Places 140
Back Creek and Hacks Neck: Catch Enough Fish
    for Dinner 145
Kiptopeke to Fisherman Island: Southern Terminus
    of the Delmarva 149

The Western Shore
Circumnavigation of Jamestown Island: History on
    the James River 153
Point Lookout: Oldsquaw at the Mouth of the
    Potomac 157
Patuxent River: Clarks Landing to Sotterly Plantation 161
Mason Neck: Bluffs and Eagles..166
Carrs Wharf: Open Space Near Annapolis.........................170
Baltimore Harbor: Stars and Stripes at Fort McHenry 173

Postscript 177
Appendices..178
Glossary 193
Annotated Bibliography 196
About the Author 203
About the AMC 204

Acknowledgments

THIS GUIDEBOOK is deeply indebted to the local knowledge of the sea-kayaking experts along the Mid-Atlantic Coast. They generously shared their knowledge and advice on tides, currents, weather, seasons, wildlife, campsites, launch spots, and land-use permission. In the New York area, special thanks go to Ralph Diaz, Bill and Janice Lozano, Andy Singer, Andy Burtsell, Rob Battenfeld, and the Hudson River Waterway Association. In the Chesapeake Bay area, I thank Chuck Sutherland, Ron Casterline, Chris Conklin, Charlie and Cindy Cole, and Bill Pettijohn. In the New Jersey area, I thank David and Chris Eden and Steve Szarawarski. Forrest Dillon, who braved the unusual February blizzards on the Chesapeake to help with on-the-water research, should also be highly commended for his patience and willingness to go along.

At Appalachian Mountain Club Books, I thank editor Gordon Hardy, who ventures out of AMC's usual mountain guidebooks into the territory of sea-kayak trips; copy editor Linda Buchanan Allen; and for production and especially maps, Carol Bast Tyler.

To all of you helpful and generous souls, may your adventures always be sound and your souls ever wakened to new experience.

Welcome to the World of Sea Kayaking

MANY PEOPLE WHO PADDLE SEA KAYAKS can trace a similar route of interest in this type of coastal adventuring. They started exploring their local waters by sailboat or by canoe. Then they witnessed a sea kayak: The sea kayak, they saw, would fulfill many needs. It could fulfill a desire to be on the ocean without the hassle of trying to anchor or moor; it provided the ability to travel great distances without the problems of windage (profile exposed to the wind) that a canoe poses, not to mention waves breaking over the gunwales; it acted as a simple key to unlock wild places close to a major metropolis; it offered a chance for camaraderie, a platform to watch and photograph nature, and a place to store gear. The sea kayak would be satisfactory on many fronts.

It is no surprise then that sea kayaking along the Mid-Atlantic Coast has developed rapidly over the past ten years. Whether bird watching, meandering in coastal creeks, surfing in breaking swells off Montauk Point, making an 11-mile crossing of Long Island Sound or Chesapeake Bay, or even a 220-mile circumnavigation of Long Island, enthusiasm and knowledge have grown tremendously and continue to develop for both beginner and expert alike.

For example, within the last two years, the New York and Chesapeake paddling communities have started creating on-water "trails" following the inspiration of the successful 325-mile Maine Island Trail (itself inspired by the Appalachian Trail). The developing Chesapeake Trail on the 200-mile-long Chesapeake Bay, and the Hudson River Waterway which documents and promotes access 200 miles up the Hudson River, are testimony to the increasing interest in waterborne exploration and along with that a need for

A kayak provides a simple key to unlock wild places. It's also more fun when you give your best friend a ride./Photo by Lesley R. Collins.

publicly accessible launching, landing, and camping in exchange for a low-impact ethic.

The Chesapeake Bay paddling community in particular has been active. It started a new sea-kayak symposium at Elk Neck State Park in 1993. It has developed sea-kayak programs consisting of nature trips to remote islands, cold-water workshops, and instructor-certification workshops. It has taken an active leadership role in teaching less experienced paddlers about the joys and hazards of the sport. Meanwhile, New York now has four sea kayak-related clubs. The Metropolitan Association of Sea Kayaking (MASK) is particularly active. Also, over the past ten years, interests have specialized. A growing contingent in the Chesapeake are interested in traditional sea kayaking, paddling Greenland-style sea kayaks with narrow-bladed paddles, and building their own boats to fit their body requirements as the Eskimos did. In New York, because many residents are apartment dwellers and interested in worldwide travel, folding boats proliferate. New Yorker Ralph Diaz has even started a specialty publication for those kayakers. The clubs' newsletters announce trips ranging from circumnavigating Manhattan to paddling the Arctic.

The Mid-Atlantic Coast is ideal for the sport of kayaking because of its historic appeal, scenery, nature preserves, working harbors, and sometimes challenging water. The strong boating interest in the area, particularly around Annapolis, on Long Island, and the New Jersey shore, has led to the proliferation of many boat-launching spots. The challenge of this guide has been to identify those spots that are particularly conducive to the self-propelled paddler.

This book covers New York, New Jersey, Delaware, and the Chesapeake Bay, including coastline along Maryland, Virginia, and the Potomac estuary near Washington, D.C. It fills a gap in the boating literature that is generally geared to cruising guides for sailors who have a different set of needs from those of the kayaker. This guide differs from *Sea Kayaking Along the New England Coast* in that by the very nature of the settled shores, it emphasizes accessible urban wilderness and lets people know where they can "get away" into a natural environment close to major cities.

How was the research done? For all trips, I relied heavily on the knowledge of those who have paddled extensively the areas described. I selected the trips based on their recommendations, then paddled nearly all the routes myself. The reader should be keenly aware that in every case, the wind and weather conditions will differ radically altering the trip's nature.

In the end, this guide is written for those in search of adventure on the water, and whose use of such will promote its preservation at a time when coastal zones are increasingly threatened. Those kayakers enjoy the companionship that sea kayaking generates. They seek and enjoy a challenge. They find satisfaction in relying on their own emotional, physical, and mental resources as well as their own judgment in the wilderness. They are ultimately aware of the risks involved.

This book is relevant for paddlers who wish to move through our marine environment quietly, intimately, and slowly enough to share the currents and moods of the sea that kayaking allows.

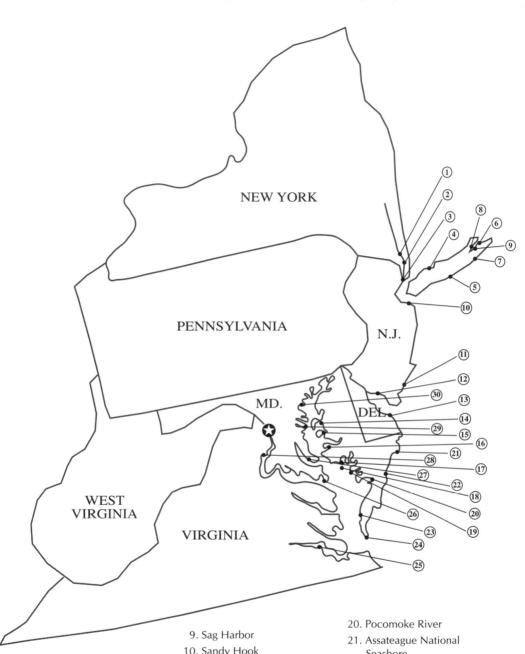

NEW YORK

PENNSYLVANIA

N.J.

MD.

DEL.

WEST
VIRGINIA

VIRGINIA

1. Hudson River Highlands
2. Hudson River Palisades
3. Manhattan
   Circumnavigation
4. Oyster Bay
5. Fire Island
6. Robins Island
7. Moriches Bay
8. Shelter Island

9. Sag Harbor
10. Sandy Hook
11. Brigantine's Wildlife Refuge
12. Dennis Creek
13. Cape Henlopen
14. Wye Island
15. Tilghman Island
16. James Islands
17. Hooper Islands
18. Deal Island
19. Smith Island

20. Pocomoke River
21. Assateague National
    Seashore
22. Cedar Island
23. Back Creek and Hacks Neck
24. Kiptopeke Island
25. Jamestown Island
26. Point Lookout
27. Patuxent River
28. Mason Neck
29. Carrs Wharf
30. Baltimore Harbor

Introduction

Sea Kayaking: An Overview

T HIS SECTION IS A GENERAL DISCUSSION of equipment, technique, safety, navigation, and camping. Readers are strongly urged to consult the other sea-kayaking books listed in the appendix for more in-depth discussion of this material. Remember, though: because sea kayaking as a sport is so individualistic, it harbors a great many biases. Any advice you receive, take with healthy skepticism. Ultimately, you need to learn what works best for you from the school of experience—the sea itself.

Choosing a Boat

When asked for advice on choosing a kayak, one experienced paddler said he has yet to find the right sea kayak—he has 10 years of paddling kayaks and his family has owned seven boats. The lesson here is not to expect a perfect solution but to decide on the best compromise.

Buying a kayak is like purchasing any big-ticket item. You will do a lot of research and probably spend much time talking to other boat owners and manufacturers. The best method is to experience the kayaks yourself. A good way to try boats is to attend a sea-kayak symposium, such as the Chesapeake Bay Sea Kayak Symposium, the East Coast Sea Kayak Symposium in Charleston, South Carolina, or the Atlantic Coast Sea Kayaking Symposium in Castine, Maine (see Appendix A). There, you can paddle a large variety of boats provided by the manufacturers and distributors. Also, you can try an outdoor retailer's demo model during the store's spring paddlefest (but the selection is much smaller than you'd find at a symposium).

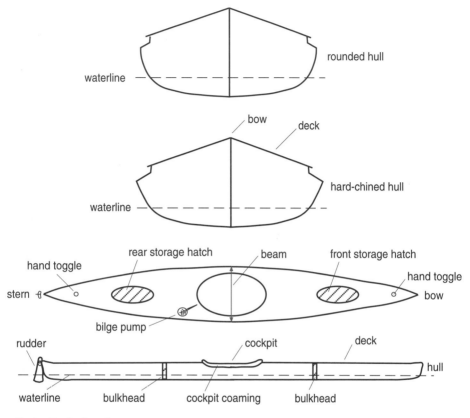

Portrait of a kayak.

Try out as many kayaks as possible to analyze each one's responsiveness on water and your comfort in the boat. How do you like the way it handles on the water? Does it weathercock (i.e. turn into the wind)? How easily does it turn? How does it feel when it is leaned over to one side? Do your feet have enough room? Is your back comfortable? How do you plan to use the boat—for long or short trips? Will you need ample storage space for many gallons of fresh water? Will you need speed to keep up with a group of paddlers? Will you need a stable platform for bird watching in the marshes? Do you want a light boat that turns easily? And finally, how do you like the look of it, its lines and color?

Kayaks perform very differently in various conditions. Try to make test runs in wind, waves, surf, and flat water. Talk to more experienced paddlers and find out what they like about their boats. Match your physique and paddling ability to theirs when assessing their preferences.

Historically, the modern kayak can be traced to two Eskimo building traditions: the Northern Canadian and Greenland single-seat skin boats used by the Inuits for hunting, fishing, and traveling; and the Aleutian *baidarka* modified by Russian fur traders to transport their loot up and down the coast. Broadly speaking, the Inuit boats led to fast, narrow, low-volume, tippy kayaks; and the *baidarka* to slower, wider, high-volume, stable kayaks, with many variations in between.

The British borrowed West Greenland styles to create skinny, sporty, easy-to-roll boats responsive to the British Isles' rough, open seas and craggy coast. These boats have rounded or shallow hulls for speed and stability, upturned bows and sterns to ride easily over

A good way to try different kayaks is to attend a workshop such as the Chesapeake Bay Sea Kayak Symposium in Elk Neck, Maryland.

waves, low profiles to minimize wind interference, and short waterlines. They sacrifice storage space for speed. Since beam measure-
ments (the width of a kayak at its widest point) are 24 inches or
less, the boats are relatively tippy and demand a greater repertoire
of bracing strokes (where you lean on your paddle for balance).
Also, while they have less initial stability (they feel tippy when you
first sit in them), their proponents claim they have more final stability because the rounded hull enables a kayaker to lean more
smoothly into the wave.

Northwest Coast boat manufacturers followed the tradition of
the Aleutian *baidarka* for protected voyaging in bays, coves, inlets,
and among numerous islands. These boats are typically wide, stable, slower, and have lots of storage space. The beam of 24 inches
or more makes them very stable initially; that is, you feel very much
at ease when first stepping in, and they don't tip over easily, but
they can be harder to roll back up when they do tip. They also provide a firm platform for wildlife photography. The cockpits tend to
be roomy, which makes them more suitable for larger people. They
have long waterlines, flat mid-sections, high-peaked decks. They
are very comfortable on long trips and can carry tremendous
amounts of gear but have a higher wind resistance. On high seas
they are said to tip and wallow because of the flat hull.

In between these two styles are a whole range of compromises,
and kayaks are constantly being designed, redesigned, and updated. The latest trend is toward shorter, 14- or 15-foot long kayaks
made of plastic, designed for touring in inlets and estuaries, taking
a great deal of abuse, and priced much lower than their longer,
fiberglass counterparts. Also popular now are hard-chined hulls
(straight-sided) from the Greenland tradition. These boats feel
very stable initially and provide another surface when leaned sideways, useful for support when side-sculling.

While there is something to be said for a nice wide, stable
boat or short, easy-to-turn craft, there is also merit to buying a
sporty boat that you can grow into as you develop stronger paddling skills. Expense divided by time used is another important
equation. How often will you use the boat? How aggressively do
you plan to develop your paddling skills? (As you become increasingly proficient, you may decide to change boats.)

More than one hundred manufacturers produce kayaks in seven countries (U.S., Great Britain, Canada, Germany, Australia, France, and Denmark), and the bulk are small operations, including one-person shops. You will find the most choice in single-person fiberglass kayaks. These range in length from 16 to 18 feet, weigh about 55 pounds (10 pounds less if reinforced with Kevlar and even less with carbon fiber), and have beams from 21 to 25 inches across.

Many manufacturers now also offer these designs in polyethylene plastic, which is less expensive than fiberglass and has been greatly improved as a building material within the last ten years. They are now stiffer and tend to flex less in waves. Loose bulkhead problems have been worked out. Plastic can generally take more abuse than fiberglass, but is heavier and offers fewer refinements in hull shapes.

The standard, single-person fiberglass designs also come in shorter and lighter models that are recommended for women. These include Pacific Water Sports Widgeon, Mariner's Coaster, Necky's Arluk 1.8, Eddyline's Zephyr, Feathercraft's K-Light 1. These

Wooden kayaks are gaining popularity. Here are Chesapeake Light models (from left to right) the Yare, Pocomoke, and Cape Charles./Photo by Chris Kulczycki.

weigh 25 to 35 pounds and are 14 to 17 feet long. Many women—and men—have found the lighter the boat, the more they use it.

About a dozen double-person, rigid fiberglass kayaks are also available. These have a safety advantage on long trips: should one person become tired or incapacitated, the other can continue to paddle. Also, they are useful when paddling abilities differ widely from one paddler to another, such as a young child and parent, and they are less expensive than buying two singles. Some family-style models are made with large hatches in the middle to carry a youngster, dog, or cooler. The drawback is that double kayaks are difficult to paddle alone.

Folding boats, which you can break down into a carrying package, are a whole other area of boats to think about. Most folding boats come packed in one to three bags, although the Feathercraft is rolled into one bag with backpack straps attached.

Typically, the folding boats have wood or aluminum tubing frames with canvas, cotton, or nylon deck fabrics, rubber hulls, inflatable sponsons (hull-length air chambers) for extra buoyancy, and rudder assembly. They are very stable, very seaworthy, and are available in single or double models. The precursor for folding kayaks—and the most well-known—is the Klepper, created in 1907 by German tailor Hans Klepper. Howard Rice made an epic journey around Cape Horn in the Klepper Aerius I. The Klepper has made two trans-Atlantic crossings (one successful) with the use of a sailing rig. Other popular folding boats include the French-made Nautiraid, Canadian Feathercraft, U.S. Folbot. Feathercraft now makes the short (13 feet) K-Light 1, which weighs only 30 pounds and is designed for gunkholing or river cruising and is very convenient to transport.

Single-purpose boats include various sit-on-top models with recessed hulls, used for surfing and racing. These include the wave ski and surf ski seen mostly in warmer waters of Hawaii, California, South Africa, and Australia. An adventurous group in northern California called the Tsunami Rangers have made surfing kayaks very popular. Racing kayaks (Doug Bushnell's X-Par Missile, Necky's Phantom, Nimbus' Sprint), are swift, light, long, well-rounded, and narrow (18 inches). Wood kayaks are gaining in popularity as a home-built economy measure, for custom-design preferences, or as works of art. They are made by a method of stitch and glue or cedar strips epoxyed together. Some are covered with Dacron or canvas. Several manufacturers offer kits. Some look too beautiful to put in the water but are very seaworthy. Bart Hauthaway's pack canoes are lightweight and designed for easy marsh poking and for rolling. Inflatables are another specialized variety on the fringe of the mainstream fiberglass rigid hull kayaks. Audrey Sutherland has given those credibility through epic voyages throughout the Hawaiian and Alaskan coasts.

Generally, longer boats travel faster than short ones, wider boats are more stable than narrow ones, round-hulled boats lean more smoothly than hard-chined or flat-bottomed boats; the more rocker (curve from bow to stern), the easier the boat turns, but the harder it is to paddle straight.

Aside from general hull design, several other details need to be considered when choosing a boat. These include the size and shape of cockpits (which is partly a trade-off between ease of entry and volume of water collected by the cockpit in a capsize); the size of hatches (the wider, the easier to get gear in and out but also more leakage is possible), the nature of hatches (how watertight); and whether the boat has a rudder (and what kind of rudder system it is). Debate often heats up between those who see rudders as valuable for helping to keep a kayak on course in a strong beam wind and those who see them as a bother—bending, catching, malfunctioning at the worst possible times and providing an ill substitute for paddling technique. A retractable skeg (a blade to provide tracking that can be lowered from a recessed box along the keel) serves a similar purpose; its design has improved greatly over the years.

Other basic elements to consider are bulkheads (buoyancy, storage), deck fittings (for emergency equipment and procedures), built-in bilge pumps, and seat-contour comfort.

Choosing a Paddle

Most people invest the bulk of their savings in a boat and treat the paddle as an afterthought. Investing in a good paddle, however, is almost as important as investing in a good boat.

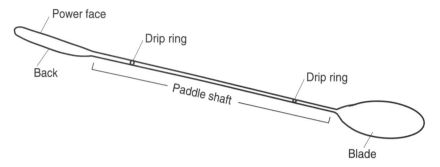

Anatomy of a paddle.

The aim of a paddle, like the paddle stroke itself, is efficiency. Lifting and holding is a waste of energy, admonishes one major U.S. paddle manufacturer. You want to choose a paddle you feel most comfortable with: How heavy and wide is it? Paddles are made of either wood or fiberglass. Wood has a pleasing aesthetic feel and more flex over the length of the shaft, meaning less tendon fatigue on a long trip. The disadvantage of wood is breakage and wear that comes from launching from rocky beaches. Fiberglass has less flex but more durability.

Shaft length is also determined by whether you are paddling a boat that is wide or narrow or how deep you are sitting in it. You need to be able to dip your paddle in the water without scraping your knuckles on the deck or shifting your weight from one side to the other too much. A shorter paddle or a narrower blade will increase cadence. (Are you conditioned for the increased heart rate?) A heavily loaded boat and wide-bladed or heavy paddle shaft can often lead to tendon fatigue and possible injury.

The other consideration is blade size and shape. The success of some paddlers' rolls is actually determined by the blade shape. Gaining in popularity is the narrow-bladed Greenland-style paddle. To paddlers trained with the modern wide-bladed paddles, the initial feel of a Greenland paddle can be a bit strange, but it reduces fatigue over long voyages and is also said to provide an easier roll. Sea kayakers are discovering a whole new repertoire of techniques with these paddles. You can customize them to the exact

George Ellis demonstrates how to make your own Greenland-style paddle at the Chesapeake Bay Sea Kayak Symposium.

specifications of hand width, forearm length, etc., so they fit you and will aid in underwater rolling maneuvers and braces in heavy seas.

Buy a spare paddle for safety and also for changing cadence, which is particularly helpful on a long trip. A good combination is a paddle with a wider blade to get you through the surf and a paddle with a smaller blade when you settle down into your long-distance stroking. A take-apart paddle is useful for storage, as probes to get you through a sandbar you didn't see, and for on-deck storage. The most important element in the take-apart paddle is a tight fit. Keep the shafts clean of grit to minimize possible looseness. Two-piece paddles generally cost more than one-piece paddles.

Much of the effort in paddle manufacturing goes into reducing the paddle's weight. The carbon-fiber paddles are particularly lightweight, a joy to paddle with, but also expensive.

Other Equipment

Spray Skirts. The spray skirt is intended to prevent water from entering the cockpit; to achieve this, it must stay in place when you lean or roll the kayak. A snug shock-cord fit on the coaming (the cockpit's raised rim) is essential, yet it should be loose enough to yank off via a grab loop if you need to get out of your boat. The spray skirt is available in different sizes to match each cockpit size and to ensure a snug fit at the waist. Neoprene versions keep out the water the best and don't allow water to pool in your lap. Coated nylon models are lighter, cooler, and less expensive but are less waterproof over time and tend to sag with water puddles. Shoulder straps keep the skirt in place. A compromise is a combination neoprene/nylon sprayskirt. A pocket can be added on to the spray skirt, to carry items such as emergency flares, suntan lotion, sunglasses, and bug repellent.

PFD. The U.S. Coast Guard requires that all kayakers have onboard an approved PFD (personal flotation device), otherwise known as a life jacket. You should wear one at all times. Most people wear the Type III PFD, designed for recreational use. Gaining in popularity is the Type V PFD, a "rescuer" vest designed with tow rope and special pockets for emergency equipment. The PFD should fit snugly so it does not float up around your ears in the water. (Not only do PFDs serve as a life-saving device, they also provide an extra layer of insulation when paddling in cold weather.)

Flotation Bags. If a sea kayak does not have watertight bulkheads, you will need flotation bags fore and aft of your cockpit. That includes folding boats. Swamped boats usually sink at one end or, if very large, become impossible to bail out. The bags should be properly fixed in your boat. Several companies manufacture them.

Gear for Self Reliance. The Coast Guard requires kayakers to shine a white light at night to avoid collision; a waterproof flashlight will do. Attach a whistle to your PFD. It's easier to blow a whistle than to yell if you need help. Also attach a strobe light for paddling at night and to help other boat traffic see you. Some put reflecting tape on their PFDs (and boats). Also carry at least three emergency marine flares (smoke flares for day use) in your PFD pocket to alert other boats that you are in trouble.

Carry a tow line and spare paddle on your back deck in case yours breaks or floats away. Many people attach a tow line to their waists with a buckle system, easier to release if need be. Also stash a paddle float and hand pump underneath your rear decklines (if a foot or hand pump is not built into your boat).

On the front deck, carry a compass, marine charts in waterproof chart case, and a horn signaling device to warn other boats of your presence in fog and busy boating traffic areas. Keep a weather radio handy. Obtain a weather check before any long crossings and check the Beaufort wind scale (see Appendix D).

Other essential items include a first-aid kit, waterproof bags, and complete set of spare clothes. Other useful items include a sponge to help bail and binoculars to determine buoy numbers from a distance. Some kayakers also carry a VHF radio to call for help. See Appendix B for list of Coast Guard stations in the Mid-Atlantic region.

You will be the best judge of how much of this gear you need to carry, depending on whether you are on an afternoon jaunt through the marshes, day-long trips, or week-long expeditions.

What to Wear

Drysuits and Wetsuits. Water carries heat away faster than air—cold water can kill you. Drysuits or wetsuits are essential for protection from immersion but are not totally effective. They simply buy you time to get out of cold water as quickly as possible to prevent death from hypothermia.

Drysuits are made of pack cloth specially coated for waterproofing. They are sealed around the neck, wrists, and ankles with latex gaskets, and have either a rear or front zipper, the latter being more convenient. A drysuit will keep you dry and warm in winter paddling conditions if you also wear a pile liner underneath for warmth and wicking perspiration away from your body. They come in one or two pieces. Kokatat now makes a Gore-Tex™ drysuit that is both waterproof and breathable so your perspiration can escape and you don't get cold and clammy. Common complaints about drysuits include overheating, fragile latex seals, and the disintegration of latex seals from perspiration, suntan lotion, or insect repellent. Most manufacturers will repair or replace seals for a fee. Also, if air gets trapped in the drysuit, you may find yourself helplessly blown across the water's surface if you come out of your boat.

Wetsuits are generally made of about 1/8-inch-thick neoprene (a lighter weight than those used by skin divers for added mobility). Generally they consist of a "farmer john," which covers legs and torso, and a jacket. Wetsuits insulate against cold water by trapping a thin layer of water that is then warmed by the body. Several companies custom-make wetsuits for a slight surcharge. Drawbacks to wetsuits include overheating or dehydrating (since they have little ventilation), chafing, and arm fatigue.

Head, Hands, and Toes. A visor works to keep the sun off and to avert salt spray from waves. Since 75 to 80 percent of body heat escapes through the head, when surfing wearing a neoprene diver's hood or heavy pile cap is a good idea for thermal head protection. A helmet should be worn for protection from rocks and the boat itself (in case of a capsize).

For hand protection, pogies, which are tubular mitts attached by Velcro to your paddle (some pile-lined), give you paddle contact but no protection should you roll over. Neoprene gloves often restrict circulation. Some paddlers use rubber dishwashing gloves over pile gloves. A neoprene, pre-curved mitt may work best. Neoprene booties are recommended for warmth and grip in winter and surf-shoes for grip in summer. Water sandals can be dangerous because a strap can get caught on your foot pedal, and you may get trapped in the boat. To save your glasses in a capsize, use a floatable security strap.

Gear for Winter Paddling. Sea kayaking in winter can be benign with calm water and lovely scenery. In crashing surf, it can be deadly. You must prepare for frigid water and air temperatures. Essential equipment and clothing include a drysuit or wetsuit (see above); for hands, fleece-lined pogies, neoprene gloves or mittens; for head, neoprene hood. Dress warmly but not too heavily so you don't overheat. A complete change of clothes should be stowed in a waterproof bag in the kayak. A stainless steel thermos (not glass) with a hot drink such as cider is also a good idea.

Charlie Cole tests his clothing for sufficient cold-water protection.

To see if your outfit is sufficient for the day's paddle, take a swim before you get into your boat. Jump in the water; if you are able to swim and float around at a comfortable temperature, then you have on the appropriate level of clothing for conditions.

Paddle Strokes

Most paddling skills are easy to learn. Your goal is efficiency of paddle stroke, not muscling through the water until your arms fall off. The paddle should act like a cocktail stirrer, held lightly in your hands swirling away in sea water.

The first step to efficient paddling technique is a solid position. Your knees should rest firmly underneath the deck, inside the cockpit. The balls of your feet lie upright against the pedals, at a 90-degree angle. The small of your back should be pressed firmly against the seat. Hold your back straight, bent slightly forward.

To find an effective paddle position, hold the paddle above your head. Let your elbows drop into a right angle and position your hands on the shaft accordingly. Keep the distance between your hands and the blade equal to help maintain a straight paddling course. To cut down on wind resistance, turn your paddle slightly, for a right- or left-hand control. (That means the control hand holds the paddle in a fixed grip position, but lightly and rotates so that the paddle enters the water at a 90-degree angle while the other hand allows the paddle shaft to turn freely.)

A basic whitewater paddling lesson can help you learn sea-kayaking strokes. The basic stroke requires moving your paddle at a shallow angle over the front of your boat (as opposed to up and down), punching out with your leading arm almost completely extended, placing the paddle blade in the water at your feet, and pulling back with the forward lower hand while pushing forward with the rear upper palm until the arm positions are reversed and you are ready to place the opposite blade in the water. The paddle should exit the water at the waist. Some say the motion represents 65 pulling and 35 percent pushing.

Your shoulders, chest, and torso should rotate with each stroke, with most of the power coming from your stomach muscles. To help rotation, push off with your feet—left foot, left stroke. Actually, your arms should do very little of the work.

When you reverse the paddle stroke, you travel backwards. Other maneuvers include the draw and sculling-draw strokes, which pull your boat sideways, and the forward and reverse sweep stroke to turn your boat. Stabilizing maneuvers include the low brace, in which the paddle is slapped flat on the water with the power face held upward; and the high brace, used in big waves, in which you hold your paddle above your shoulders (but not above your head) and jab the paddle, power face down, into the wave as you lean into it. Normally you lean into oncoming water. The exception is when crossing a strong eddy line. Here you lean downstream. Otherwise water will wash over the deck and possibly capsize you.

Depending on wind, current, and heading, you will need to correct your strokes. If you are paddling without a rudder or retractable skeg to help keep a straight course in a side wind, you can lengthen the paddle shaft to one side by adjusting your hands and thereby provide more leverage on that side. In a following sea, when the waves are coming from behind, your boat will tend to surf in one direction or another. By dragging the back of your paddle to one side, you can keep the boat tracking, prevent it from broaching (turning sideways) and possibly capsizing, and surf forward. That's a quick overview of the technique. Read David Seidman's *The Essential Sea Kayaker* for a more detailed explanation of paddling and maneuvering techniques (see Annotated Bibliography).

Sea-kayak symposiums, held in South Carolina, Maryland, and Maine in the spring and summer, offer paddling instruction from experts. Many outfitters now offer high-quality instruction. Outdoor shops or clubs may offer sea-kayaking classes. Since no U.S. umbrella organization monitors sea-kayak instruction in the United States, ask an outfitter if the organization follows the guidelines of TASK (Trade Association of Sea Kayaking), a professional organization of sea kayak manufacturers, dealers, and experienced kayakers, based in Seattle, Washington (see Appendix A).

Rescue Techniques

One of the biggest controversies among sea kayakers is whether it is necessary to know how to execute an Eskimo roll, in which following capsize, you right yourself by using your basic paddle stroke on top of the water and lift your body to the surface without coming out of the boat. The basic Eskimo roll has many variations, the most common of which are the C to C, Pawlata, Put-Across, Screw, and Steyr. For a complete discussion of the technique, see Derek Hutchinson's *Eskimo Rolling* (see Annotated Bibliography).

Some kayakers begin their argument by saying they have never tipped over during the years they have been sea kayaking. However, they have probably stayed away from breaking waves, avoided headlands, or paddled only in fair weather. You may tip over, but you will not be trapped if you have learned a basic wet-exit technique (which you should).

In any case, the aim is to get out of cold water as soon as possible. The Eskimo roll is the most efficient method for doing so. The energy exerted in rolling back up is much less than that of twisting back into the boat and pumping out an unstable water-filled boat that can tip you over again. As one kayaker has noted, learn the

Eskimo roll, and it will improve your bracing technique to such an extent you may not need to know how to roll.

Clubs often hold pool sessions in winter or spring to practice rolling and deep water rescue techniques. Hofstra University on Long Island even offers college-level courses in the Eskimo roll and other survival techniques.

The paddle float is another self-rescue technique. In this technique, a paddle float, foam block, or even PFD is tied to the paddle blade, providing flotation to simulate an outrigger. This allows you to crawl back onto and into your boat without tipping over the boat. Other self-rescues use Sea Wings, two inflatable sponsons that can be attached quickly to either side of the cockpit after capsize and provide stability while you climb back in and pump out the boat. Still another is the re-entry and roll, in which you ease yourself back into the cockpit of your overturned kayak and roll back up sometimes with the use of a paddle float to provide extra leverage.

In group rescues, the rescuers collect the boat and stray paddle, raft up (bring boats parallel to one another and lay paddles across the deck) next to the capsized colleague, and pull the boat up on one rescuer's deck to empty the water. Rescuers secure the boat by holding tightly onto the cockpit coaming while the colleague pulls himself onto the rear deck by grabbing the cockpit rim and the paddles that have been placed behind the coaming of the rescuer's boat. The rescuers continue to hold the boat while the water is pumped out. This rescue can also be performed by only one rescuer, but don't hesitate to take advantage of two other paddlers by placing the swamped boat in between their boats. The video *What Now?* by Maine Sport guides Shelley Johnson and Vaughan Smith, shows these rescues in detail (see Annotated Bibliography).

In an Eskimo-bow rescue, the capsized paddler remains upside down, usually after a failed roll, and pounds the kayak's upturned hull to attract attention. Then the capsized paddler moves both hands in the air back and forth on either side of the cockpit until the rescuer nudges his or her boat up to the extended hands. The paddler then pulls to the upright position while holding onto the bow of the rescuer's boat. This saves the capsized the bother of wet-exiting. Obviously, this technique requires proximity to—and earlier practice with—the paddling companion.

Practicing rescues with your colleagues in calm water is good preparation for real-life capsizes.

Swimming to shore, if you are near the shore, alone, or when your self-rescue is not effective, is another possible rescue technique. Although kayakers are drilled to stay with their boats in capsize, such a course is not always the wisest. However, strong swimming abilities will not save you when hypothermia from prolonged exposure to the water sets in. It's good to have a survival container that you can clip onto yourself if you do abandon your kayak and swim to shore. It should include food, metal cup, flares, matches, signaling mirror, orange signal flag, and Jell-O, a good survival drink when mixed with hot water.

The point is, you should have your safety covered with a first line of defense for deep water rescue; that is, an efficient technique such as an Eskimo roll, followed by a series of techniques that definitely work for you as a second line of defense. In addition to these, many more sea-kayaking rescue techniques exist. For more on those techniques, read John Dowd's revised edition of *Sea Kayaking* or David Seidman's *The Essential Sea Kayaker* (see Annotated Bibliography). Also read the sea kayaking journals, *Sea Kayaker, Atlantic Coastal Kayaker,* or *ANorAK* for updated accident reports, from which much can be learned.

Navigation

Equip yourself with NOAA (National Oceanic and Atmospheric Administration) charts or USGS (United States Geological Survey) maps and a compass, both mounted on your deck, and know how to use them. Maps will help you follow a meandering shoreline that has few visual clues. One paddling companion pencils bearings directly on charts he will be using on routes planned carefully back at the kitchen table.

Most coastal paddlers in the mid-Atlantic find a 1:40,000 scale suitable although a 1:20,000 gives greater detail particularly for harbors and in vast tidal marsh. The ratio is inches of sea and land to inches on the chart, i.e. a 1:40,000 scale means that 40,000 inches of sea appear as one inch on the chart. The larger the second number, the smaller the scale. Some paddlers prefer the USGS 1:250,000 scale. This allows them to see distant points for correct orientation and navigation and to avoid paddling off one chart and onto another too quickly. You can buy charts in most marine stores or you can order any chart of any place in the world over the phone and have it sent COD from New York Nautical Instruments in New York City. For "Chart Kits," contact the Better Boating Association (See Appendix A).

For tides and currents, consult the annual *Eldridge Tide and Pilot Book,* by Robert E. White (see Annotated Bibliography). The book is particularly useful for New York Harbor and Sandy Hook.

Be aware that headlands pose the greatest challenges for sea kayakers. Here, the current runs strongest and closest to shore, and winds can stir up a chop and create turbulent conditions way out to sea. Wherever water narrows into a passage, particularly if it has come from a very large body of water, be aware of strong currents and possibly whirlpools or overfalls.

Also, don't forget to look over your shoulder frequently to see what the coastline will look like on your return trip. Mark in your memory any outstanding landmarks, such as a lone tree or rocky outcrop.

In order to familiarize yourself with navigation, read David Burch's *Fundamentals of Kayak Navigation* (see Annotated Bibliography).

Safety Considerations

Hypothermia. The biggest danger posed to kayakers is hypothermia, a rapid loss of internal body heat that can totally debilitate the kayaker and lead to death. Most kayaking deaths can be attributed to hypothermia caused by prolonged exposure to cold water and the body's inability to heat itself. The American Canoe Association issues the following warning about hypothermia:

> Hypothermia can develop rapidly if an individual is not properly dressed for immersion. Survival time in the water is roughly 3 hours at 50 degrees Fahrenheit and 1 hour at 41 degrees Fahrenheit without proper clothing (wetsuit/drysuit). Signs of hypothermia include slurred speech, uncontrolled shivering, failure to respond to questions, illogical reasoning and deteriorating reflexes. Action must be taken when these signs appear. Get the victim into dry clothing and a sleeping bag if possible. Make yourself familiar with the details of treating hypothermia.
>
> Following a capsize, your partners should be able to get you back into your boat in no more than a few minutes. In 10 minutes your boat should be pumped 'dry.' You should be dressed to withstand accidental immersion. Wear a wet suit that is designed for paddlers or a dry suit plus some warm clothes inside it. Carry spare dry clothes, a thermos of hot liquid, and a one-burner stove. Have a sleeping bag in the group in case severe hypothermia is encountered.
>
> In general, when risk factors on your trips increase due to cold, sea conditions, etc., do not fail to take measures necessary to compensate for the increased risk.

People seem to capsize most often because they stop paddling when another person in the group has tipped over. When you stop paddling, the dynamic balance you had established while paddling is disrupted, possibly causing you to upset. Capsizes also occur often late in the afternoon when paddlers are tired, during launching and landing, in overfalls or tide rips, and in surf. However, when surfing, paddlers usually expect to capsize a time or two.

Learn to anticipate potential capsizes; they usually occur because of the momentary conditions or the skill level of one or more paddlers in the group.

Finally, note that in sea kayaking, because of instant immersion, the victim can go into something called cold water shock, bypassing the usual hierarchical order of symptoms for hypothermia. An environmental physiologist in Washington, D.C., Moulton Avery, has developed his theory of cold water shock, which many a kayaker is now familiar with. He developed this theory from his experience in the Chesapeakein the spring with warm air and cold water conditions.

Water can take heat away from your body 25 times faster than air. Shock responses begin at water temperatures of 50 to 55 degrees. You have a series of shock responses, according to Avery. After capsizing in cold water, your ability to control your breathing is completely lost and you involuntarily gasp for air. If you're underwater when you gasp, you drown. Other responses include hyperventilation, breathlessness, inability to hold your breath, inability to synchronize breathing, and panic. Also, you have a constriction of blood vessels over a large skin area so the blood pressure gets corked, and you get a pressure spike.

All this leads to disorientation, inability to function, and possible drowning through inhaling water. In other words, the paddler runs a high risk of drowning way before hypothermia sets in. The best way to avoid cold water shock is to dress for the water and not the air, even on a balmy spring day, which comes early to the Chesapeake.

Group Dynamics. One of the keys to safety, especially when paddling in groups, is communication. It's a good idea to have a meeting onshore before the trip begins. The group should have a paddling plan. Decide where you plan to go, where you plan to gather, where you plan to turn around, and what to do in case of an emergency. These decisions are much easier to make beforehand, on land, than they are on water during a crisis. File a float plan (see Appendix C) with a responsible friend or relative back home.

Designate one person in your group to be leader, and another to be sweeper (the last boat); frequently switch positions to maintain morale. Paddle to accommodate the ability of the weakest or slowest paddler. Establish group horn or whistle signals such as one for attention, two to raft up. Also set up paddle signals in the event of group separation—a common occurrence when the weather turns bad or conditions intensify.

Be aware of how well you know the person or people with whom you are paddling. Do they know how to do self or group rescues? How often do they go kayaking? How will they react if the wind and waves kick up?

Self-Reliance. You may feel safe because you are in a group. This is a false sense of security. The most important thing to remember is that you are solely responsible for your own safety. You need to be self-sufficient, know your limits, have your own gear, and, most of all, exercise sound judgment. Don't go out if you are worried about weather conditions; be aware of bail-out points; go with an experienced group.

Keep yourself within a safe boundary. You may want to keep things exciting and push your limits, but by the same token be cautious about waiting conditions out for a day or two if weather deteriorates. You can't afford to be on a deadline to get somewhere.

On Shore. Be aware that many grassy areas harbor the deer tick, a tiny mite that carries a virus that can cause Lyme disease, a debilitating illness that can lead to arthritis and even heart disease. Always wear boots or pants tucked into shoes when walking in the grass. Apply insect repellent to skin, socks, and pant legs. Check for small dark spots on your skin. Should you develop a circular rash or flu-like symptoms, seek medical attention immediately. Lyme disease is curable in its early stages.

Regulation. Sea kayaking has been a free activity that has encouraged self-reliance and self-education. That is one of the beauties of the sport. Many kayakers attend to safety in order to keep the Coast Guard out of regulating the sport. So far, that approach has worked and will continue to work if kayakers continue to take precautions, learn more, and exercise sound judgment.

Get the free "Coastal Kayaking" brochure put out by the American Canoe Association (ACA) in cooperation with the U.S. Coast Guard, which lists in detail major safety considerations. Write to the American Canoe Association (see Appendix A) for a copy.

Camping

The great advantage of sea-kayak camping over backpacking is that you can carry lots of gear and not have to worry as much about weight. A heavily loaded boat can actually enhance the kayak's stability. You can carry luxury items such as sun showers, lanterns, fresh food, nature books, and camp stools. Unless you have watertight hatches, you will need waterproof bags available in various sizes. For an excellent discussion on general provisioning, read Linda Daniel's *Kayak Cookery* (see Annotated Bibliography).

On shore, always carry your boat above the high-tide mark and tie it in place so it won't blow away at night. Cover your cockpit to keep out sand fleas and other unwanted creatures and also to prevent rescuers from needlessly searching for you should your kayak float away.

The following is a basic equipment check list. It can be adjusted for your personal needs.

Equipment Checklist
Safety items
   PFD (personal flotation device), required by federal law
   Tow rope
   Spare two-part paddle
   Repair kit for either fiberglass or plastic boat
   Paddle float
   Airhorn
   Smoke signals
   Flares
   Whistle
   Waterproof flashlight and extra batteries (required by law
      at night)
   Strobe light

Hand pump
Sponge
Wet/drysuit
Spare warm, dry clothes
Compass
Marine charts and chart case
Tide tables
Weather radio
Thermos
Stove
First-aid kit
Fresh drinking water
Sunglasses
Sunscreen
Hat for rain/sun

Boat Gear

Kayak
Paddle with drip rings
Spray skirt
Float bags for both ends
Waterproof storage bags
Deck lines

Clothing

Drysuit
Wetsuit jacket and pants
Neoprene booties
Nylon paddling jacket
Neoprene gloves, mittens, or pogies
Polypropylene or fiber pile jacket
Polypropylene or fiber pile pants
Polypropylene top
Complete change of clothes
Swim suit and towel
Rain jacket and pants

Security strap for glasses or sunglasses
Quick-drying shorts
T-shirt

Day-Trip Items

Emergency shelter
Insect repellent
Sitting pad
Drinking cup
Camera/film and dry bag or box
Toilet paper
Litter bag
Windbreaker
Lunch/Snacks
Drinking water

Overnight Items

Tent
Sleeping bag
Sleeping pad
Stove and fuel
Cooking pot
Eating utensils
Pocket knife
Waterproof matches and container
Personal toilet items
Biodegradable soap
Extra flashlight batteries

Miscellaneous

Sneakers
Binoculars
Fishing gear
Bird-identification book
Notebook
Camp stool

Explanation of Trip Data

THE SUGGESTED ROUTES for the following thirty trips are not meant to be definitive. Wind and wave conditions are the ultimate route deciders, and many interesting islands, peninsulas, riverbanks, thoroughfares, inlets—not to mention wildlife or unusual boats—can easily draw you away from the main route. Rather, these are general routes that have been tried by me and other kayakers.

Note that the trips are not rated according to paddler's abilities. Sea kayaking is a sport that can appear seductively easy but is highly dependent on weather conditions. Seemingly benign conditions can change rapidly when winds or storms (such as the infamous Chesapeake afternoon thunderstorms) suddenly appear. A smooth passage when you are paddling with the tide will become a major battle when wind and tide oppose one another—this is particularly true in the inlets on Long Island and in New Jersey. Therefore, the general trip data includes an entry on Caution Areas, of which all kayakers, however experienced, should take heed. It is up to you to judge your abilities in regard to each trip.

Note that the maps in this book are illustrations and should not be used for navigation. You should supply yourself with the recommended marine chart or USGS map of the area.

The following is an explanation of data provided.

Charts. The recommended maps are marine charts issued by the National Oceanic and Atmospheric Administration (NOAA). Most kayakers find the scale of 1:40,000 suitable. If you paddle long distances at a good pace, then the standard 1:250,000 USGS topographic maps are useful, despite their lack of the usual navigational aids found on the NOAA charts.

Trip Mileage. The mileage is an estimate from the charts and does not take into account detours into inviting inlets and bays or how far inshore or offshore you might travel. If you calculate the average sea kayaker travels 3 miles per hour, you can reasonably estimate how long it will take to get from point A to point B, assuming favorable winds and tide.

Getting There. Normally only one or two access spots are described, but note that many more are usually available in any given area. For more information on public launch spots, consult various sources given within the discussions of access for each state.

Camping. Where available, ocean-side camping (which is limited) is mentioned, but many mainland campgrounds that are handy to the launch area are noted. As this sport grows, we hope more government agencies in the Mid-Atlantic will cooperate in making coastal camping available. Meanwhile, don't forget to observe the rules of low-impact camping: pitch your tent in designated areas, carry out all your trash, use a camp stove rather than an open fire, walk on established paths to and from shore to avoid erosion and sensitive vegetation, and leave the site in a natural state.

Tidal Range. This refers to the average measure in feet of the rise and fall of tide over a year's time as provided by Eldridge Tide and Pilot Book (see Annotated Bibliography). Where no figure is available for a specific area, the closest recorded range is given. Remember that specific tidal range varies throughout the lunar month, seasonally, and according to wind direction and barometric pressure, as well as spring river run-off.

Caution Areas. Often, these are narrow inlets, tide rips, shoals, major boat channels, and generally rough areas. In summer, heavy boat traffic is *always* a consideration if not a major hazard when considering caution areas, and is not always referred to specifically in the guide. Always use your judgment and be aware of your surroundings.

Chapter 1
New York

SEA KAYAKING around one of the world's biggest cities—the New York metropolis has a population of 8 million people—can be full of adventure considerably different from the freedom of heading off to the wild shores of Maine so many of us have come to enjoy. Compare paddling around Manhattan to going around Beal Island at Appalachian Mountain Club's Knubble Bay Camp in Georgetown, Maine, for example. The only similarity is that they both have gates called Hell, which each can run upwards of 3.5 knots. From there, however, the similarities end.

New York has skyscrapers instead of spruce-topped granite; pigeons and cormorants rather than eider ducks and black guillemots; barges to contend with as opposed to lobster boats; murky water versus crystal clear views; the aroma of container ships versus the waft of pines. Still, for the prepared, paddling around New York can be full of surprises, a great way to leave the tensions of city life behind.

New York paddling divides itself into roughly four geographic areas. The Hudson River offers new sights, sounds, boat traffic, layers of history, not to mention good restaurants, each and every mile. New York Harbor (one of the world's busiest) is dominated by the Statue of Liberty. Long Island offers a great variety of trips from the harbors on the north shore in Long Island Sound to the long beaches, shallow bays, and surfing inlets on the south shore.

Public Access

Virtually all waterside access in New York is tightly protected by private ownership as well as city and town, county, state, or federal government. In the mid-1980s several kayakers—catalyzed by Chuck Sutherland—began working to secure federal launch sites in the Gateway National Recreation Area around New York Bay. After much effort, cartop boat owners were granted five sites, including those at Floyd Bennett Field on Jamaica Bay, Great Kills Park on Staten Island, and Breezy Point on the Rockaway Peninsula in Queens. Unfortunately the canoe and kayak launch program is still considered an experimental project. As of now, only one Gateway site in New York is open, and that is Floyd Bennett Field in Jamaica Bay at the seaplane ramp behind Hangar B. You can obtain a cartop permit (free) at the Floyd Bennett Field (718-338-3828) office. On Staten Island, the Great Kills site is closed due to construction, possibly for the next few years.

Meanwhile, Sutherland was unable to come to any agreement with the state government, due to insurance complications, even though surfers and fishermen were already allowed access to the waterside.

However, the City of New York Parks and Recreation Department has developed eleven official launch sites for canoes and kayaks in New York. You can get a permit for the launch sites for a $2 annual fee at any Parks Department office in the five boroughs. In Manhattan, the address and phone number are: The Arsenal, Central Park, NY 10021; (212) 360-8133. The application process is designed to ensure that you comply with safety requirements. You can also get city permit applications at several retail stores in the area, including Klepper in Park Ridge, New Jersey, and Campmor in Paramus, New Jersey. In New York, the South Street Seaport Book Store and the Metropolitan Canoe and Kayak Club (see Appendix A) also issue permits. The permit season runs from April 1 to December 1, dawn to dusk.

City launch sites include Riverside Park, Inwood Hill Park, and 79th Street Boat Basin in Manhattan; Clason Point, Ferry Point Park, Pelham Bay Park in the Bronx; Bayside Marina in Little Neck Bay; Marine Park and Canarsie Park in Brooklyn; and Alice Austen House Park and Conference House Park on Staten Island.

Also, the Sebago Canoe Club has a clubhouse and launch at Paerdegat Basin in Jamaica Bay and is well worth the high initiation fee for membership for the storage space and launch area it provides.

Folding kayaks are convenient for city paddling, where apartment space and launch-site parking is a problem. A good source on folding kayaks is *Folding Kayaker* newsletter, published bimonthly by New Yorker Ralph Diaz (see Appendix A).

On Long Island, access is problematical without local knowledge. During the high season (from Memorial Day to Labor Day) you need a town or county sticker on your car to park and launch from most beaches, so it's best to paddle in the off-season. Consult with one of the clubs to find the best local launches (see below for more details).

For the Hudson River, launch sites are more readily available, and the newly formed Hudson River Waterway Association is working hard on securing overnight camping. An excellent source for launch sites on the Hudson is the new *Hudson River Waterway Guide* by Ian Giddy. Finally, the *NYNEX Boaters Directory* for New York and Connecticut also lists launch sites (see Annotated Bibliography for both).

Clubs

Sea-kayaking clubs in New York are popular, borrowing from a long tradition of canoe clubs here. Paddlers started the New York Canoe Club in 1871, and in the early twentieth century hundreds of canoeists took to the Hudson from more than twenty canoe clubs.

Following the principle of safety in numbers, sea-kayaking groups have eddied through Hell Gate and zoomed under the Verrazano Bridge at the Narrows. They've charted new territory, begun new relationships with the Coast Guard, and had experiences from the uneventful to the hair-raising. Gradually a great fund of local knowledge has been growing and generously shared by fellow club members.

The Appalachian Mountain Club's New York-North Jersey chapter has an active canoe committee with trips to the Pine Barrens and around Manhattan. The Sebago Canoe Club has a clubhouse on Jamaica Bay. The Metropolitan Canoe and Kayak Club is more recently involved in the sport under the tutelage of Dieter Stiller, owner of the Klepper America shop in Park Ridge, New Jersey.

There are four major sea kayaking clubs in New York: Metropolitan Canoe and Kayak Club (M.C.K.C.), Metropolitan Association of Sea Kayakers (M.A.S.K.), Mad American Kayaker (M.A.K.), and Paumanok Paddlers. All of these groups have done much to introduce new people to the sport and share local knowledge of New York waters via trips, newsletters, and hotlines.

Hudson River Waterway

As you paddle the Hudson River, don't expect to find any boater-oriented camping facilities at all. That's what Bob Huszar discovered when he took twenty-one days in 1990 to paddle his Klepper kayak up the Hudson from Manhattan's north tip to Lake Champlain, a distance of about 200 miles. Much of the riverbank is privately owned or deeded to the railroad right of way. As a result of his and others' frustration, Huszar and Craig Poole helped to form the Hudson River Waterway Association, one of the most rewarding efforts of the New York paddling community, and well worth joining if you plan to paddle the Hudson (See Appendix A).

Huszar found a kindred spirit in John Middlebrooks, a regional program specialist with the Taconic Parks Department, when Huszar was presenting a talk at the L.L. Bean Sea Kayak Symposium. A productive partnership between the state government and HRWA has developed as a result of that meeting.

Paddlers officially formed the Hudson River Waterway Association in 1992 to create a river trail from the mouth of the Hudson River at New York Harbor to Troy, then onward through the canal system to Lake Erie and Lake Champlain, open to all "small beachable boats," and providing a variety of overnight facilities every 10 to 12 miles.

HRWA encourages an ethic of conservation and responsible, nonpolluting use of the Hudson River, promotes access, and maintains the trail through local river stewards. HRWA publishes the *Hudson River Waterway Guide,* a trail guidebook for small boaters, with points of interest, launch points, camping areas, and bed-and-breakfast establishments (B & Bs) along the river, is invaluable for river trips and can be obtained through HRWA.

As of 1993, the association had succeeded in gaining the right of river-based camping at three locations: Norrie Point just north of Poughkeepsie, Iona Island south of the Bear Mountain Bridge, and Croton Point south of Haverstraw. More are being negotiated. Attempts to include Turkey Point and Athens Flats in the camping trail have to date not been successful. HRWA encourages those considering longer trips to use riverside (or near-river) B & Bs or low-cost hotels and advises bringing along collapsible transport wheels as well as a locking device for kayaks.

The Hudson has many interesting day trips, some reachable by train on the Metro North railroad from Manhattan. Some of the more popular include trips in Tivoli Bays, 90 miles north of New York with views of the Catskills' high peaks; Catskill, where you can launch from Dutchman's Landing to paddle to Rogers Island and the Hudson-Athens Lighthouse; and riverside camping at Mills-Norrie State Park, 4 miles north of Hyde Park, for excursions to Esopus Lighthouse and Island.

For the latter, look for the Norrie Point State Park sign on NY 9 in the village of Staatsburg, 9 miles north of Poughkeepsie. The state launch is on the north side of the Indian Kill River, where HRWA has built a boat rack for paddlers. Contact Mills-Norrie State Park, Rte. 9, Hyde Park, NY 12538; (914) 889-4646 or call the NY State Parks Reservation system at (800) 456-CAMP.

Charts

You can buy NOAA charts at most local marine stores. New York Nautical in New York has charts for all of New York as well as places all around the world (see Appendix A).

For the Hudson River, NOAA Chart #12343 covers the lower Hudson, #12347 the middle Hudson, and #12348 the upper Hudson. NOAA #12327 covers New York Bay. Waterproof Chart #57 covers the Hudson River and #62 covers New York.

For most of Long Island's south shore, use NOAA #12352 and for Peconic and Gardiners Bays, NOAA #12354. For the northwestern Long Island Shore, use NOAA #12364. The latter two are useful for Long Island Sound crossings.

Safety

When in Manhattan, you are paddling in one of the country's busiest harbors, and your major concern is large boat traffic—barges, container ships, freighters, ferries and tugboats. Stay out of major channels. Use a marine navigation chart to identify them, and make crossings swiftly, in a group (don't get strung out), and at a right angle. Look behind you at regular intervals to see what is coming that you might not be able to hear. Captains of large freighters and barges can't see you and even if they could, would not be able to stop or avoid hitting you. Be prepared to pull over or to wait to see where a freighter is headed before you cross.

Remember the rule of Red Right Returning: Boats returning to the harbor, or going upstream, keep red buoys to their right (starboard) and green buoys to their left (port).

Bill and Janice Lozano of Atlantic Kayak Tours regularly take clients into New York Harbor without incident, but they know every single schedule and path of the six ferry lines in the bay and what the tide is doing. Ferry slips are active from the Staten Island and Governor's Island ferries. You have a 10-minute window in which to cross the ferry path.

"New York Harbor is a very intense place, but if you live in the city and buy a boat, that's where you're going to go," says Bill. The harbor has lots of confused waves bounding off vertical seawalls. The water is almost always bouncy and full of undulations.

Do not cross a ferry landing when a ferry is approaching or leaving. If you see a ferry heading for a berth, wait for it to dock. It travels very fast. Be aware of large wakes and of ferry washes, which create strong eddies that can easily tip a kayak over if you don't lean away from the eddy line. Also watch out for submerged pilings of derelict docks; there are many of these in the harbor.

The good thing about paddling in a settled area with a folding kayak is if conditions get rough, you can pull out, fold up your kayak, and take a taxi home. (It's a good idea always to carry taxi money.)

At night, Manhattan lights up and is very appealing to paddle around. Groups often launch from South Street Seaport. However, more than one kayaker has had a confrontation with an unlit garbage barge. At night, look for two (or three) yellow lights over one another: That's a tug pulling or pushing a barge. By law, you must show a white light to all approaching boats at night. A head-lamp qualifies, but you might want to attach a lightstick to your stern to help others see you.

Eldridge Tide and Pilot Book, published annually, has detailed diagrams of New York Bay currents and complete tables of daily current predictions for Hell Gate at Mill Rock on the East River in Manhattan and The Narrows in New York Harbor, and is well worth consulting before a harbor cruise.

The 310-mile-long Hudson River is tidal as far as Troy, about 150 miles from its mouth, and has very strong currents, so it's best to time your trips with the ebb and flood of those currents. *Eldridge* provides times of current change at various points from New York Harbor north to West Point based on The Narrows. For points above West Point, consult *Hudson River Tides and Currents.* See the discussion of the Hell Gate and tip of Lower Manhattan below. The currents are affected by winds, heavy rains, and spring run-off. In the spring, generally the ebb current is much stronger than that indicated on the tables. The river floods for five hours and ebbs for seven hours, according to the *Hudson River Waterway Guide.*

On Long Island, the major safety concern is narrow inlets between barrier beaches on the south shore. Here an ebb tide can sweep you out an inlet, and if you have opposing wind and tide, you get immense standing waves. This is also true in areas in Peconic Bay and in Plum Gut at Orient Point. In south shore beach launchings and landings, you may have to contend with steep and powerful surf.

Trip Planning

The following trips range from 4.5 miles to 33 miles and can be handled by beginners in benign conditions except the Manhattan trip, which is very long for someone not used to sitting in a kayak for ten hours. On all trips, winds will greatly alter the conditions you find, from millpond to raging, capsizing seas.

With the exception of Fire Island, which allows primitive camping in its wilderness area, all are day trips due to lack of water-side camping facilities. That is not to say that kayakers don't extend their trips. Many cruise around Shelter Island and the Peconic Bays for a few days or more. Bob Huszar made a twenty-one-day journey up the Hudson River, overnighting where he could. The rule in those cases is to practice low-impact camping and always check with owners of private land before camping there.

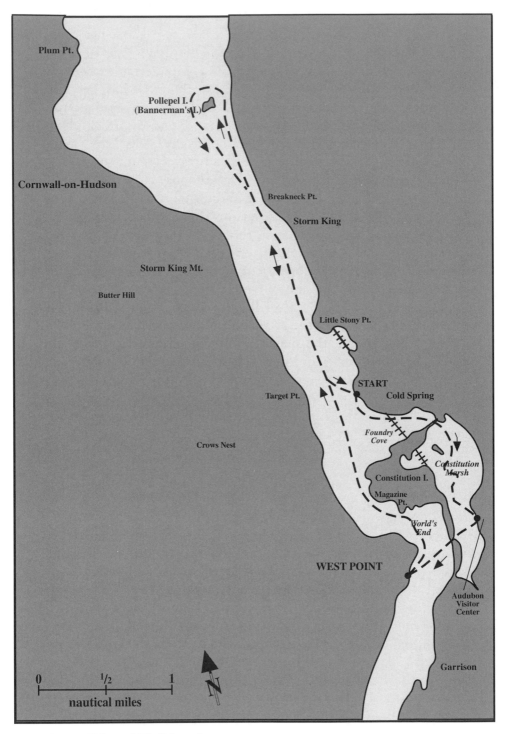

Plum Pt.

Pollepel I.
(Bannerman's I.)

Cornwall-on-Hudson

Breakneck Pt.

Storm King

Storm King Mt.

Butter Hill

Little Stony Pt.

START

Target Pt.

Cold Spring

Foundry
Cove

Crows Nest

Constitution
Marsh

Constitution I.

Magazine
Pt.

World's
End

WEST POINT

Audubon
Visitor
Center

Garrison

0   ½   1

nautical miles

N

Hudson River Highlands

Hudson River: Goblin-filled Hudson Highlands

Charts: NOAA Chart #12343, Middle Hudson River

Trip Mileage: 9.5 nautical miles

Getting There: From the north, from U.S. 84, take NY 9 south to Cold Spring. Turn right onto NY 301/Main Street to the village of Cold Spring. Follow Main Street toward the river. Turn left onto Lunn Terrace just before iron fence that separates Main Street from the railroad. Follow road over bridge. Bear right (arrow on sign, "To River"). Go straight. Turn toward the river at stop sign. Follow Main Street to gazebo (Hudson House is on the right).

By train: Metro North Railway Station at Cold Spring. From the train station, walk down the short dirt road to left of the Chapel of Our Lady of Restoration. It leads to a mud and gravel put-in not far from the gazebo.

Alternate launches: From West Point, take NY 9W to Highland Falls, then turn at the United States Military Academy main gate to South Dock Road. Launch sites can also be found in Newburgh or Beacon, Cornwall-on-Hudson, and Little Stony Point.

Camping: Iona Island, seven miles south of Cold Spring and just south of the Bear Mountain Bridge on the river's east side. Camping is limited to the Hudson River Waterway Association site, marked by a sign, just north of Round Island. Access is from a small beach at the southeast end. Camp in the grassy area between the road and seawall or up on the hill just slightly to the west and above the road. Drinkable water is available at east end of island from a pipe marked "potable water" (on road, north of buildings). Porta-johns are located just north of the camp site.

Tidal Range: 2.8 feet at West Point

Caution Areas: At World's End, just south of Constitution Island, the Hudson River, 1 mile wide just above in Newburgh Bay, funnels into a narrow passage, the current speeds up, and you can't see northward around the corner to oncoming traffic.

The Hudson Highlands is a beautiful spot on the Hudson River, romanticized by the Hudson River School painters, celebrated by the Knickerbocker writers, and pursued by health-spa seekers and millionaires. Here the river has pressed through several high bluffs of the Appalachian mountain range, creating the deepest point in the river (175 feet) at World's End. You glide below steep, rugged cliffs of gneiss and granite, some of the most ancient rocks in this region. You paddle through the splendid Constitution Marsh, by West Point Military Academy, and up to the strange Bannerman's Island. Always, you experience a mixture of the picturesque and the rugged.

Start from Cold Spring, about 50 miles north of Manhattan. Here the Hudson is still tidal, so time your trip with the ebb and flow. At slack tide, the current is still, and at flood tide, the tide overtakes the current so that the current actually reverses. Consult your weather radio or *Hudson River Tides and Currents*.

Cold Spring is a pretty nineteenth-century village that slopes down to the river. The town got its name during the Revolutionary War when on a visit to his troops, George Washington stopped here for a drink at the spring and so named the town. The spring is

A lazy meander through Constitution Marsh, near the Hudson River, yields a wealth of wildlife activity, particularly at sunrise.

marked by a sign next to the Cold Spring Depot restaurant, which overlooks the railroad tracks.

The West Point Foundry, which manufactured armaments including the famous Parrott Cannon for the Union Army during the Civil War, operated in Cold Spring from 1818 to 1911. The Foundry smelted iron from ore found in the nearby hills, and for its workers built cottages that still line the village streets.

Main Street has a variety of shops, including antiques, crafts, galleries, delis, ice-cream parlors—even a clock repair shop and doll hospital—as well as restaurants, small inns, and B & Bs. Manitou Realty invites customers in with a sign, "See us about other Hudson River Castles and Mansions"—a reminder of the mansions built in the surrounding hills by New York millionaires.

Main Street ends at the river (after a jog over the railroad bridge) and the public boat launch is located on a beach just south of the gazebo, across the street from the Hudson House, a handsome B & B and restaurant with an inviting porch overlooking the river. You can park along the street here.

Put in at the gazebo and paddle south past the Cold Spring Boat Club and the Chapel of Our Lady Restoration Church, a Greek Revival chapel built in 1834 for the Catholic workers of the West Point Foundry. Perched on a promontory with dozens of swans swimming below, it is evocative of a Victorian landscaper's fantasy. Paddle under the railroad trestle into Foundry Cove. Bear right into Constitution Marsh, a National Audubon Society Wildlife Sanctuary.

The 160-acre Constitution Marsh is one of five large, productive marshes left on the Hudson, and like the others, helps "keeps things working," according to the sanctuary manager, James Rod. The marsh pumps thousands of pounds of detritus into the river and provides nursery grounds for shrimp, crabs, and other small fauna that many of the Hudson's 204 species of fish feed off, says Rod. As a result, the water appears to be dark brown "beef bouillon."

In a 1990s drama of nature versus industry, however, the Environmental Protection Agency (EPA) has targeted Foundry Cove as a Superfund site, slated for clean-up after several decades of dumping by the nearby, federally funded Marathon Battery Factory. At this writing, EPA had dredged 14 acres in a 30-acre hot spot of cadmium and nickel settled on the cove's muddy bottom. The spot is located below an offending outfall pipe and was considered one of the world's most heavily polluted cadmium sites. EPA had planned to complete the project by summer of 1994. Until that time, EPA has closed Foundry Cove to boaters.

Constitution Marsh is a tidal marsh, ranging from freshwater to brackish. It is a critical habitat for fish, crabs, muskrats, turtles, wrens, herons, egrets, osprey, swallow, and water fowl. Cattails, arrow arum, and arrowhead dominate the marsh, and bird life is abundant (paddle here at dawn for the greatest variety). A favorite is the marsh wren, identifiable not by sight (it tends to hide in the cattails) but by sound—a "liquid gurgling sound ending in a mechanical chatter," according to *The Audubon Society Field Guide to North American Birds*. Like most wrens, these build "dummy" nests, often hidden in dense marsh grass. Look also for the most unusual visitors, the Virginia rails and least bitterns, which are easier to see at low tide, according to Rod.

One of the best times to visit the marsh is in the fall when 50,000 to 100,000 swallows swoop around about fifteen minutes before sunset then roost in the cattails. The most common are tree and barn swallows but you will also see cliff, bank, and rough-wing swallows.

The marsh is almost a mile long, with several channels branching off at right angles from the main, straight channel. Henry Warner dug the channels in 1837 in an ambitious project to turn the marsh into a wild rice farm. He couldn't keep the cattails at bay, however, and abandoned the plan even though some of his wild rice is still growing today.

The channels have stayed open for 150 years because they are 5 feet deep at high tide. At low tide, the marsh empties, so be sure to get out at least one hour on either side of low tide.

Chinese carp thrash in the weeds of Foundry Cove. The species that was introduced in 1870 as a food fish has now multiplied to nuisance levels. When spawning, they rout around disturbing the sediment, which kills the growth of aquatic vegetation. Also, a kayak paddle may crunch on what seems to be a rock. More likely, it's one of the hundreds of snapping turtles that live in the marsh. The snappers are mostly vegetarian, much too slow to rely on a fish diet, and are primarily scavengers for the remaining part of their diet. Be careful, though; they can be vicious when provoked (this happands most often when they are on land rather than in the water) and have powerful jaws and a dangerous bite.

Follow the main current until you reach the straight, long channel. Go to the end and turn left (west), then immediately right (south) and come out at the east end of the dyke. Paddle west to the opposite shore, follow the shoreline until you spy Indian Brook. Turn left (west) up the brook. Pull up your boat and hike up to Constitution Marsh's Visitor Center, which has several good exhibits on local flora and fauna. Hike up the hill and over to the boardwalk for a great view of the marsh. The Hudson's water quality is improving all the time, so the middle Hudson is a pleasant place to paddle. It's even swimmable, like much of the rest of the Hudson, because no sewage treatment is released into the water. According to Jim Rod, forty to fifty years ago fish would run into the Albany pool and die. Now many of the fish stocks are on the rise. SAV (submerged aquatic vegetation)-covered tidal flats provide underwater jungles for the little stripers and shad when they swim up the river to spawn. They also feed on the algae that grows on SAV. The larger fish have no big marine predators but tons of food.

The Hudson is the only major North American estuarine river that has not lost its native stocks of fish. Hudson is now producing 75 percent of all of North America's striped bass (even though the commercial bass fishery has been shut down). There's still room for improvement, however. The Department of Environmental Conservation puts out advisories for which fish are safe to eat, which excludes any fish that spends its entire life in the river.

Several other factors contribute to the Hudson's overall health. The Hudson's limestone bed buffers acid rain, causing less distress to the river ecosystem so dramatic drops in pH do not occur even if a pulse of acid rain hits the river. The river banks are well forested, so run-off from farms and nonsource pollution are minimal.

The Hudson's mixture of fresh and saltwater make the river an estuary. As the flow drops throughout the summer, the saltwater advances farther north bringing the blue crabs with it all the way to

Albany. These are just some of the dynamics of the Hudson River, many of which are explained at the visitor center.

After a hike in the sanctuary, head west toward the railroad trestle on the south end of the marsh. You may be able to paddle under the bridge toward the low end of the tide. Otherwise, portage over the railroad tracks just to the south side of the bridge. Watch in both directions for frequent, fast trains.

Paddle over to West Point. A public launch spot is located just below the south end of the huge, castle-like structure across from a green corrugated building. Here you will find picnic tables and a public rest room. After a rest, paddle back across the river to Constitution Island, site of Fort Constitution during the Revolutionary War. The Revolutionary Army built a steel chain across the river here from West Point to deter British war ships. It's now owned by West Point, which offers tours to the public.

Now you're at World's End, where you get a full sense of the conditions that made the Highlands so feared by colonial sailors: whirlwinds, unpredictable currents, changing weather, tidal action as the Hudson narrows and forces itself through the gorge. These conditions led to much folklore such as that recounted by Washington Irving in the legend of *The Storm Ship:* a little bulbous-nosed Dutch goblin with a speaking trumpet in his hand gives orders for fresh gusts of wind in the midst of stormy weather. He is followed by little imps who tumble head over heels down Thunder Mountain, signaling the worst of the storm. The goblin's jurisdiction ended at Pollepel (otherwise known as Bannerman's) Island.

Then paddle along the east shore of the Hudson, past Cold Spring. Just around the corner at Little Stony Point is a public beach where you can stop for lunch. You will probably share it with many powerboaters, particularly on the weekend. Just north of Little Stony Point is another public launch spot. Pass by Breakneck Point, just below Breakneck Ridge (1,196 feet high), a height with the most improbably placed graffiti.

Next head for Pollepel (Bannerman's) Island in Newburgh Bay. You'll pass The Catskill Aqueduct stone building (built to cover a manhole over the aqueduct that went under the Hudson River, and then through a mile-long tunnel under the mountains,

an amazing feat when it was engineered in 1912 to bring water to
New York City).

Bannerman's Island is the site of a structure that resembles a
red sandstone Indian palace but was in fact a munitions factory,
built by arms dealer Francis Bannerman in 1908 to hold his arsenal
of second-hand military equipment. The castle held his stores until
1920 when it exploded. Landing is not allowed because of unex-
ploded munitions.

As you turn south again, expect a shift in current and tide.
Enjoy the view of Storm King Mountain (1,355 feet) and at the
south end Crows Nest (1,403 feet) at the Northern Gate, the
favorite view of the Hudson River painters. Here, you can contem-
plate the seventeen-year-old ordeal of Storm King's proposed
hydroelectric project. It started in 1962 when Con Edison decided
to blast a part of Storm King Mountain to build a pumping storage
plant to cover peak-use electricity needs of the growing New York

*Storm King Mountain provides a dramatic backdrop for the ruins of
Bannerman's Castle.*

metropolis. Nationwide public protest and a band of conservation-
ists finally won the fight to save Storm King.

After paddling, you have several options. You can go in style
and eat on the porch of the Hudson House overlooking the river
(hamburgers run $6 at lunchtime) or for a large group try the
Cold Spring Depot. Karen's Kitchen is also recommended. Main
Street also has several pizzerias, delis, and ice-cream parlors so you
have a wide choice. The Salgamundi Book Store on Main Street
has a good selection of books about the Hudson River. You can also
see some of the Hudson River School paintings on view at the But-
terfield Memorial Library.

Cold Spring has several B & Bs and small hotels, none of
which is inexpensive. The historic Hudson House (914-265-9355) is
a handsome inn right on the river. In town are the Olde Post Inn
(914-265-2510) built in 1820 and Pig Hill Inn (914-265-9247),
located above an antique store. Or contact Cold Spring Area
Chamber of Commerce (914-265-9060).

In all, this is a lovely part of the Hudson with easy public
transportation from New York City, welcoming launch spots, spec-
tacular scenery and history, great natural sanctuary, and a charming town, all just 50 miles from Manhattan.

Hudson River: Majestic Palisades from Englewood to Piermont

(Note: This description contributed by Ralph Diaz.)

Charts: NOAA #12343

Trip Mileage: 20-nautical-mile roundtrip, shorter distances possible

Getting There: Launch from Bloomers Beach at north end of Englewood marina, New Jersey, which is accessible from Palisades Interstate Parkway, exit 1. Follow the steep road down to marina. The parking fee is $3, May to October. Restrooms and water are available. Alternate put-in is across the river near the north tip of Manhattan side at Tubby Hook, an official New York City kayak launch site.

Camping: No designated camping areas

Tides and Currents: 7 feet, maximum ebbs average 2.5 knots and flood currents around 2.0 knots, faster in heavy winds.

Caution Areas: Sandy beach put-in turns to mudflats at low tide. There are also submerged pilings from old ferry docks at recreational facilities that once lined shoreline along the cliff's base. Water is shallow on western side as Hudson forms a new delta. Boat wake from barges and speedboats can cause 2 to 3 foot waves as they hit the shallows.

Rarely does a major coastal metropolis find its proud man-made structures outdone by a nearby natural monolith. New York City has its rival in the Palisades, a magnificent 10-mile stretch of massive igneous rock cliffs that reach skyward more than 500 feet above the western bank of the Hudson River within sight of the city's towers.

The Palisades get their name from their characteristic tall columns of rock that the Dutch thought looked like the palisaded walls of Iroquois villages. Targeted for massive quarrying to meet the needs of a booming city, the cliffs were saved from destruction by the action of women's clubs that in 1900 led to the creation of the Palisades Interstate Park Commission.

The Palisades are best viewed from the mile-wide river. Dwarfed by the many-hued cliffs, a paddler can forget the city for awhile, lost in speculation about discoveries made along the way:

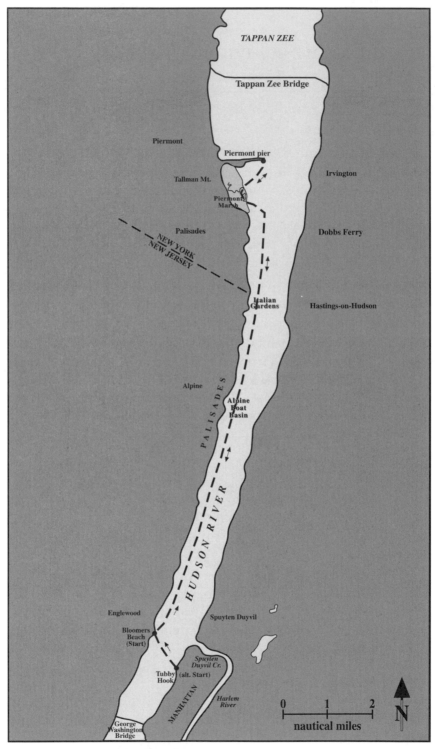

Hudson River Palisades

*The Palisades cliffs reach more than 500 feet skyward above the western bank of the Hudson River./*Photo by Ralph Diaz.

How were these rotting pilings once used? What is that old ruined stone structure? Why this mile-long pier? How were the Palisades themselves formed?

The Palisades formed 195 million years ago, during the last collision of continents. Molten rock pressed upward and cooled under 2,000 feet of crust. Over millions of years, wind and ocean waves removed this blanket, shaped the monolith's face and shaved off 700 feet of height. The final product, a solid diabase rock mass, rests on sandstone that is visible in spots along the river. The formation is an elongated, rectangular "box" 1 mile wide that parallels the river and tilts toward the sea to disappear finally under Staten Island.

While the Palisades parallel the mighty Hudson, the river had little to do with shaping them. In fact, at one point the Hudson ran on their western flank, following what is now the Hackensack River into Newark Bay.

The Hudson is both an estuary and a fiord. An estuary is any river mouth where fresh water meets and mixes with salt water. The Hudson is an estuary 60 miles up, although it is tidal much farther, up to the Troy dam. A fiord is a river, its bed is below sea level, and the banks are mountains. The Hudson is a true fiord in the Hudson Highlands where the banks are mountains for 15 miles, from Anthony's Nose to Storm King. However, it is not a fiord at the Palisades because it has "mountains" only on one side and because the Palisades don't drop straight into the water.

This drowned topography gives the tides great sway over the Hudson. Ocean currents drive well upriver. Even 80 miles north of the city, maximum flood currents average 1.8 knots. The astute paddler can take advantage of such ebbs and floods for a free ride.

The waters are much cleaner now than they were 30 years ago. Environmental laws, on both the federal and state levels, have helped resurrect the river from ecological doom. Fish and fowl are thriving once again. Between fishing forays, cormorants by the dozens now sit on pilings that once supported busy recreational docks. If it weren't for the shifting silt, you would likely be able to see several feet down.

Begin your trip at Bloomers Beach at the Englewood marina. Plan to put in just after flood begins. This will give you a leisurely five hours to make it to Piermont, 11.5 miles north, with exploratory stops along the way. Be conscious of wind. If it is blowing strongly from the north, the wind will wipe out the flood current completely. If it is blowing strongly from the south, you will be hit by strong breaking waves on the way back as wind and current clash.

Within a half-mile of Bloomers Beach, you will find the remains of a stone building fronting a sandy beach. This was once the Undercliff recreational pavilion for a popular swimming beach during the 1920s and 1930s. It was replete with amenities including toilets, changing rooms, a food concession, and even a dance floor. Watch out for pilings from its former dock.

At mile 1.5 you come to Canoe Beach, a north-facing cove. Three quarters of a century ago, on any summer weekend, hundreds of canoes would be pulled up on its shore after crossing the Hudson from Manhattan; the immediate woods would be filled with frolicking picnickers.

As you paddle along, keep looking up at the Palisades. The colors and slices in the rock face depict nature's work. The tall columns were formed when the molten rock of the Palisades was still cooling under the earth. Cuts in the rock and rock slides are recent phenomena caused by the constant freezing and thawing of water in cracks in the rock. Lighter colors show recent split-offs of rock. Darker colors mark older ones where the high iron content of the rocks has rusted. The deep gorges here and there are caused by seismic faults in the earth's crust.

At mile 2.6, you will see one dynamic result of such a fault, Greenbrook Falls. At 300 feet these falls are almost twice as tall as Niagara Falls. While nowhere as powerful, these falls can be stunning after a spring rainfall. Stop and take a look; pull your boat up on the small beach just to the south.

As you proceed, you will come across remains of piers and obvious landings. Many of these predate the park's creation, going back to the time when Dutch farms dotted the foot of the cliffs accessible only from the river. Imagine the farmhouses and their hard-won grain and vegetable plots.

Look north. Up ahead you will see Bombay Hook, a prominent spot high up on the cliffs that looks like a fish hook. Its name comes from the Dutch word for "little tree." The views north are stunning as rows and rows of 500-foot cliffs stretch out to the horizon.

At mile 5 you will reach Alpine Boat Basin. Here you will find the restored Blackledge-Kearney House, built in 1750. Reportedly it was used by General Lord Cornwallis in November 1776. He and 5,000 of his troops made a daring night-time amphibious assault across the river from Dobbs Ferry, 5 miles upstream. As Cornwallis napped, his soldiers hauled cannon and horse up the dock road in an attempt to catch an off-guard General George Washington at Fort Lee, 7 miles downriver. But the rebel general escaped by just fifteen minutes; his capture would have likely ended the war right then and there.

The house is open during the summer weekends, and is well worth visiting since it continuously shows silent films depicting Canoe Beach in its heyday and swimmers and dancers at other recreational facilities along your route. Land your kayak at the beach at the north end of the marina. Water and toilets are available.

Within a mile of Alpine, the shoreline beaches die off and landing becomes more difficult. You'll find more remains of docks but with an exciting new development: the beginning of a return of salt marshes. Salt marshes once lined both sides of the river down to the Battery. They were prime breeding grounds for scores of fish species but disappeared as civilization advanced along the shoreline. At mile 7.5, Forest View, the grandest of the earlier recreational landings, is almost completely taken over by salt marsh. This is another sign of the rebirth of this mighty river.

You will now be off shore of a massive, half-mile wide rock slide caused thousands of years ago. In among the talus lie boulders as big as trucks. At the northern end of the slide, there is a good resting spot at a small beach near a rock marked by the graffiti "Joe." At mile 8.5 you will see a rusting fence that marks the New Jersey/New York border, which is almost the end of this stretch of the park. Just a few hundred yards north are columns and ruins of the Italian Gardens, a summer home built at the turn of the century, where you can view a seasonal waterfall.

Within a mile is Palisades, an exclusive town with no landing permitted. Push on and you soon come on to the beginning of Piermont Marsh at mile 10. The marsh, which survived human intrusion, extends for over a mile along the river. You can explore it through two breaks in the marsh wall. The first, at about Mile 10.5, has numerous meandering channels. Enter only when the tide is on the high side. Be prepared to have to back out of spots since there is little room in which to turn around. The next opening to the marsh is almost at the Piermont pier. This marsh channel meanders into the town of Piermont.

The Piermont pier, a man-made narrow peninsula that juts out a mile into the river, was built in the 1800s. The West Hudson railroad was not chartered to cross the New York/New Jersey border, so the railroad used the pier to transfer its cars onto barges that ferried them down to the city. During World War II, the pier was a major terminus for the movement of troops to Europe. Remains of the barge and ship slips abound these days in twisted steel that dots the waters and shore. You can land but not launch from the pier; a special sticker is required to drive out on to it. This is your turnaround point for catching the ebb current back to Englewood.

Manhattan Circumnavigation: Urban Wilderness

Charts: Waterproof Chart #62 that combines NOAA charts for the main harbor and environs including most of the East and Hudson Rivers, and both the Upper and Lower Bays.

Trip Mileage: 29 nautical miles

Getting There: From I-78 (New Jersey Turnpike), take exit 14B (Liberty State Park) in Jersey City. Turn left after the tollgate and follow signs for Liberty Park. The launch is from a pebble beach at the first parking lot on the right as you enter. You need to park your car in the next parking lot down. Upon return you can paddle right to your car if you're willing to climb over some rocks. An alternate on weekends is to park at the empty factory across the street from the launch site. That way, you can keep on eye on your boat while parking.

Camping: None

Tidal Range: 4.5 feet at the Battery

Caution Areas: Although the whirlpool-filled, boat-eating Hell Gate at Mill Rock on the East River is often considered the most challenging part of the circumnavigation, in fact confused currents and refracting waves around the Battery in lower Manhattan can be more troublesome.

Over the past eighteen years, various clubs have been leading trips around Manhattan for the beginner and intermediate paddler, so this trip has become a yearly institution for the twenty or so boats that participate. Typically the trip starts from a parking lot in Brooklyn, across from lower Manhattan. Some leave from South Street Seaport and paddle over to join those on the Brooklyn side.

You ride the tide up the East River to Hell Gate while the tide is still flooding. You pause at Mill Rock at Hell Gate. You come up through the Harlem River, typically the trip's most sluggish part. You stop at Columbia University's boat house next to Inwood Hill Park, about 17 miles into the trip, and wait for the tide to turn and ride down the Hudson. Under the George Washington Bridge, you raft up by the Little Red Lighthouse, the subject of a well-known children's book. At Forty-second Street, you congregate by the air-

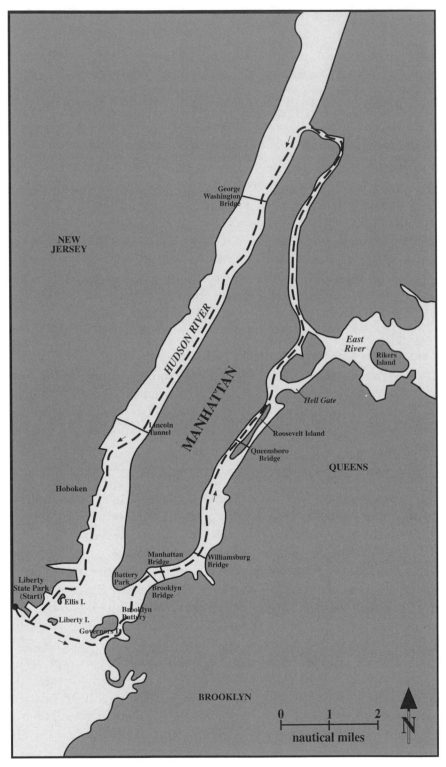

Manhattan Circumnavigation

The group paddles by the skyscrapers of lower Manhattan on their way to the Brooklyn Bridge.

craft carrier *USS Intrepid*. A strong southwesterly wind will make paddling down the Hudson tiring. You've spent nearly ten hours in a boat. At this point, you can opt to paddle to the Statue of Liberty, about 2 or 3 miles. Or you can continue around the toe of Manhattan back to South Street Seaport or Brooklyn.

I accompanied the Metropolitan Association of Sea Kayakers on a spring circumnavigation of Manhattan. The trip averages ten hours with only two breaks, at Mill Rock and Columbia. You can always expect something unusual, such as a hailstorm or heat thunder. There's always something to talk about, but the aim is to have a good trip and to learn about the harbor.

New York Harbor has 750 miles of shoreline with docking space for more than 250 ships. It is said that an ocean-going vessel enters or leaves the port every 28 minutes, so this is an extremely busy place to paddle.

Liberty State Park on the New Jersey side is a good place to launch to see the Statue of Liberty at the trip's start. We paddled from the launch along a long slip and into what is known as the Upper Bay (the Lower Bay lies south of the narrows crossed by the Verrazano Bridge) and headed directly to the south side of the

The Statue of Liberty provides a dramatic backdrop to a New York Harbor paddle.

Statue of Liberty. She faces away from the harbor as if still welcoming the twelve million immigrants who passed through nearby Ellis Island to the United States. We followed the channel markers, because little boat traffic was about, but it's possible to stay out of the channel. Typically, this is a bumpy ride across the Upper Bay to Governors Island, with many waves bouncing off seawalls and confusing wakes.

We passed between Governors Island (a military reservation with two forts) and Brooklyn through the Buttermilk Channel into the East River. Here I tried to cross the East River from Brooklyn to the South Street Seaport Museum to see the 100-year-old *Lettie G. Howard*, one of the last Gloucester fishing schooners. It is docked among one of the largest fleets of historic ships in the world, including the four-masted bark *Peking* built in 1911, and the iron-hulled, full-rigged *Wavetree* built in 1885. So swift was the current that I passed South Street on my ferry across, and with 23 miles to go, I didn't paddle back to it.

The trip is long but passes quickly when the tide is with you. You feel like you are zooming by the shore most of the way. Currents run swiftly, particularly in the East River—up to 3.5 knots just north of the Battery at South Street Seaport and at Roosevelt

Island, where the river constricts into two narrow passages around the island. The mile-wide Hudson has uniform currents that reach 2.8 knots. Only the Harlem River tends to be sluggish. In short, this is a fast trip in which you cover a lot of distance.

We had the tide with us the whole trip, thanks to the planning of leader John Rashak. The group of fifteen boats stayed together until the George Washington Bridge on the Hudson River when wind and fatigue caused us to string out.

To lend some historical perspective to the trip: William Shurcliff, a physicist from Cambridge, Massachusetts, made a 29-mile solo circumnavigation of Manhattan in 1935. He started from a "mudbank beside a disreputable pier on the New Jersey shore of the Hudson River," and paddled his two-person kayak across the Hudson to the lower tip of Manhattan, then turned north up the East River. "Here the swift current was with me, and I progressed one city block each 17 seconds. Arriving at the Harlem River, I was staggered to find the swift current to be against me—and further staggered on discovering that this river was much more than 100 blocks long, a long way to go against such a current. (Fortunately, this kayak, 25 ft. long and only 19 inches wide, was fast - perhaps the world's fastest kayak). Arriving, tired, at the Hudson River, I found that here too, the current was against me. Making my way to the George Washington Bridge was a long struggle, as was the final leg of the trip back to the starting point, where I had parked my car." Amazingly, even with the tides against him, Shurcliff made the trip nonstop in seven hours.

New York City has turned its back to the water with seawalls, bulwarks, and apartment buildings that drop right into the river. Riverside parks, walkways, and marinas are limited. The situation is a little better on the Hudson side with Riverside Park, but generally the city doesn't encourage casual interaction between river and city on a human level.

You get your bearings not by buoys but by skyscrapers: the Empire State Building (34th Street), third-tallest building in the world; the Chrysler Building (East 43rd Street), its top reminiscent of the 1929 Chrysler radiator cap; the octagonal MetLife Building (the former Pan Am Building on East 44th Street), one of the largest civilian office buildings in the world (50 acres of offices);

*Venerable stone-and-steel bridges span the Harlem River./*Photo by David Eden.

the Citicorp Building (54th Street), with its sloping crown; and the 110-story-high Twin Towers of the World Trade Center (second tallest in the world). Even from the water, your senses are assaulted by the city: screeching car brakes, the acrid smell of river water, the sudden appearance of the Circle Line or a barge.

You pass under seventeen bridges, but my favorite is the mile-long Brooklyn Bridge, second-oldest bridge in the city (1883) after the Harlem River's High Bridge. You can paddle right by either one of its two massive masonry towers and admire the network of huge cables draped between them.

On our trip, after passing under the Brooklyn Bridge, we floated by the United Nations and toward Roosevelt Island (called Welfare Island more than thirty years ago, when it was the site of four city hospitals). Roosevelt Island is now occupied by a huge apartment complex reached by aerial tramway. There's a lighthouse at the north end and the shell of one of the hospitals at the south end. The current runs very fast, and a confrontation with a couple of barges and a confused slop of waves reflecting off the bulkheads at the northern tip of Roosevelt led one of our trip members to remark, "Was that the Hell Gate?"

By contrast, the mouth of Hell Gate, about 10 miles from Liberty State Park, was anticlimactic. Nearly one hundred years ago, the Hell Gate was a twisting, rocky, treacherous channel, where

Long Island Sound's waters constricted into the East River. Through dredging and landfill, it has become less dangerous. The "shallows" are 4 feet deep at low tide, but the current is still strong creating whirlpools and riptides. Maximum current is about 6 knots, producing standing waves 1.5 feet high, but there's a way around them. (The nightmare about getting swept down the East River past City Island out Long Island Sound doesn't exist.)

It's best to aim to reach Hell Gate while the tide is still flooding. Slack tide (weak current) has a small window of thirteen to twenty-two minutes depending on velocity (see *Eldridge*). We went through at just about slack and had our bows pushed around a bit by whirlpools. We sat on Mill Rock (best landing is on the rocky beach on the north side) for about a half hour to wait for the turn of the tide up the Harlem River. Sometimes paddlers wait longer, and sometimes people choose to battle the ebb tide anyway.

After steady progress up the Harlem River, passing under some scenic bridges, we stopped for lunch at Columbia University's boathouse, about 17 miles from the put-in and a little more than half way. You can land at the floats and use the restrooms in the boathouse.

After an hour's rest, we reentered our kayaks and continued the short distance up the rest of the Harlem River. We passed under the Spuyten Duyvil ("spitting devil") railroad bridge, so named by the Dutch for the fast tides, and into the wide Hudson River with a grand view of the Palisades. Under the George Washington Bridge and past the little red lighthouse, out into the middle to follow the swiftest current, down to the *Intrepid* on the West Side, and across to New Jersey in some increasingly turbulent water, those still feeling fit made a break for the finish while others took a more leisurely pace. We paddled by Ellis Island, made the critical right-hand turn to return directly to Liberty State Park instead of going south of the Statue of Liberty. Ten hours after launch, we landed with spaghetti legs.

It's best to do this trip with paddlers who know the area well. The Metropolitan Canoe and Kayak Club and the Metropolitan Association of Sea Kayakers lead trips around Manhattan in summer. The Sebago Canoe Club holds the Hell Gate Hop for experienced paddlers only in the early fall.

Long Island

The poet Walt Whitman never lost his lifelong yearning to return to his birthplace in Huntington. He called Long Island "fish-shaped Paumanok." The 120-mile-long fish tilts southwest, the snout pokes into New York Harbor at Brooklyn to the east, and the fintails open up into Gardiners Bay to the west.

Although Whitman would be horrified at what has happened to his beloved pine barrens, hills, and shores—Long Island has largely been dredged and paved over by housing developments, shopping centers, and highway—he would still find some wild places to fire a poet's inspiration.

Those spots hearken back to Long Island's native origins when no fewer than thirteen Algonquian tribes farmed its fertile land, hunted abundant wildlife, and caught fish and dug for shellfish by canoe in shallow bays. Names like Massapequa, Patchogue, Shinnecock, and Montauk were the places where those tribes lived. Long Islanders can roll these names off their tongues as easily as names like Westhampton or Riverhead.

Some intrepid kayakers have circumnavigated Long Island's 220-mile coastline averaging 20 to 30 miles a day. First was a group of firemen who made the trip in twelve days. Then came a young man named Thomas Carroll who paddled the trip in eleven days. The journey is a good way to describe the different areas of Long Island to paddle.

Long narrow bays protected by barrier beach form the south coast. You can travel through Great South Bay and Moriches Bay to Shinnecock Bay, nearly the entire southern coast, without having to exit to the Atlantic Ocean through one of its turbulent inlets, which are few and far between. It's 30 miles along the barrier beach from Fire Island Inlet to Moriches Inlet, much of which is Fire Island National Seashore. The 7 miles from Watch Hill to Smith Point are a designated wilderness area and constitute a kayaker's paradise for those who make the effort to cross Great Bay to the primitive camp sites along this stretch. This is what Fire Island looked like four hundred years ago to the Algonquian natives.

Out east, Shinnecock Inlet is nothing short of ferocious, with strong tides and steep standing waves. Kayakers are advised to stay close to the inlet's west shore when crossing.

In the Hamptons, enclaves of summering New Yorkers, beach clubs, and restaurants overshadow the humble history of the early colonists who were fishermen, farmers, whalers, and tradesman. At the tip of the southern fork is Montauk and its fabulous high bluffs ending at the brown and white Montauk Lighthouse. Montauk is a great surfing and fishing spot, and people have spotted great white sharks off the point.

The fintails of fish-shaped Paumanok open up into Gardiners Bay, 19 miles from the South Fork at Shagwong Point to the North Fork at Orient Point. In the middle lies Gardiners Island, 9 nautical miles offshore, privately owned by the same family since the 1600s. It is a destination only for the most hardy because of the open-water crossing and the fact that no landing is allowed. Westward is Shelter Island, then Little and Great Peconic bays divided by the jewel of the Peconics, Robins Island.

It's a rough 7-mile crossing from Gardiners Island to Orient Point owing to the currents of Plum Gut, which separates Orient Point and Plum Island and links Gardiners Bay to Long Island Sound. Plum Gut is a deep open-water channel that runs more than 4 knots, causing fierce riptides. The Cross Sound Ferry arrives from New London, Connecticut at Orient Point.

To the east of Plum Gut lie several small, rocky islands including the very important Great Gull Island. Great Gull has colonies of more than 6,000 pairs of common terns and about 1,200 pairs of roseate terns, the second largest breeding colony of this endangered species in the United States, according to U.S. Fish and Wildlife Service biologists. Fishers Island and Fishers Island Sound lie beyond Great Gull.

At Orient Point, Long Island's north shore begins a long, graceful sweep toward Port Jefferson. The rocky shore with high cliffs are glacial erratics (there is no bedrock exposed on Long Island) and are quite a contrast from the South Shore's long, flat, sandy beaches.

The widest part of Long Island Sound occurs at Wading River, 30 miles across water from New Haven, Connecticut. Farther west, the sound is 18 miles across, from Port Jefferson to Bridgeport, Connecticut. You can cross here and take the ferry back. Deeply indented bays with high hills lie beyond Port Jefferson. Rocky headlands alternate with sandy beaches in shallow bays, and sandy areas expose boat-crunching rocks at low tide. A popular paddling spot is Stony Brook (Stony Brook University is the site of an active sea-kayak education program).

Continuing your theoretical trip, you cross the wide Smithtown Bay to Eatons Neck and the Three Harbors area—Lloyd Harbor, Cold Spring Harbor, and Oyster Bay. You can go from Lloyd Harbor to Cold Spring Harbor without paddling the 5 miles around Lloyd Neck by carrying your kayak over the causeway at West Neck. The Three Harbors area is an important spot for wintering and migrating sea ducks. Here are some of your shortest paddling stretches across Long Island Sound, such as from Glen Cove to Mamaroneck—4 miles.

To finish the circumnavigation you pass the deep indentations at Glen Cove, Great Neck, and Little Neck to the Throggs Neck Bridge, which marks the end of the sound and the start of the East River, which then carries you via the Hell Gate to Manhattan and to New York's Upper Bay.

Kayakers should be aware of water-temperature variations in the area. Although Long Island waters are blocked from the full benefit of the warm Gulf Stream by the "cold wall" of the the Labrador Current, enough mixing occurs to warm the frigid New England waters. On the southern coast, a weather shift can push the warmer waters offshore. (The water off Fire Island can drop to 60 degrees on a hot day in August.)

Public Access

Town beaches, village beaches, hidden beaches, ocean beaches, bay beaches—there's a great variety on Long Island, but most require parking permits issued either from the town or the county. (The fine for illegal parking here averages $50.)

The nicer the place, the harder it is to find public launching on Long Island. Still, a few spots offer public access even if you don't have a resident sticker or are unwilling to pay $35 to launch your boat. (These spots are listed below in the trips described.) You can also get local launch information through clubs, and launching is generally more convenient during the off-season, from September to May. Some beaches that allow off-road vehicles (ORVs) provide ample space to park and opportunities to launch. The New York Department of Environmental Conservation provides some launch sites such as the one at Moriches Bay (see below).

Camping

For state parks throughout Long Island, call the New York State Parks Reservation System at 800-465-CAMP. Hither Hills State Park, located on Old Montauk Highway in Montauk, has oceanside campsites, but they're difficult to book in summer. The state won't book sites more than ninety days in advance. If you call 800-465-CAMP around 8 A.M., you should be able to get a booking for ninety days from the date you call. Spaces are available on shorter notice from September through November.

On the South Shore, primitive camping is allowed in Fire Island National Seashore's wilderness area (see below for details). On Eastern Long Island, the county has four campsites between Riverhead and Montauk; however, these are sometimes reserved for county residents only. The sites include Indian Island in Riverhead, Sears Bellows in Hampton Bays, Cedar Point County Park in East Hampton, and Montauk County Park in Montauk (four-wheel drive vehicle needed).

Surfing

Eastern Long Island has some excellent surf spots, including Ditch Plains off Montauk, which has an outside break on a rock reef, giving consistent waves. Other good spots are Ponquogue Beach just outside Hampton Bays, Moriches and Little Pike Inlets in Moriches Bay and Shinnecock Inlet in Shinnecock Bay. For more information on Eastern Long Island surfing, contact Lars Svanberg at Main Beach Surf & Sport in Wainscott (see Appendix A). For a daily beach and surf report, call 516-537-SURF.

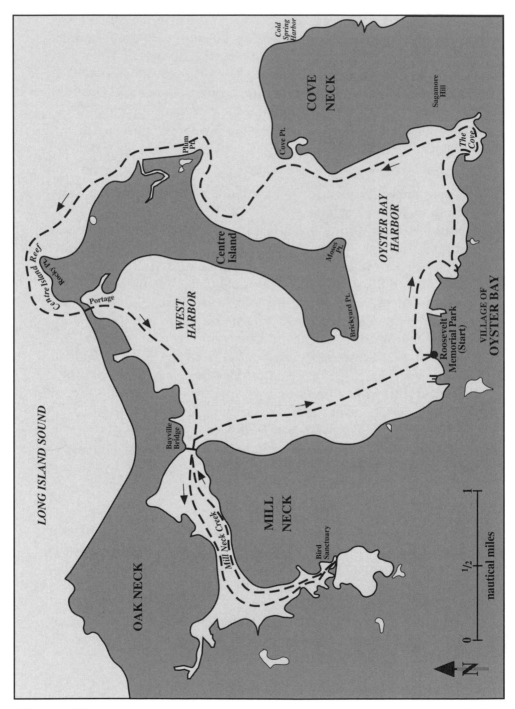

Oyster Bay

Oyster Bay: Paddling Under Sagamore Hill

Charts: NOAA #12365

Trip Mileage: 9 nautical miles; 13 nautical miles with a trip into Mill Neck Creek

Getting There: From the Long Island Expressway, take exit 41N to NY 106 North, into Oyster Bay. Follow South Street to West Main Street. Turn left. Follow West Main to Larrabee Avenue. Turn right. Go to the end, cross the railroad tracks at Shore Avenue to Roosevelt Memorial Park, owned by the town. Use the pebble beach to the east of the boat ramps. Off-season, there is no charge; in season (Memorial Day to Labor Day) the fee is $7 for a resident and $35 for a nonresident. An alternative is to follow West Main Street past Larrabee Avenue to Bayside Avenue. Turn right. Cross the railroad tracks and turn left at West End Avenue. Park outside the gate. This gives you access to Beekman Beach, where there is no lifeguard or ticket booth.

Camping: None

Tidal Range: 7.2 feet at Oyster Bay Harbor

Caution Areas: Rocky Neck Point has several submerged boulders.

Oyster Bay is located on the western north shore of Long Island, within commuting distance of Manhattan. It provides an interesting variety of environments: dense forest on high bluffs surrounding the bay and marsh, which open to Long Island Sound and sand beaches. Because of the presence of 3,000 acres of Oyster Bay National Wildlife Refuge in the bay, which includes Mill Neck Creek, Oyster Bay has rich wildlife for such a heavily settled area.

A circumnavigation of Centre Island in Oyster Bay is a pleasant three-hour outing. You paddle through the two prongs of Oyster Bay—Oyster Bay Harbor and West Harbor. While gliding under the high, leafy bluffs of the bay (including renowned Sagamore Hill, the home of Theodore Roosevelt) you will see many sleek yachts and a working oyster fleet. Dutch settlers supposedly named Oyster Bay for all the fine oysters they found there in the 1630s and it is still one of the most important oyster-producing waters in New York state. The oysters are generally found in waters greater than 6 feet, and many of those underwater beds are leased for commercial purposes, marked by flagged sticks throughout the bay.

After the American Revolution, Oyster Bay flourished as a farming community, then during the mid-1800s wealthy New Yorkers began to settle here with their families. These new residents built country villas and estates along the shore, so Oyster Bay became known as the Gold Coast. You see many of these mansions as you paddle under the bluffs.

Time your trip to the tides. Follow the outgoing tide out past the Sagamore Yacht Club and a wharf where several oyster-dredging boats are moored. The Oyster Festival is held the first weekend after Columbus Day.

As you continue, you pass a few elaborate private docks including one where a Chesapeake Bay oyster skipjack is moored. Paddle into The Cove and along Cove Neck under Sagamore Hill, where from 1901 to 1909 Theodore Roosevelt established the summer White House. Roosevelt used to row around Oyster Bay in a skiff for

Passing the Sagamore Yacht Club on the way toward Sagamore Hill.

relaxation and enjoyment either alone or with his wife. You can see his on-water photos at the Sagamore Hill National Park, 1.5 miles out of Oyster Bay Village. The federal government has just completed a thorough renovation of the Victorian mansion and grounds, and hours are 9:30 A.M. to 5 P.M. Grounds close at dusk.

Cross the harbor over to the Seawanhaka Corinthian Yacht Club, said to be the second-oldest yacht club on Long Island. Cold Spring Harbor veers off to the north, and if you care to extend your trip, a paddle into this lovely harbor is worthwhile. Cold Spring was once a major whaling port. From 1836 to 1862, it supported a nine-boat whaling fleet that sailed all over the world.

At Rocky Point, you now have a full view of Long Island Sound. To the north you can see the buildings of Stamford, Connecticut, and Larchmont, New York is right across the water. Watch out for submerged boulders at Rocky Point. Land on the beach on Centre Island just south of the boulders and just beyond the guard house and carry your kayak over the causeway (about 100 yards at mid-tide) into West Harbor. This is a good picnic spot.

Head down West Harbor back to Roosevelt Park or paddle under the Bayville Bridge, marked by white lanterns, into Mill Neck Creek, a protected marshy area with several important species of birds. The embayments around here, including Oyster Bay, have a high concentration of migrating and wintering ducks including greater scaup, black duck, American wigeon, canvasback, red-breasted merganser, common goldeneye, bufflehead, and old-squaw. On your way back you'll pass Nickerson Boat Yard, which used to manufacture tugboats.

All the beaches in this area—Oyster Bay, Bayville, Locust Valley, Glen Cove, and Hempstead—are town beaches and require a parking sticker during the summer. From Labor Day to Memorial Day, however, you are free to park and launch.

Theodore's at 1 East Main Street is a good post-paddle spot in Oyster Bay. The restaurant has a large menu and varied specials. (Roosevelt had the place built in 1903 to serve as summer White House offices.)

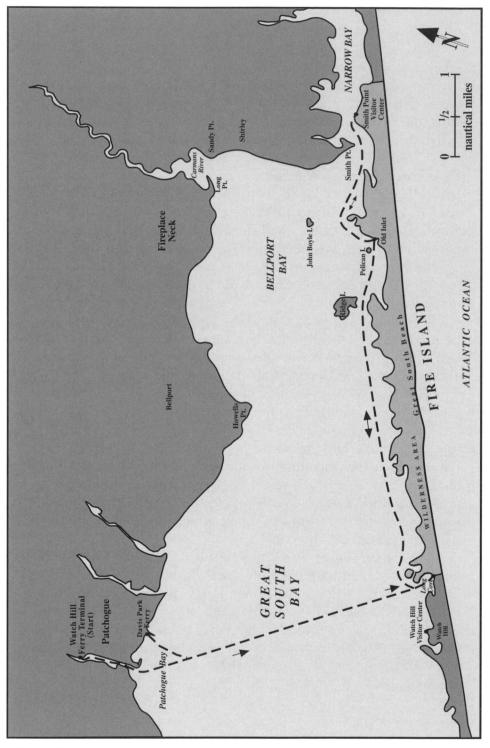

Fire Island

Fire Island: Wild Beach

(**Note:** This description contributed by Ralph Diaz.)

Charts: NOAA Small Craft Chart #12352

Trip Mileage: Wilderness area is 7 miles long between Watch Hill and Smith Point. Crossing of Great South Bay varies from 1 to 4 nautical miles.

Getting There: For leisurely day trips use the Smith Point parking lot (no overnight parking permitted) on the eastern flank of the National Seashore Wilderness Area. The put-in is located at a small beach at the eastern end of the parking lot. You can also paddle across from Patchoque (a four-mile open-water crossing). Leave your car at the Davis Park ferry parking lot (around $12 per day; overnight stays allowed) and put in on a small beach at the north end of the marina dock, next to the parking lot. In season (May through October), you can park free at the National Seashore Watch Hill ferry terminal (overnight parking permitted), but the put-in is tricky here, and you may want to shuttle a car to the marina at the foot of South Ocean Avenue. A paddle across from other spots on Long Island is possible from waterfront sites, but be careful to observe any local restrictions on overnight street parking if you plan to camp on Fire Island. If you have a folding kayak, you can get to the area by public transportation. The back end of the Long Island Railroad station at Patchogue is located a few hundred feet from the Watch Hill ferry. Cross on the ferry and assemble your boat at Watch Hill.

Camping: Camping in the wilderness area requires a backcountry permit. There are limits on numbers of campers and locations of campsites. To obtain a permit, go either to the Visitors Center Station at Smith Point (516-281-3010) or the Fire Island National Seashore office in Patchogue (120 Laurel Street, Patchogue, NY 11772; 516-289-4810). Camping is also available at the public campground at Watch Hill (May through October). Sites are awarded on a lottery basis arranged prior to the season. However, because of cancellations, you can usually get a site if you just show up.

Tidal Range: 3 feet on the bay side, 5 feet on the ocean side. Currents are below 1 knot except in heavy winds.

Caution Areas: Great South Bay may look benign, but it can turn to a mini-version of the North Sea when heavy winds blow across its shallow waters. Fog can obscure crossings. Extremely heavy pleasure boat traffic, particularly nearer the Long Island shore requires that you stay alert. Keep in mind that Fire Island is heavily infested with ticks that can transmit Lyme disease; you should plan to take necessary precautions (see page xxxi).

The Fire Island National Seashore Wilderness Area offers the paddler a world of splendid isolation just 40 miles from the heart of New York City. It is a treasure trove of shifting dunes and storm-stunted pine forests with wildlife-filled salt marshes on its bay side and pounding surf on its Atlantic Ocean beaches.

An act of Congress in 1980 wrested the 7-mile stretch of shore from Watch Hill on the west to Smith Point on the east from the encroachment of civilization, designating it as wilderness. This part of Fire Island is as different from the well-known beach communities as paddling a canoe or kayak is from running a power launch. The wilderness area, which never did experience extensive development as did other parts of Fire Island, is being allowed to return to a wild state. There are no roads; the only amenities are on its flanks at Watch Hill and Smith Point.

The Wilderness Area is your chance to see nature at work on a compelling phenomenon: barrier beaches, which run roughly parallel to shore and are separated from shore by a body of water such as a bay, lagoon, or marsh. Fire Island is a 50-mile-long barrier island protecting Long Island from the ravages of the Atlantic. It is a dynamic environment that has changed greatly from the time five thousand years ago when sea levels stabilized and the Atlantic reshaped glacial sands and gravel runoff from the Hudson Canyon to form the island.

Every year brings noticeable change. Take Old Inlet, an area about 2 miles west of Smith Point that borders on a fine camping spot among secondary dunes overlooking the bay. It was formed when the legendary hurricane of 1938 filled in an ocean inlet to Great South Bay, thus the name. The same storm also created Moriches Inlet, about 6 miles east of Smith Point. (See the trip on

Moriches Inlet.) In storms in 1992 and 1993, the Old Inlet area was breached once again temporarily. Several hundred feet of 30-foot-high primary dunes were washed out, leaving that part of Fire Island vulnerable to future further intrusion by the sea.

Such displays of raw power will leave you in awe and draw you back to the area again and again. What you will hardly notice, unless you spend a lifetime at it, is the movement of the whole barrier island itself toward Long Island proper. Fire Island is advancing north at a rate that will have it collide with Long Island's south shore within two thousand years.

There is more to see. The marshes and dunes are the playground for many animals. Deer are everywhere. You may surprise them as you land on the bay-side marshes or see their white tails bouncing as they lope away across dunes through pine thickets. Less obvious are the red fox that could poke around your campsite at dusk. Bird life abounds. On the shoreline, you may see herons and egrets as well as tiny sanderlings scurrying about. Mockingbirds, catbirds, and brown thrashers flit among the dunes and forests. In the fall, Fire Island is a time-honored stopover for migratory birds that blanket the bay waters and small forests.

As you roam around the island, you will find some signs of previous human settlement. Before the area was designated a protected wilderness, it was home to fishing and hunting shacks as well as "squatter" vacation retreats during much of this century. Piles of building siding, old water pipes, and electric wires are left behind. Even earlier, this was a haven for pirates; their fires gave the place its name. Captain Kidd frequented Fire Island to bury treasure. (Perhaps a storm will unveil some for you.)

The remnants of what is called the Burma Road lie up the spine of the island. The National Park Service is encouraging its overgrowth and disappearance. Park service vehicles do not use the road, but patrol the dunes and swale by horseback.

Kayaking offers a special perspective in this area. Shallow-draft boats allow you to move quietly along the bay side of the island and into salt marshes along the way. Natural channels and mosquito drainage ditches give access to the marshes. (The drainage ditches were carved out on the mistaken notion that they would drain the marshes and help insect control in preparation for planned development of the area. The ditches are slowly filling in but traces allow you into some otherwise inaccessible areas.) The largest of the marshes is located in the eastern section of the Wilderness Area. Be careful not to get caught "high and muddy" in a receding tide.

The marshes do make it difficult to exit your kayak in many places. You either face poor marshy footing or impenetrable thickets of thorny bushes, spartina grass, and gnarled trees. The landscape is so changeable that access spots come and go. As you paddle, though, you will find some. First look for any of the sandy beaches. Walk along, dropping into a crouch every so often, to locate deer trails. (Deer regularly swim the bay and follow definite paths to favorite berry bushes.) Or follow the mosquito ditches at high tide; they often lead to a way ashore without many obstacles.

If you are stuck for a landing spot, you can paddle to the midway point of the wilderness area. Here you will find about a half-mile wide section that has been "grandfathered" by the 1980 law as a beach for the town of Bellport, across the bay. It is a sandy area with boardwalks. By taking out here, you can roam on foot either

A mosquito ditch leads to a good camping area just west of Old Inlet in the Fire Island National Seashore Wilderness Area./Photo by Ralph Diaz.

into the western or eastern section of the wilderness area. You are not allowed to camp here.

The best camping is located at two areas. The first is in the eastern section of the wilderness, just west of Old Inlet as mentioned earlier. Access is through a mosquito ditch (see photo on page 42). Follow it to a spot where you can get out on to reasonably good footing and then take deer trails through a few feet of berry bushes. Here you will find several sand bowls among the secondary dunes in which to pitch a tent. These will shelter you from the wind and provide great views of the primary dunes and town lights twinkling across the bay. Watch the primary dunes change color throughout the day, with their most striking hues at dusk and dawn. Keep still, and you will soon discover how much bird and animal life is all around you. *One caution:* Be certain to pull your kayak to high ground and tie it to a tree or bush to avoid losing your craft at times of spring tides.

The other good kayak-camping area is in the western section of the Wilderness Area, near Long Cove. Access here is difficult. You have to find one of the few deer trails off the sandy beach through the thicket. Paddling Fire Island tests your skills to move slowly and with open eyes to find these precious cuts. This camping location allows you to pitch your tent among pine trees or up on one of the small secondary dunes in the area. If you have a hankering for civilization, it is only about a 3-mile hike along the beach to the night life at Davis Park.

Whichever camping site you choose, obey all rules regarding the area. Do not walk on the primary dunes. They are fragile and the only line of defense this barrier island has against the harsh sea. Even a quick walk over them will kill some grasses and lead to erosion of an inch or two of sand. That small groove will broaden as the wind blows through and what was a slight indentation can quickly become a foot-deep breach. Of course, do not set open campfires; use a camp stove. Follow all the good common sense on minimal-impact camping, and carry out trash when you leave.

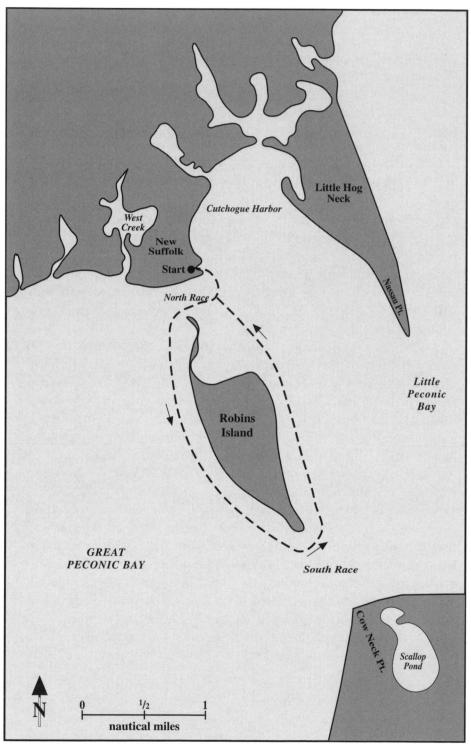

Robins Island

Robins Island Circumnavigation: Jewel of the Peconics

Charts: NOAA #12358 or #12354 Long Island Sound eastern part

Trip Mileage: 6 nautical miles

Getting There: From NY 25, turn right at Mattituck onto New Suffolk Road and go about 3.5 miles to the end (it becomes Main Street). Launch ramp into Cutchogue Harbor in New Suffolk next to the Ho Seafood Shanty and Saloon. Parking is available nearby. An alternate launch is located in West Creek just to the west of New Suffolk.

Camping: Camping is available at Indian Island County Park (516-852-3252) in Riverhead, about 15 miles away. This is a county park, normally reserved for county residents, but the ranger may allow you to camp if space is available. Rates are $16 per night for nonresidents. From the west, take the Long Island Expressway to the end at exit 73. Drive east on NY 58 for 4.5 miles, then turn right (south) onto County Road 105. Watch for the entrance sign.

Tidal Range: 2.6 feet at New Suffolk

Caution Areas: North and South Race, narrow channels off north and south points of the island, can have large standing waves in conditions of opposing wind and tide.

Located in the middle of the North and South forks of Eastern Long Island, Robins Island is a wild, undeveloped island known as the Jewel of the Peconics. Circumnavigating this *jalapeno*-shaped island from Cutchogue Harbor is a leisurely three- or four-hour paddle. The island is privately owned so no landing is allowed.

Robins is a dividing island between Great Peconic Bay to the west and Little Peconic Bay to the east. The island blocks the flow and ebb of the tide so currents at what are known as the North Race and South Race are strong, and you can get large standing waves when the tide is running. This is *not* a place for beginning kayakers. The South Race, about two knots at maximum flood, is stronger with healthy tide rips near nun #26, also marked by a lighted bell. Neither currents are insurmountable, however, but you may want to time your trip so you are paddling around the south end near slack tide, or you can land at the long sand spits off to the north and south spits and carry your kayak over.

It is miraculous that Robins Island has remained totally undeveloped except for the keeper's dock on the north end for so long. The island has naturally nesting osprey, hawks, deer, and fox. A sandy beach rings the island with a wooded interior about fifty feet high. The Indians named the island Anchannock, or "place well wooded." Ruins of an old hunting camp lie in the interior. The camp was established in the 1800s for the shooting of quails, pheasants, and wild turkeys raised on the island.

Much legal wrangling has taken place over Robins' preservation. In the 1980s the Prince of Monaco tried to buy the island as a refuge for a reputed $5 million, but he decided it lacked sufficient privacy. In the winter of 1993-94, Robins finally found a savior when Louis Moore Bacon, a successful Wall Street trader, swiftly bought the 445-acre island for $11 million from the German corporation that had purchased Robins in 1979. So came to an end the longtime conflict between Suffolk County, private developers, and previous owners over the fate of this remarkably undeveloped island. Bacon indicated he planned to work with The Nature Conservancy to preserve the island in a natural state and allow public access while using a portion for a family compound. As of this writing, no public access agreement had been worked out so the old rule of "no landing" still applies.

You have panoramic views up and down both magnificent bays. Until the mid-80s, shellfishing was a multi-million-dollar business for the baymen here, but because of algae blooms (probably due to sewage overflow), the shellfish have all but disappeared. The federal government recently declared Peconic Bay a national estuarine reserve, giving it new credence as an important ecosystem to be studied and preserved.

Even though we are suggesting launching from Cutchogue Harbor on the North Fork, you can launch from either fork. On the South Fork, you will find launch sites at Conscience Point in North Sea Harbor, or North Sea Beach at the end of North Sea Road. After paddling, try the Ho Seafood Shanty and Saloon in New Suffolk on Cutchogue Harbor, right near your launch. It serves fresh Robins Island oysters and local Little Neck clams when available.

Moriches Bay: Atlantic Ocean Has Its Way

Charts: NOAA #12352

Trip Mileage: 5 nautical miles

Getting There: Access is from the parking area next to the Group Moriches Coast Guard Station in East Moriches. If you are coming from the west, turn right off NY 27 onto NY 46, then immediately left on NY 27A, which becomes NY 80. Turn right (south) off NY 80 just after the sign to the Coast Guard Station, onto Atlantic Avenue. Go 1 mile to Moriches Island Road and turn left. Watch for signs for Moriches Bay Waterway Access Site (about 0.5 mile beyond the turn-off). An alternative launch site may be found along Dune Road in Westhampton. This would avoid crossing Moriches Bay.

Camping: None

Tidal Range: 2.9 feet at Moriches Inlet

Caution Areas: Moriches and Little Pike's inlets can be very rough, with high standing waves and strong currents difficult to paddle against. Exercise extreme caution going in and out of these inlets.

If you are going to explore the shallow bays behind the barrier beaches of southern Long Island, Moriches Bay is a good choice because it's on a smaller scale than Great South Bay and just a short crossing to Westhampton Beach. Moriches Bay is very shallow, measuring 2 to 6 feet. It is about 8 nautical miles long and connected to Great South Bay to the west by Narrow Bay and to Shinnecock Bay to the east by two canals. The Long Island Intracoastal Waterway goes down the middle of Moriches Bay and averages 6 feet deep, but mariners are warned to obtain local knowledge before navigating the waterway due to frequent shoaling. (Fortunately, kayakers don't have to worry about shoaling except to be prepared for disturbed wave action—and all the motorboats that use the channel.) The waterway is marked by frequently spaced cans.

A somewhat mundane trip can become a lesson in the frailty of humankind and the strong regenerative power of nature. From the put-in in Hart Cove from a beach that had miraculously

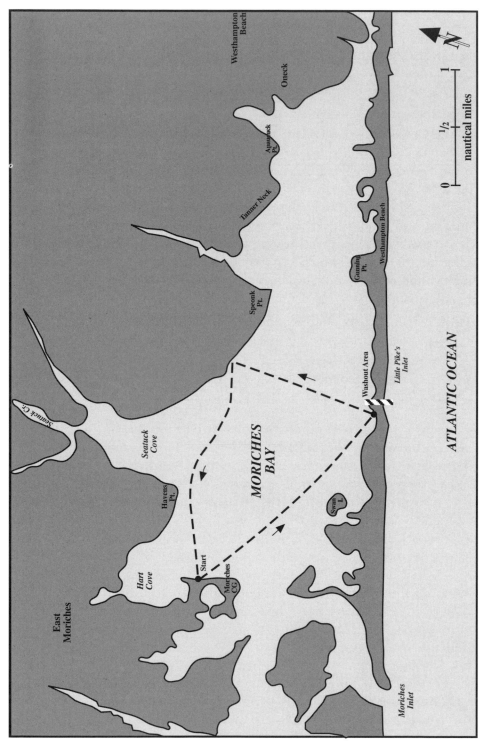

Moriches Bay

appeared over the winter, I paddled southeast to Westhampton Beach to view the washout that had occurred during a severe winter storm in 1992.

The storm destroyed forty homes and opened two new inlets. Pike's Inlet was the westernmost opening, measuring 1,000 feet across and 6 feet deep, and has since filled in. Little Pike's Inlet, the smaller inlet to the east, has grown since the storm. At one point, it was 0.25 across and 14 feet deep. With the help of Army Corps of Engineers dredging, Little Pike's comes close to closing up, then reopens again in the next storm. So it is unclear at any time whether this break will exist (as of this writing it had been filled in). Little Pike's has a fierce current and eddies. Submerged pilings can't be seen, and paddlers should use extreme caution in approaching the area.

Also because of the two inlets—Moriches and Little Pike's—several strong currents are set up, and you need to be wary of getting caught in the cross currents. NOAA considers it unsafe for mariners to negotiate Moriches Inlet at any time and the Coast

Summer homes awash from the 1992 storm on Westhampton Beach left much flotsam, including porch chairs, along the beach.

Guard doesn't bother to maintain buoys in the inlet. Experienced paddlers consider both inlets excellent local surf spots.

As we paddled out of Hart Cove across the bay and came closer to Westhampton Beach, it became eerily apparent that none of the hundreds of summer homes set on stilts were occupied. The closer we got, the more ominous it became. We discovered that the storm had obliterated many of the houses.

We landed and saw debris—chairs, a child's plastic castle, a sink, beams, barbecues, bits and pieces of Dune Road, then a wide-open space of dunes that in less than six months had been completely taken over by hundreds of nesting terns and plovers. We stayed well away from the area roped off by wildlife officials but irate terns still attacked us.

Meanwhile, the horseshoe crabs were in a breeding frenzy, and one even clasped a sandal as we stepped out of the boats. Sandpipers and gulls were eating the eggs of the crabs, and we picked our way among the horseshoe crabs that had turned over to die.

Then we started seeing more devastation. The sand dunes were all spotted with furniture, cement blocks, wiring, asphalt. Barely surviving houses stood precariously on stilts in the pounding surf. Nature had conquered Westhampton Beach. Meanwhile, environmentalists and town officials worried that the ecology of Moriches Bay would be altered by the increased amount of tidal wash and salinity that could destroy the shellfish.

Despite the caution needed in the inlets, Moriches Bay is a pretty place to paddle. You can cross to the eastern and non-developed end of Westhampton Beach and have the place to yourself. Bird life is plentiful. The water is clear and green. The beach is less crowded than at Great South Bay. It has less boat traffic, no ferries, and a very agreeable launch spot. An alternative for the return trip is to cross to the mainland and paddle by Seatuck and Hart Coves. After paddling, try the Fish Net in Hampton Bay, a rustic spot with great seafood.

Circumnavigation of Shelter Island: Ospreys and Clear Water

Charts: NOAA #12358 or #12354 Long Island Sound, eastern part

Trip Mileage: 19.5 nautical miles

Getting There: Coming from New York, take the Long Island Expressway about 120 miles from Manhattan to just south of Riverhead, then get on NY 25. From NY 25, turn onto Manhanset Avenue in Greenport, travel past the Stirling Marina and Brewer Yacht Yard, then turn right onto Beach Road. Go all the way to the end. Parking area and launch are next to a marina at Stirling Basin. Also inquire at Preston's marine store for launch spots.

New Englanders will want to reach the East Forks or "Out East" by the New London ferry, otherwise known as the Cross Sound Ferry, which goes from New London, Connecticut, to Orient Point, New York (516-323-2525). The price is $28 for car and driver, $8.50 for an adult passenger one way (1993 weekend prices). You can also leave your car behind in New London and launch right from the ferry slip at Orient Point and make your way down to Greenport and Shelter Island.

Camping: Eastern Long Island Kampground, Queen Street, Greenport

Tidal Range: 2.4 feet at Greenport

Caution Areas: Beware of fast-moving boat traffic when crossing the north and south passages between Shelter Island and Long Island. The ferries at the north and south end go back and forth nonstop in the summer, and never turn their motors off, so you need to stay alert and give the washes good berth.

Gardiners Bay is a long stretch of water, and the eastern shore can be very exposed in an easterly wind. Beware of currents speeding up around exposed points and bluffs.

Shelter Island sits snugly between the two eastern forks of Long Island, connected by ferry at the island's northwest shore (from Dering Harbor to Greenport) and at the south shore (from Smith Cove to North Haven Peninsula). Like all islands, it seems a decade

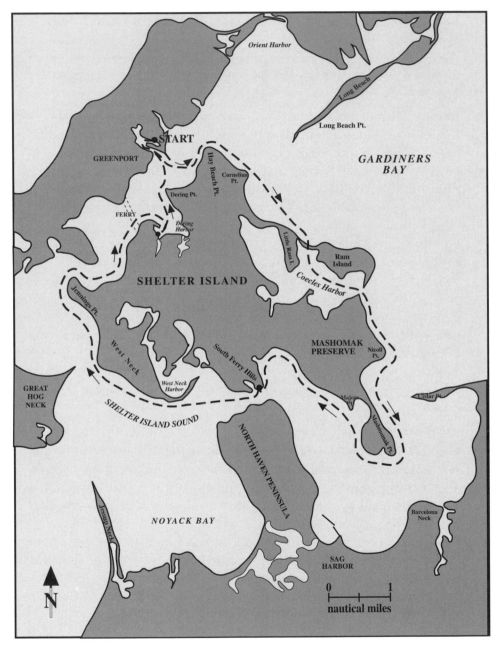

Shelter Island

or two removed from the hustle of either fork. The island has high, leafy green bluffs with hills and lots of conservation land.

What makes Shelter Island so special is that nearly 10 miles of coast are preserved as part of the Nature Conservancy's Mashomack Preserve. The entire southeastern peninsula from Sungic Point at Coecles (pronounced "cockles") Harbor down to Mashomack Point to South Ferry Hills is untrammeled shoreline. In all, Mashomack encompasses 2,039 acres, a former private hunting preserve bought by The Nature Conservancy in 1980. The preserve supports one of the few naturally nesting colonies of osprey in the northeast.

The coastline is indented with five harbors, which adds to visual interest. The main settlement is Dering Harbor, a mile across from Greenport, on Long Island's North Fork.

Boat traffic is the main caution of this trip. Very large powerboats ply the north and south passages. Fortunately, with a circumnavigation you only have to cross the passages twice. Otherwise, you can hug the shore and keep to the shallows. If the large powerboats prove too ominous, you can always take the North Ferry back to Greenport. Call (516) 749-0139 for the schedule.

At Greenport, put in at Stirling Basin, a protected area, which provides immediate access to the deep channel between Greenport and Shelter Island. People have seen and (in earlier times) caught whales in this channel, which reaches depths of 94 feet.

Follow the breakwater off Young's Point. Stay out of the channel to avoid powerboats and sailboats going in and out of Stirling Basin. Then make the half-mile crossing to Shelter Island just northeast of Dering Point. This is a high bluff with several mansions. As you round Hay Beach Point, you will probably spy your first osprey nest (a collection of dead sticks sitting on top of a high pole or platform). Shelter Island is said to have more ospreys than any other place on Long Island, second only to uninhabited Gardiners Island in the middle of Gardiners Bay.

You will also get a full view of the bay dominated at this end by Bug Light off Long Beach Bar. To the southeast 9 nautical miles lies Gardiners Island, privately owned by the last of the Gardiners family. Lion Gardiner of East Hampton bought the island called Manchonant in May, 1639, from Yovowan, sachem of Long Island

Dering Harbor on Shelter Island is a welcome stop near trip's end.

(the deed still exists), but was careful to secure ownership also from Charles I of England in March, 1639. With this generation of Gardiners, the property will be removed from trust status, which has both developers and environmentalists edgy. Gardiners Island is an undisturbed breeding ground for thousands of colonial birds. Bald eagles along with harbor and gray seals settle here during the winter, as does a large population of osprey. The island also has several forests that have never been cut.

Paddle along the settled shoreline of Shelter Island to Cornelius Point, which brings a change of direction and wind shift. A fish weir is located just off Ram Island. You can carry your kayak over the causeway at Coecles Harbor which lies just south of Ram Island, to get a flavor of the harbor. It has a pleasing landscape indented far to the south. Head for sandy Sungic Point, where you may see another occupied osprey nest, and out the mouth of the harbor with the tide. *Caution:* This could be a fairly nasty place in opposing wind and tide. Follow the pristine sand beach (lined with "No Landing" signs to protect nesting piping plovers and terns). The whole run from Sungic to Nicoll Point to Mashomack Point is a very pretty, sandy shore, backed by dune grass and woods and filled with dozens of terns fishing off the points. You look over to the high dunes of Cedar Point. You may get a wild ride around Nicoll Point due to water speeding up around the point.

Rounding Mashomack Point and heading northwest up the peninsula, you have a full view of the dramatic Barcelona Point cliffs. If you get an opposing wind and tide, you may want to stay close to shore past Majors Point where you'll find shallower water, less current, fewer waves. You can land at the beach at the Manor House, owned by The Nature Conservancy, and follow one of several hiking trails (for more information and to obtain *The Nature Conservancy South Fork and Shelter Island Preserve Guide* call 516-749-1001. TNC has a sea-kayak program in the adjacent, protected Bass Creek. You can also land at the South Ferry dock, which has a short stretch of pebble beach and a small shady park behind the ticket office.

As you paddle through Shelter Island Sound past West Neck Harbor, you can look down to the wide broach of the Peconic bays and tantalizing cliffs of Little Hog Neck. Huge sailboats ply the waters.

West Neck is fairly settled. Rounding Jennings Point (the green can is not visible until you actually round the corner), you are greeted by high bluffs and calm water, if the wind is blowing from the southeast. Paddle by the ferry dock and around the corner to Dering Harbor, the island's main harbor, where you will find a fine collection of sailboats and a yacht club. Pull up along the wall on the causeway and walk into the small town down the main street. Dering Harbor has a chandelry, The Dory restaurant, a few clothing shops, a Mobil gas station (public restroom), a liquor store, and Helena's Kitchen, where you can sip tea or cappucino and eat scrumptious cookies.

For your return to Stirling Basin, set your bow toward the twin white towers of the memorial to lost Greenport mariners. If you paddle along the Greenport waterfront, you will pass the ferry slip and new maritime museum, the schooner *Regina Maris*, and Preston's, which sells local charts. *The Spirit of Massachusetts* berths here on its way down to the Virgin Islands in winter. Claudios is a popular post-paddling spot. Also try the Chowder Pot Pub for chowder, fish sandwiches, or fresh catch of the day. It is located next to the

Shelter Island ferry dock on 3rd Street and has tables overlooking the water.

The commercial fishing port of Greenport has always enjoyed the reputation of being more mellow, rural, and family-oriented than South Fork towns like the Hamptons. Long Island's North Fork has many wineries, several with wine tastings between 11 A.M. and 5 P.M. Check the local newspaper, *The Suffolk Times,* for listings of these.

Other Access: You may also want to put in at Orient Harbor. Just out of Orient Point, on Long Island Sound, you will find the Oyster Ponds Department of Environmental Conservation "Marine Recreational Access Site." It has seven spaces for nontrailered vehicles and one space for handicapped drivers. Or at the eastern end of the seawall, limited parking on the causeway lets you launch into Orient Harbor.

Sag Harbor to Barcelona Neck: Marsh and High Dunes

Charts: NOAA #12358

Trip Mileage: 4 nautical miles roundtrip

Getting There: From NY 27, at Bridgehampton turn north on Route 79. Follow that road into Sag Harbor. At the end of Main Street, turn into the Long Wharf parking lot next to the John Steinbeck windmill, Sag Harbor's tourist information center. Turn right. To the left is a small public beach from where you can launch. You don't need a sticker to park on Long Wharf Promenade, although you will need to get here early on a weekend morning to find a parking spot. There's also a municipal lot on Main Street, which you can park in after you've dropped off your boat.

Camping: Cedar Point Campground (516-852-7620) in East Hampton overlooking Gardiners Bay, $12 a night unreserved, $14 a night reserved. From Sag Harbor, take NY 114 south. At the stoplight, turn left on to Stephen Hands Road. Follow signs for Cedar Point; it's 4.8 miles from the turn-off to the campground.

Tidal Range: 2.5 feet at Sag Harbor

Caution Areas: When the wind is out of the south or southwest and the tide is coming in, beware of freestanding waves and rough conditions.

During the nineteenth century, Sag Harbor was one of the major whaling ports in the United States along with Provincetown, Nantucket, New Bedford, Fairhaven, and New London.

Whaling started here in 1760, but when the brig *Lucy* set out in 1785 Sag Harbor's reputation really grew. By 1839, Sag Harbor had thirty-one ships and was the third-largest whaling port in the world. The whaling industry shifted to the Pacific Ocean in the 1840s. In the 1850s, the California Gold Rush eclipsed whaling as a fortune-seeking interest, and the whalers who were settled in Sag Harbor went to California, leaving the town depleted in population and importance. The Sag Harbor Whaling Museum tells part of the story.

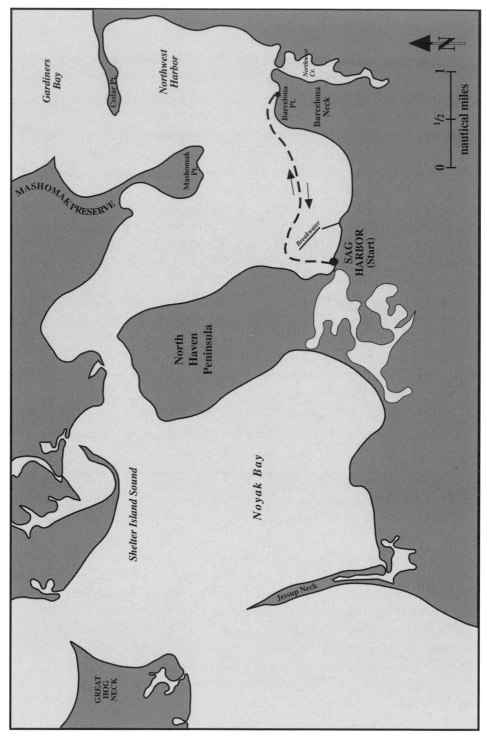

Sag Harbor

It is a short trip from Sag Harbor to Barcelona Neck. Paddle past the moored yachts and out the breakwater parallel to North Haven Peninsula. Turn right (east) and follow the sharp curve of the shoreline offshore. Your view is across Northwest Harbor to the lighthouse at Cedar Point and over to Mashomack Point on Shelter Island. Northwest Harbor is considered one of the most productive shellfish environments in the state because of the circular motion of the tides here. In winter and early spring, you're bound to see many harbor seals resting or playing on several rocky outcrops.

Barcelona Neck is a 341-acre New York State preserve that was rescued from residential development in 1986. It has a 40-foot-wide beach that meets a beautiful 80-foot-high dune. This is a good spot for sunbathing, swimming, exploring on trails within the preserve, and collecting shells. Just beyond the neck, you can poke into the peaceful Northwest Creek, a marsh with many interesting wading birds such as herons and egrets.

Beware of tides and currents, which can be particularly strong in opposing wind and tide. When the wind is out of the south or southwest and the tide is coming in, look for freestanding waves and rough conditions, especially out in the middle. A tremendous amount of water moves through narrow passages from the Great and Little Peconic Bays into Gardiners Bay and back. If you stay out in the channel, your watery path is well buoyed with no fewer than eight cans. The upside of this fast water is that the water is brilliantly clear.

Trip options include a circumnavigation of North Haven Peninsula through Sag Harbor Cove with a carry over Short Beach or a paddle over to Shelter Island and back by way of Cedar Point. Sag Harbor, a major summer tourist town, has several restaurants for post-paddling refreshment.

Chapter 2
The New Jersey Shore

NEW JERSEY'S SEACOAST stretches 120 miles from Sandy Hook to Cape May. The barrier beach that runs most of the state's length gives paddlers miles of exposed Atlantic shoreline and protected bayside waters. Add the many trips up the little rivers and creeks that start in the bays, and the paddling possibilities on the New Jersey shore are endless.

Barrier beaches backed by miles of tidal salt marsh play host to thousands of migrating birds on what is known as the Atlantic Flyway. During spring and fall migrations, more than three hundred bird species stop along this coastal corridor to rest and feed. The Cape May peninsula has the second-largest concentration of shorebirds in the United States, and 80 percent of the hemisphere's red knots and ruddy turnstones make their only stop here on their 6,000-mile migration from the Arctic to South America. The Cape May Observatory is world renowned for bird watching.

At the north end of the coast, Sandy Hook is a 6-mile-long peninsula that is part of Gateway National Recreation Area run by the National Park Service. The area also includes Jamaica Bay, Breezy Point, and parts of Staten Island in New York City's boroughs. Sandy Hook juts north into Lower New York Bay and is a popular destination for paddlers making the 8-mile bay crossing from Staten Island.

About 25 miles down the coast from Sandy Hook, the Intracoastal Waterway enters bay waters at the Manasquan River north of Point Pleasant Beach, and continues all the way to Cape May through the long bays and marsh behind the beaches. Barrier beach begins at Bay Head, protecting Silver and Barnegat bays.

Thousands of acres of Barnegat Bay's tidal marsh are protected by the Edwin B. Forsythe National Wildlife Refuge (Barnegat

Division), which is a favorite paddling spot for birdwatchers, especially during spring and fall migrations. The bay is also popular with duck hunters. Long Beach has many public launch spots.

Continuing south, next come Little Egg Harbor, Great Bay, Little Bay, and Reeds Bay. Miles of marsh constitute the Brigantine division of the Forsythe Refuge, another area rich in birdlife. Together Brigantine and Barnegat protect 39,000 acres, one of the largest wildlife refuges on the Northeast coast. Atlantic City, an old ocean resort reborn as a gambling mecca, lies 9 miles south of Brigantine.

Barrier beach, marsh, and smaller bays reach south to Cape May, a popular resort for generations of New Yorkers and Philadelphians. Cape May has many grand hotels and several hundred restored Victorian homes. From here the Cape May-Lewes Ferry (800-64-FERRY) crosses Delaware Bay to Delaware in about seventy minutes and can save hours of driving.

The Intracoastal Waterway passes through these bays and creeks behind the barrier beach, so kayakers setting out for a secluded jaunt in the empty marsh will soon find themselves in the company of powerboats, waterskiers, and jetskiers.

Heading up Delaware Bay, gentle surf laps against marsh and beach interspersed with small coastal villages like Reeds Beach at Bidwell Creek or Bivalve and Shell Pile on the Maurice River, once the center of the Delaware Bay oyster fishing industry. You can still see several oyster boats, one-hundred-year-old schooners converted to diesel, their sawn-off masts rotting at the wharves at Bivalve and Shellpile.

The Pine Barrens are also a great place to paddle. Located inland from Barnegat Bay, the barrens constitute 750,000 acres. A good local source for trips is the Metropolitan Association of Sea Kayakers, which offers regular trips into the Pine Barrens, and Kayak King, Inc., in New Gretna, which rents kayaks (write or call PO Box 171, New Gretna, NJ 08224; 609-296-8002).

Note that the Garden State Parkway is usually jammed in the summer, and some of the beach parking lots fill up by late morning. Get to your launch spot early.

Public Access

The *Boating Almanac,* Vol. 3, published yearly, is a source for public launch ramps. It covers New Jersey along with Delaware Bay, Hudson River, Erie Canal, and Lake Champlain. You need to wade through all the private marinas, but the almanac provides the addresses of the municipal (public) boat ramps. Also, Ocean County Parks (609-971-3085) welcome kayakers at several of their locations. Jersey Paddler, located in Brick, New Jersey, is a good source for put-ins along the mid-New Jersey coast.

Safety

A dozen inlets interrupt the 120 miles of New Jersey coastline. Some are more benign than others, so local knowledge is essential. Six do not require extreme caution and calculation of wind, tide, and current. From north to south, these are Shark River, Manasquan, Great Egg, Absecon, Townsend, and Cape May, also known as Cold Spring Inlet. Inlets that can be quite dangerous are Barnegat, Little Egg, Beach Haven, Hereford, Corson, and Brigantine. Most of these are plagued with shoaling nearly all the way across their mouths, so it's hard to find a way through.

Some have shoaling to either side of the inlet, and you get a deep channel in the middle with quieter water but have to surf and brace through the waves on either side. If you plan to go in and out of these inlets, it's good to have a large-scale (1:40,000) NOAA chart, which gives the depths in detail.

The breaker-choked inlets have strong tides and standing waves, and you will need to negotiate wave refraction around shoals, reflection from groins, clapotis, and overfalls (see glossary for definitions). The quieter inlets get plenty of boat traffic and chaotic wakes. Be aware of whether the tide is ebbing or flooding and if the wind is opposing the current, in which case you will get turmoil. Six-foot waves or larger are not uncommon. Listen to your NOAA weather radio for small craft advisories (15-MPH winds or above, which means it's probably not a good time to paddle the inlets). Finally, for those with bracing and surfing skills who enjoy wild water, it's best to go through the inlets when the water is warm so you can enjoy them. If you plan to be surfing, be sure to wear a helmet.

Needless to say, the surf on the Atlantic side can be quite steep. You'll need to punch out of the surf line, keeping your boat pointed directly into the oncoming surf, then paddle beyond the breaking waves. Upon return be prepared to run your boat up on the beach on an incoming wave even though it will grind the bottom. That's better than getting sideswiped by your boat at shoreline.

Perhaps the single biggest deterrent to summer paddling, however, is bugs, particularly greenhead flies. If you are paddling in July or August, try to do so on a breezy day. Bring plenty of bug dope. Also, don't forget the sunscreen and visor; there's little shade.

Trip Planning

Starting at Barnegat Inlet, eight barrier beaches form long, skinny islands south to Cape May. They make good day-trip circumnavigations, giving you a taste for the swell-filled Atlantic and the inside bays, lagoons, and mazelike marshes linked by thoroughfares, all fun to explore. Long Beach, the northernmost island, is 17 nautical miles long (which would entail about a 35-nautical-mile trip).

One popular trip is circumnavigating Peck Beach at Ocean City. You can put in at Corson's Inlet State Park, go out Corson's Inlet, head north up along the shore, then into Great Egg Harbor Inlet, through Great Egg Harbor, and back to your put-in. Peck Beach is about 7 nautical miles long; a circumnavigation is about 16 nautical miles. Beware that kayakers have dumped in Corson's Inlet's wild surf.

An alternative is to paddle up the many creeks and rivers that indent the shore—some of the more scenic include Reedy Creek, Cedar Creek, Bass River, and the Mullica River. Consult Ed Gertler's *Garden State Canoeing: A Paddler's Guide to New Jersey*. Another option is to circumnavigate Cape May using the Cape May Channel and paddle out in the Atlantic with the porpoises past the famous Cape May Lighthouse, about a 15-mile day trip.

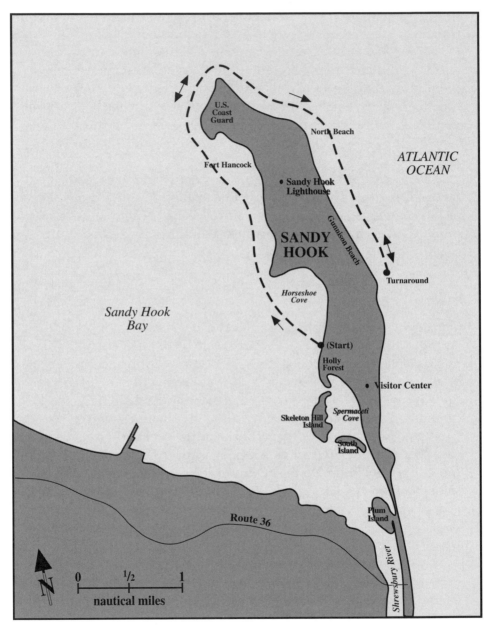

Sandy Hook

Around Sandy Hook: History and Shifting Sand

Charts: NOAA Small Craft Chart #12324

Trip Mileage: 12 miles roundtrip

Getting There: From the Garden State Parkway, take exit 117. Watch for the highway sign for Sandy Hook National Recreational Area. Get onto NJ 36 and head east. Follow signs for Sandy Hook. Cross the Highlands Bridge. After entering the park, parking is at Kingman and Mills, site of two gun battlements and an old campsite. To reach Kingman and Mills, go 0.25 mile past the Ranger Station and turn left at Parking Area F. Summer weekend fee is $5.

Camping: Cheese Quake State Park, Matawan, N.J., 6 miles S.E. of Perth Amboy, N.J., Garden State Parkway, exit 120; 50 sites; (908) 566-2161, $10 a night.

Tidal Range: 4.6 feet at Sandy Hook

Caution Areas: The north tip can have major wave action in opposing wind and tide.

Sandy Hook is a long, slender sandbar peninsula that stretches 6.5 miles north into lower New York Harbor from New Jersey's northeastern shore. Its strategic location at the New York Harbor entrance made it an important navigational landmark and a key defense site to protect New York City from enemy attack from the American Revolution through World War II. It was also remote enough to be used as a site to test military weapons.

The trip's main interest is seeing what wind, tide, and current offer at the north end. Although many paddlers would prefer to time their trip with slack tide and minimum current going around the tip, others in search of wind and waves will deliberately choose maximum ebb or flood for surfing. And good surfing they will get. Even in calm conditions the north passage can feel lumpy. Add the motorboat wakes of summer weekend anglers using the Sandy Hook channel, which parallels the north tip, and you are guaranteed some chop. Longtime New Jersey-area paddler Bill Lozano has reported 6-foot-high waves in which all visibility of other boats is lost.

According to *Eldridge,* at low tide at the Battery in New York, the Sandy Hook channel gets a current of about 0.4 knots, which by contrast reaches 2.3 knots at maximum flood. Meanwhile, you have five different currents at work—going in and out of Sandy Hook Bay, Raritan Bay, the Atlantic side, New York's Lower Bay, and Jamaica Bay. This is a very interesting place.

Sandy Hook is part of the Gateway National Recreational Area, so called because of the "arms" of New Jersey and New York that reach toward each other, forming a natural gateway through which millions of immigrants entered America. Congress created the park in 1972 and appointed the National Park Service to run it. The aim was to preserve recreational parkland in one of the most urbanized areas in the world. Several kayakers made an effort about ten years ago to get launching for five sites in Gateway National Recreation Area. Currently, only one—at Floyd Bennett Field on Jamaica Bay— is available. Often kayakers launch from a city site—Alice Austen Park on Staten Island—to cross the lower bay to Sandy Hook.

Sandy Hook is a low-lying, mid-Atlantic white-sand beach backed by a thick growth of cedars. Its engineers have tried to keep it in place with seawalls and groins because Sandy Hook itself is nothing but shifting sand. The hook has shifted a mile north within the last two hundred years, leaving the famous Sandy Hook lighthouse well inland from the shoals it was supposed to mark. An aerial view of Sandy Hook shows an amoebalike landform with long arms of beach stretching out into the Atlantic held in place by groins.

The trip combines protected paddling on Sandy Hook Bay, open ocean paddling on the eastern side, and many natural and historic sites. You pass beaches, historic Sandy Hook lighthouse and Fort Hancock, and one of the largest holly forests on the Atlantic seaboard.

Park and launch from the parking lot at Kingman and Mills, a short drive from the entrance. Head north from your launch site. First you pass the many yachts moored in Horseshoe Cove, a popular stop for those sailing the Intracoastal Waterway before they travel the 20 or so miles down the New Jersey Coast. Next come several battlements, fish weirs, and jetties before you reach a ghostly complex of deserted yellow-brick military officers quarters surrounding a parade ground, and the Sandy Hook Lighthouse beyond. These quarters are part of Fort Hancock, a group of various fortifications and embattlements. As you paddle around, you can see several gun batteries, two on the Atlantic side and one dramatically slabbing off into the bay just before Horseshoe Cove. The government started building the yellow brick quarters in 1899 (you can read about Fort Hancock's history in the museum across the parade ground).

Pass a Coast Guard Station (which forbids landing) and around the north tip of Sandy Hook. Here you may see perhaps a thousand terns feeding on the shore just beyond the "bell." Ruddy turnstones, oyster catchers, and black skimmers join them. Across the point you might discern gray ships looming out of the haze from the naval base in Raritan Bay.

Turning out of the protected bay with its still water and steamy summer haziness is like entering a whole other world. The north end current is strong and the water choppy; boat wakes may further confuse the waters. Big surf breaks off a shoal off the northwest tip. This would definitely be a place for the prepared paddler to go out and play, given minimal boat traffic. It can be amusing for an experienced paddler, but the tide and currents here do not make this a beginner trip.

When you turn the corner at the north tip, you might expect to have a clear view of Sandy Hook's eighteenth-century light-house. Not so. When first built, it stood 500 feet from the tip of the hook; now it's nearly a mile and a half south down the spit because so much extra sand has been carried north by the prevailing north-ward longshore currents. In more recent years, the dredging of Sandy Hook Channel has slowed the spit's growth.

In the great age of sail, when ships coasted up and down the coast as the modern-day equivalent of trucks, the narrow Sandy Hook Channel provided the only safe entry through the treacher-ous shoals of New York Bay into New York Harbor. To keep the ships from running aground, government officials built a light in 1764. It's said to be the oldest light in continuous operation in the United States. They installed a Fresnel lens in 1856, which greatly magnified the lighthouse's oil-burning lamp. The same lens now transmits the light of a 1,000-watt bulb nearly 20 miles.

Once you pass the north end of Sandy Hook, continue on around the tip and follow the shoreline south, staying beyond the swimmers' buoys. The Atlantic Ocean's water quality is less clear here than you will find farther south.

Just south of Gunnison Beach is a "naturist's" (nudist's) beach. Here the unclad stroll along an area that has been roped off for nesting terns and plovers. You also pass many surf fisherman, and you need to stay well offshore away from their lines. Gunnison beach's off-boat limits swimming area takes you away from shore, off area F.

The federal goverment closes long stretches of beach for nesting terns and plovers in spring and summer, so you get nice uninterrupted views of wild beach, and literally thousands of terns. The three species that nest here are the common, least, and rarer royal tern, according to a visitor center volunteer. Most fishing boats are parked peacefully for their morning's fishing. By afternoon, however, much traffic is astir, which means that early morning weekend paddling is a good plan. You mark the end of the hook by all the boats heading east or west in the channel passing the north end.

The next highlight along the route is the visitor center, a shingled-towered building that served as headquarters for the U.S. Lifesaving Service, an operation designed to save drowning victims before the U.S. Coast Guard came into service. Weekend evenings, the park rangers put on a demonstration of the breeches buoy system, with which marooned sailors were transported to shore via a rubber tire on a pully connecting a ship to a landward tower.

If you keep heading south, you pass by more public beach and you can go down as far as Parking Areas C or B to the entrance gate. Ideally, if the park rangers would let you, you would land on the Beach at Parking Area B and carry across the road back to the bay for a wonderful 12-mile circumnavigation of Sandy Hook. Unfortunately, at this writing, park rules did not allow launching or landing on the Atlantic side in order to protect swimmers and wildlife. That being the case, you should return to you start by retracing you7r route around the northern end of Sandy Hook.

Once you return to your starting point, you can explore the southern end of Sandy Hook Bay. If you paddle south from the Kingman and Mills launch area in the bay, you will reach Skeleton Hill Island, so named for victims buried there in a cholera epidem-

Officer's quarters line the parade ground at Fort Hancock near the lighthouse on Sandy Hook.

ic in the 1800s. In this marsh environment, little fish jump, terns fly overhead, and herons stalk: the bottom is shallow and warm, covered with periwinkles, seaweed, and swimming crabs. Spermacetti Cove is so named because that species of whale washed up there once.

An option is to paddle up the Shrewsbury River, which has strong currents, and under the twin historic lights located on one of the highest bluffs along the Atlantic.

If you still have time, you can drive north up the hook to the Visitor Center and museum. Sandy Hook Museum traces the development of the nation's first concrete gun batteries, counterbalanced gun carriages, rapid fire gun batteries, and the first official proving ground. Here at Sandy Hook, the government also tested the Nike Air Defense Missiles, developed to replace antiaircraft guns after the Korean War. In 1974 the army phased out the Nike Hercules nationwide and deactivated the missile units at Sandy Hook. The fort closed altogether in 1974 and became the Sandy Hook National Recreation area, except for the Coast Guard station at the tip. As you paddle around Sandy Hook, you will be struck by what strange bedfellows recreation and military defense make. For more information on Sandy Hook, call (908) 872-0115.

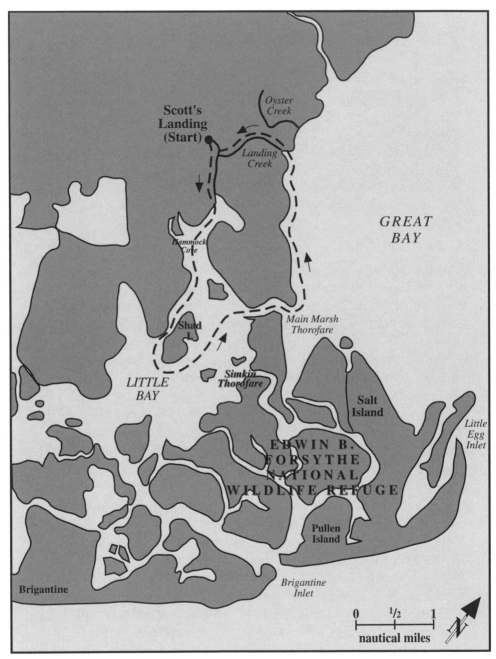

Brigantine's Wildlife Refuge

Brigantine's Wildlife Refuge: Egrets and Casinos

Charts: NOAA #12316

Trip Mileage: 9 nautical miles

Getting There: In Leeds Point, from NJ 9, turn onto Moss Mill Road. (Route 561 Alt.), which turns into Oyster Creek Road at Hammock Road (at sharp curve). From Moss Mill Road, it's 1.5 miles to Scott's Landing Road. Turn right and follow that road 0.5 mile to Scott's Landing launch ramp. The launch is federally owned by the refuge so there is no fee. A big parking lot is located in the woods. You will share the ramp and dock with crabbers.

Camping: Bass River State Forest. From south New Jersey, take exit 50 and turn left at the exit. From north New Jersey, take exit 52 (first exit after New Gretna) and bear right. Go one mile and take a right. Follow signs for Bass River State Forest, one mile on left. First come, first serve basis. $10 a night. Open until midnight. 609-296-1114.

Tidal Range: 3.6 feet at Absecon Inlet at Atlantic City

Caution Areas: If you are paddling out into the Atlantic, beware that Brigantine and Little Egg inlets can be quite rough in conditions of opposing wind and tide but not as rough as Beach Haven Inlet just to the north. Also watch out for getting stranded in the marsh channels at low tide.

The trip gives you an intimate feel of the vast, wide, empty, and low-lying marsh that consumes the landscape behind Atlantic City. So minimal is dry ground, you can expect to stay in your boats the entire trip. Much of the marsh is protected under the Edwin B. Forsythe National Wildlife Refuge (Brigantine Division) and the Absecon Wildlife Management Area, so birdlife is rich and abundant, making this a very special trip for birdwatchers.

Bays and thorofares separate the marsh islands. These thorofares require attentiveness. Many smaller channels can lead you astray, but if you stick to the main current and mentally note your route back, you can muddle through. You will muddle less by paying close attention to your chart as you move through the marsh channel. If it's not too hazy, you can see Atlantic City's casino towers, in the distance, 9 miles away.

From Scott's Landing, launch into the straight creek to the right (southeast) and bear right (southeast) at the first Y. Soon you will notice the thick brown soup you are paddling through and the plethora of blue crabs who dance away right under the water line on the muddy banks as you pass by. You will also see thousands of fiddler-crab holes and in some places hundreds of their inhabitants. Keep bearing right (southeast) in the channel. If you launch near low tide as we did, you will not be able to see over the top of the marsh, but low tide is the best time for watching the wading birds that feed on the mud banks on crabs and clams. If you are lucky, you may see herons, egrets, osprey, terns, hawks, swallows, and gulls. Muskrats and diamondback terrapins also abound in this refuge.

The creek broadens and leads you into Hammock Cove (pronounced "hommock," according to a local clammer), otherwise known as Dry Cove, marked by the old dredger barge with a windmill. You will pass by hundreds of clam-seed stakes, empty branches stuck into the mud at regular intervals. Watch out at low tide that your paddle doesn't cut the netting laid over the beds to protect

Crabbers try their luck in the creek near Scott's Landing, part of the Brigantine Division of the Edwin B. Forsythe Wildlife Refuge.

them and prevent fish from eating the little seed clams, which take two to three years to mature.

In the distance, you can see Shad Island, its height gained from mud and sand dredged from the main channel. Shad's bluff is covered in phragmites (tall marsh reeds), and the entire island is surrounded by marsh grass, so the only possible place to land is on the south side. The spot is quite wet and muddy, so landing is best for emergency use only (it's also a wildlife refuge).

When we visited we circumnavigated Shad and were rewarded with the sight of a black skimmer dragging the tip of its bright orange lower mandible on the water's surface to scoop up fish. The skimmers like areas with newly dredged sand fill (officials are constantly dredging the Intracoastal Waterway) before much grass grows, which is one reason why they might be in this area.

Cross Little Bay to the Main Marsh Thorofare to Great Bay. If you're feeling adventurous, you might want to proceed east through one of the thoroughfares around one of the marsh islands or to Brigantine Inlet and around Pullen Island, back through Little Egg Inlet to Great Bay. Both these inlets, however, are considered quite rough.

Otherwise, at the end of the Main Marsh Thorofare, turn left (west) up Great Bay. The third large creek on the left is Landing Creek. Although the creek entrance is unmarked, you can tell Landing Creek by your first clear view of the row of gray houses at Oyster Creek. Also, note the channel marker that denotes the opening to Oyster Creek, the next creek north.

Wind your way back. Bear left (east) at the first Y, then continue to bear right (west). Follow the main current.

If you still have time, take the 8-mile Wildlife Drive around the Brigantine refuge, just a few miles away off Route 9. The refuge is almost 90 percent tidal salt meadow and marsh, interspersed with shallow coves and bays. The refuge manages water impoundments by "diking" and so has created more than 1,000 acres of both fresh and brackish water marsh habitat. The diversified wetlands attract and support a wider variety of wildlife than salt marsh would alone. Thousands of ducks and geese, wading birds and shorebirds, stop off here during spring and fall migrations to feed and rest. The first week of November, more than 100,000 ducks and geese congregate in the refuge pools, which makes it a good time to paddle here. Atlantic brant and black ducks overwinter here. A seasonal bird list that identifies 289 species found at Brigantine and Barnegat is available at the visitor center.

An alternative to the itinerary above is to paddle the north side of Great Bay. From NJ 9, take Great Bay Boulevard straight down to Little Egg Inlet. Look for launch spots along the creeks or all the way at the end at Little Egg Inlet. You can make a circle through the marsh or head across the channel to the Seven Islands. The best time is mid- to late September, when the marsh is full of migrating birds including curlews, oyster catchers, and clapper rails. According to longtime New Jersey paddler Chuck Sutherland, "For bird watchers with a little bit of diligence, it's possible to dig out a little bit of everything."

Note that the greenheads can be severe in July and August. Be sure to bring bug repellent or wait until the fall.

Dennis Creek to Reed's Beach: Marsh That Time Forgot

Charts: NOAA #12304

Trip Mileage: 10.5 nautical miles

Getting There: Going south on NJ 47, 1.5 miles beyond the turn off for NJ 587, you will see a sign for Jakes Landing Road and boat launch ramp. Turn right. It's 1.6 miles to the ramp.

Camping: Belleplain State Forest, Woodbine, NJ. From NJ 47, turn onto NJ 587. Go three miles on NJ 587 to NJ 550. Turn left at the flashing light. Go .5 mile. Entrance to state forest is on left. There is a $10 fee. Phone 609-861-2404.

Tidal Range: 5.6 feet at the Dennis Creek entrance

Caution Areas: Be sure to follow Dennis Creek's main channel so you don't reach a dead end.

To get to Dennis Creek on Jakes Landing Road in Dennis, you drive through a shaded pine forest whose deep pleasing aroma is abruptly replaced by a wild, salty one as you cross from forest to marsh. All you can see for miles is a flat expanse of green marsh, wide sky, and a haze of more pine forest on the horizon. Welcome to the east shore of Delaware Bay, a place which time and the human hand seem to have forgotten.

That's not altogether true. When we visited we encountered two trucks in the parking lot belonging to the mosquito control division, which indicated something not too promising to human beings. A couple of miles into our trip, we saw a dredger digging foot-wide ditches designed to drain the still water and prevent mosquito breeding. But we were lucky: no mosquitoes prevailed that second week in August, just a few greenheads that were not particularly bothersome. The major challenge of this trip was lack of shade—just a wide, sun-blared expanse of marsh.

Dennis Creek is protected by the Dennis Creek Wildlife Management Area and is much more rural than other parts of New Jersey. The creek has high banks, so your vision is limited to water, marsh, and sky. But with a fresh breeze at your back and an outgoing tide pushing you out to Delaware Bay, you feel like you are

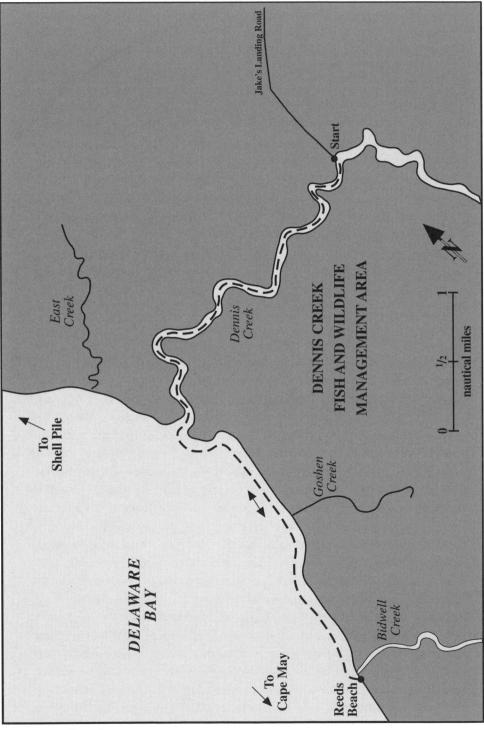

Dennis Creek

A kayaker gets ready to launch into Dennis Creek from Jake's Landing.

moving swiftly and going somewhere. You just need to make the right twists in the creek and not end up in a dead end.

Bear left (south) at any incoming channels and follow the widest channel and swiftest current. It is highly advisable to time this trip with the tides. After about 3 miles (one hour), you reach Delaware Bay. Because of all the suspended nutrients in the mahogany-colored bay, it is hard to tell whether the water is 6 inches or 20 feet deep. If you turn right, you can land on a beach just to the north. Turn left and continue to follow the Dennis Creek Wildlife Management Area. The shoreline is sand beach slabbed in mudbanks and backed by marsh. The trip's highlight is watching the abundant shorebird life along the edge. Bring your binoculars and just drift. The second week in August, the shorebirds head south and wading birds gather for migration. You might see plovers, terns, egrets, ruddy turnstones, glossy ibises, and yellowlegs. Most of the birds to be found here are migratory. Check with the Cape May Bird Observatory to see which unusual species you might see at other times of the year.

Another observation is the mysterious gray heads, which poke up when your kayak gets within about 20 feet of the creatures, look at you for a boat length or two, then disappear. When you paddle over them and try to stick your paddle into them, all you see is muddy water. We found out later they are diamondback terrapin turtles, which are common here.

Paddle to Reed's Beach at the mouth of Bidwell Creek. Lots of fishermen cast off the jetty. Reed's Beach is not the most scenic place, but a beach behind the jetty provides a place to land and eat lunch. Many dead horseshoe crabs lie on the tideline, testimony to the thousands of horseshoe crabs that mate and spawn on the beaches here in May and June. Delaware Bay has the world's largest population of horseshoe crabs in the world, according to U.S. Fish and Wildlife biologist Karen Day. The crabs crawl up the beach in high tide to lay their eggs, but about 10 percent get stranded on the beach when the tide goes out and die due to an inability to turn over, weakness, or disease. Those many crabs lying dead on the beach actually represent only a tiny fraction of the Delaware Bay population.

Paddle back along the shore, which is much more interesting than the waters farther out. Look for the green marker at the mouth of Dennis Creek. You can't miss the creek. It has a wide mouth, which the current flows in and out of quite strongly.

This is a very rural part of the state, containing large areas of forest and marsh and sleepy towns with little industry. A few small farms grow produce such as watermelon and tomatoes sold road-side with the owner sitting under an umbrella.

But this corner of southern New Jersey is also the site of a defunct major oyster industry, signs of which are visible on the Maurice River just to the north. A trip up the Maurice River starts at Shell Pile where there is a public dock, goes to Port Elizabeth, and returns for a total of about 12 nautical miles. At Bivalve (where a root beer still costs 50 cents) and Shell Pile along the river, you can see 100-year-old schooners with their masts sawn off and converted to diesel, lining the river, many still in use.

Chapter 3
Delaware Bay

THE 110-MILE DELAWARE COAST follows the Delaware River, Delaware Bay, and Atlantic Ocean. It starts north of industrial Wilmington and ends just shy of the high-rise hotel strip of Ocean City, Maryland. Inland, sleepy towns surrounded by fields support Delaware's major industry of farming—soybeans, corn, and chickens. Although development is taking over much of the coastal farmland, you can still find plenty of sand dunes in pristine state beaches and substantial coastal wetlands protected by the national refuge system at Bombay Hook (15,000 acres) and Prime Hook (9,000 acres) as well as much state parkland.

Thirty miles at its widest, Delaware Bay was once known worldwide for its oyster fishing, but shellfish disease invaded the bay in the late 1950s and has all but wiped out oystering. Crabbing and commercial fin-fishing industries are still fairly healthy operations.

Delaware Bay has been historically a busy place for commercial boating traffic. Yearly, thousands of cargo ships and oil tankers make their way up the Delaware Bay and River to Wilmington, Philadelphia, and Camden. They are led by pilot boats from Lewes (pronounced lou-is), Delaware, which navigate the ships through the deep channel up the middle between the bay's many shifting sandy shoals.

Delaware is perhaps best known as the place where Du Pont chemical company, inventor of nylon and Kevlar, started operation. Wilmington is headquarters to three major chemical corporations: Du Pont, Hercules, and ICI Americas. Between frequent oil spills from tankers and toxic effluent from manufacturing, Delaware Bay has had an undisputed reputation for pollution, but that is slowly turning around. The bay looks better than it has in years, according to an official at the University of Delaware Marine Study center.

That is due in large part to the federal Clean Water Act and efforts of the federal Delaware Bay Estuary Program, which is trying to identify and halt major polluting sources. Many people are now canoeing the Delaware River up to the Philadelphia waterfront. The Philadelphia Canoe Club is a good source of information for such trips.

Paddling possibilities along the coast are numerous, ranging from trips to historic sites, large wildlife preserves, and long, sandy beaches. You can find much useful information on launch sites from *The Delaware Estuary Public Access Guide* available from The Delaware Estuary Program. A good source for landward access to some of those sites is *Day Trips in Delmarva, A Guide to Southern Delaware and the Eastern Shore of Maryland and Virginia* by Alan Fisher. Delaware occupies the Delmarva Peninsula, consisting of Delaware, Maryland, and Virginia. It is such a distinct ecological region that the Delmarva fox squirrel, a federally endangered species, lives here and nowhere else in the world.

Several river inlets that open onto Delaware Bay provide interesting possibilities such as the Smyrna, Leipsic, St. Jones, and Mispillion. At the Leipsic in Smyrna, you'll find Bombay Hook National Wildlife Refuge (302-653-9345), three-quarters tidal marsh. The refuge is a labyrinth of creeks, all good for exploring by kayak—you can paddle from one end of the refuge to the other—especially from September through March when it is host to high concentrations of greater snow geese, Canada geese, and ducks such as black duck and pintail.

About two-thirds of the way down the coast in Milton, Prime Hook National Wildlife Refuge (302-684-8419) has a public launch spot into the marshes of Prime Hook Creek and the Broadkill River behind barrier beach. You launch next to the ranger station into a ditch, which then opens up into a beautiful spot. It's a full-day trip, all in calm water among overhanging trees with mistletoe, evocative of the Florida Everglades. Specifically, you reach Prime Hook Creek (closed to boaters during duck hunting season) by Headquarters Ditch. From here you have several possibilities. You can paddle a 2.5-mile circuit using ditches and the creek; 11 miles roundtrip to Waples Mill Pond; or 8 miles roundtrip to Beach Plum Island Nature Preserve, a lovely 2-mile long sandy peninsula preserved by the state. Birders have identified more than 260 species that frequent the wildlife refuge—you can pick up a bird list at the refuge headquarters.

Another great place to paddle is Trap Pond State Park (302-875-5153) in Laurel, Delaware, just to the west of Cape Henlopen. The 90-acre pond is accessible by a state boat-launch ramp and is good for rolling and rescue practice, then exploring one of the northernmost bald cypress swamps on the Atlantic Coast by a canoe trail at the end of the pond.

On Delaware's south border lie 25 miles of Atlantic beach and enormously popular seaside resorts such as Rehoboth and Bethany Beach, to which Washington, D.C. flocks in summer.

Indian River and Rehoboth bays, south of Cape Henlopen, are good paddling spots here. These inland bays are located behind the 7-mile-long sand dunes of Delaware Seashore State Park, open to the Atlantic only at the narrow Indian River Inlet. The inlet gets very strong currents to paddle against if you're going in or out and gets whipped into swirling, frothy water if you're paddling across it.

You have several state-run launch spots. On Rehoboth Bay, you can launch from a gentle sandy beach at the Towers Road Bayside exit at the north end of the park. You will share this small beach with swimmers and windsurfers.

On Indian River Bay, you can launch from the Indian River Marina on the south end of the park, about 4 miles north of Bethany Beach. This ramp gets very crowded with powerboats in summer, however. A better choice is Holts Landing State Park on the bay's south end. From any of these launch spots, you have plenty of beautiful creeks that don't require advanced paddling skill to explore.

A great place for a full-moon paddle is on Salt Pond, behind Bethany Beach. Every October, Charlie and Cindy Cole of Millpond Paddlers (see Appendix A) in nearby Millville hold a Delmarva Paddlers Retreat at Camp Arrowhead on Rehoboth Bay. Held at a church camp, the retreat offers a beautiful site with pine trees and bright, white sandy beaches. This has become a major gathering to share Inuit paddling techniques and to mix with a host of experienced instructors.

Meanwhile, the inland waterway will take you from Cape Henlopen by way of the Lewes and Rehoboth Canal into Rehoboth and Indian bays and into Little Assawoman Bay by way of the Assawoman Canal, and so on down to Assateague and Chincoteague Bays. Here you will contend with mosquitoes and mud at low tide. Be prepared for a long journey.

One major reason to paddle Delaware Bay is to witness the spectacle of spawning horseshoe crabs. Each spring during the high tides of the new and full moons, thousands of horseshoe crabs crawl ashore to spawn. The smaller male attaches itself to the female who then digs holes in the sand to deposit as many as twenty thousand eggs. The male fertilizes the eggs as he is pulled over the nest. With the spawning finished, the crabs leave the beach but often in the process flip over and can't right themselves with their sharp, pointed tails. When walking the beach in the spring, one always feels the urge to turn the horseshoe crabs over so they don't get eaten by predators.

Cape Henlopen: Wild Surf and Porpoises

Charts: NOAA Chart #12216

Trip Mileage: 5 nautical miles

Getting There: From Lewes, drive east on Business Route 9 across the canal. Continue .4 mile to an intersection with Henlopen Drive, then turn right onto Henlopen Drive and go 1.5 miles to the park entrance, passing the Cape May-Lewes Ferry Terminal on the left. After the ticket booth at the park entrance, take an immediate left and go to the fishing pier. The launch is from the beach next to the fishing pier.

Camping: Cape Henlopen State Park, 42 Cape Henlopen Drive, Lewes, Del. 19958; 302-645-8983. The rate is $13 a night. The 159 campsites are available from April 1 to October 31 on a first-come, first-served basis. Camping here is nearly impossible in summer because it is so popular; it's best to camp here off-season.

Tidal Range: 4.1 feet at Cape Henlopen

Caution Areas: The stretch between the north tip of Cape Henlopen and Harbor of Refuge Breakwater gets whirlpools and standing waves. The cape itself gets whirlpools and strong currents not necessarily related to the ebb and flood of Delaware Bay. Hen and Chicken Shoal gets standing waves in a strong northeast or southeast wind.

Each day the waters of the Atlantic Ocean and Delaware Bay, which meet off Cape Henlopen, have an entirely different look, and you never get tired of it, notes Charlie Cole, a man who has sailed, waterskied, and kayaked off Cape Henlopen nearly his whole life. If you stand on the dunes, you look out on waters that appear very innocent and inviting, but in fact they are very complicated and should not be undertaken except by the most skilled and prepared paddler.

Cape Henlopen is a distinctive, sandy hook that juts northward into Delaware Bay. A state park, it is a popular beach spot for flocks of Washingtonians seeking relief from the summer heat. It is located just south of the Lewes-Delaware Ferry Terminal outside Lewes, Delaware.

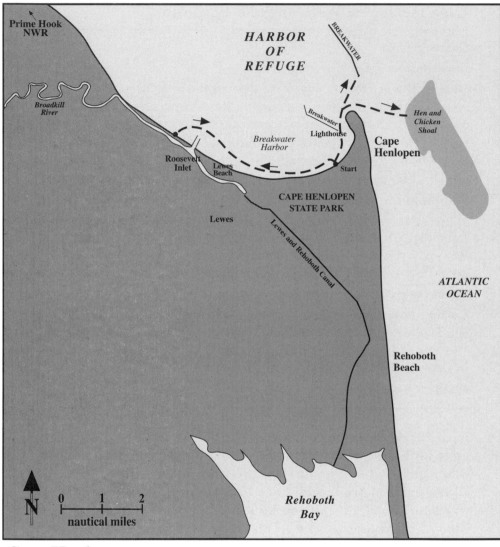

Prime Hook
NWR

Broadkill
River

HARBOR
OF
REFUGE

BREAKWATER

Breakwater

Breakwater
Harbor

Lighthouse

Roosevelt
Inlet

Lewes
Beach

Start

Cape
Henlopen

Hen and
Chicken
Shoal

CAPE HENLOPEN
STATE PARK

Lewes

Lewes and Rehoboth Canal

ATLANTIC
OCEAN

Rehoboth
Beach

N

0   1   2
nautical miles

Rehoboth
Bay

Cape Henlopen

The best launch is from the beach next to the fish pier, into Delaware Bay within the hook. Rangers charge an entry fee for out-of-staters (free for Delaware residents), but the real problem is a jammed parking lot in summer. The best time to paddle here is spring, fall, or winter.

The fishing pier launch puts you into Breakwater Harbor. A pilot boat uses the channel that runs from the ferry terminal, by the fishing pier and parallel to the hook, east toward Cape Henlopen and out to an anchorage area in Delaware Bay. Here the pilot boat directs trawlers from throughout the world up Delaware Bay. Often the pilot boat goes out hourly. It has large shark teeth painted on the bow and not only looks menacing but is menacing to kayakers. Be sure to watch out for it.

Breakwater Harbor and Harbor of Refuge (2 miles out), are protected by two long breakwaters. Cape Henlopen has long been an important stop for ships traveling up and down Delaware Bay. Federal officials built the Delaware or Inner breakwater in 1828 to provide a ship's refuge, then refortified the protection in 1901 by building the Harbor of Refuge breakwater 2 miles farther offshore. The two breakwaters now provide 1,000 acres of the Harbor of Refuge, although shoaling is beginning to cause problems as the cape expands northwestward.

From Breakwater Harbor you have several choices. You can go straight out to the inner Delaware breakwater, around the light and the backside of the pile and out to the point. More experienced paddlers can go right by the point to the outer Harbor Refuge breakwater and light. Between the cape and Harbor Refuge breakwater, you will encounter whirlpools, swells, and extreme current caused by the flood or ebb of Delaware Bay, so it is best to time your trip with slack tide.

At the spoon-shaped point of the cape, it doesn't matter if the tide is coming or going because the water swirls all around it, creating its own current, reports Charlie Cole. It gets all kinds of whirlpools, with currents, standing waves, and rips that are extremely powerful. However, if you run right along the shoreline at a distance where you could reach out and touch your paddle on the sand, you can find calmer water. Once around the point to the Atlantic Ocean side, you enter more ocean-like conditions, and here you move from shore past the wave break line. Head toward the #7 green can and Hen and Chicken Shoal.

The shoal gets breaking waves in a strong northeast or southeast wind because the water measures 5 to 17 feet deep while the surrounding water is 25 to 53 feet deep. You can see the break as you round the point, however, and judge accordingly. In summer, many porpoises feed on Hen and Chicken Shoal, and you get a fabulous porpoise show daily.

In spring and early summer, much of the beach along Cape Henlopen is closed for the protection of the nesting of piping plover, a federal threatened species. No landing is allowed from the last fishing pier all around the point on the inside of the hook, and rangers patrol the area. Be aware that often the current washes away the closure signs. After the plovers migrate in mid- to late summer, the rangers allow four-wheel-drive vehicles to park along the beach on certain days of the week, and the beach becomes very crowded with the anglers. Many of those fishing have a long cast—up to 50 yards—and getting bonked in the head by a sinker is not out of the question. Give the anglers wide berth.

If Cape Henlopen is too treacherous, head northwest from the fishing pier up Lewes Beach. This is a very beautiful spot with barrier island and uninhabited sand dunes. Pass the ferry terminal to Roosevelt Inlet. Just to the north of the inlet is a partially submerged wreck of a 150-foot-long wooden steamship, on which you can climb. You can pull up on Lewes Beach and have lunch. Going this route, you need to watch out again for the pilot boat and also for the Lewes-Cape May ferries going out of the terminal. The inlet has a lot of current, which is not insurmountable (not as bad as Indian River inlet to the south), but you do need to stay within the channel markers because nearby submerged pieces of metal could rip the bottom of your kayak. Also stay to the sides of the channel, away from the many commercial fishing charters coming out of Lewes.

Roosevelt Inlet leads to the Broadkill River. If you go down to Lewes on the river, the current is negligible, but if you head north, you will probably have to run the eddies. Either way you will encounter a lot of boat traffic.

An alternative to paddling open water is going through the 7-mile-long Lewes-Rehoboth Canal starting in Lewes. The canal connects the Broadkill River in Lewes to Rehoboth Bay at Rehoboth. The current can be strong, particularly at the railroad bridge where the canal narrows, but nothing that a kayak can't handle. The canal is a beautiful place to paddle because it's all part of Cape Henlopen State Park with no settlement until you reach the out-skirts of Lewes or Rehoboth. A good plan is to paddle down about halfway, then return.

In Lewes, you can launch from Lewes Municipal Landing on the southwest side of the canal just north of the Inn at Canal Square and across from the Anglers Seafood Restaurant. A good post-paddle spot, open all winter, is the Rose & Crown Restaurant and Pub on 2nd Street in downtown Lewes. It has English beers on tap and serves nightly dinner specials such as half-price burgers and English Cottage Pie.

Historical Lewes, first settled by the Dutch in 1631 as a whal-ing station, is an attractive town and major summer resort with many restaurants, B & Bs, and fishing-charter boats. The Zwaanen-dale Museum, housed in a Dutch brick building, tells part of its his-tory. Lewes is located at the terminus of the Cape May-Lewes Ferry service, which started in 1964. The ferry crosses Delaware Bay in 70 minutes on a frequent summer schedule. Unlike the Cape May side, you can walk from the ferry terminal into town, so Lewes is a popular day trip for tourists. For a ferry schedule, call 800-64-FERRY. The Lewes terminal phone number is 302-645-6346. A round-trip ticket is only $8.50 (1993 prices) for an adult passenger. Car and driver costs $18 one way (1993 prices). It is possible to carry your kayak on board. You will be charged the bike rate of $8 one way, and it is best to call ahead of time to let the ferry know. The boat goes on the car deck.

In all, Cape Henlopen is a beautiful place to paddle, but so many little things can get you into trouble that it is a very complicat-ed, if intriguing, spot. A situation may look insignificant, but it could be much more of a challenge than you expected and could be fatal. Cold-water kayaking specialist Moulton Avery once lost his boat at Cape Henlopen and often retells the tale on the lecture circuit as an example of a truly humbling experience. Many choose to go out with the Coles's Millpond Paddler operation (see Appendix A) first, to get to know the waters before negotiating them on their own.

Chapter 4
Chesapeake Bay

CHESAPEAKE BAY STRETCHES 200 MILES north to south, from just 9 miles shy of the Pennsylvania line to Hampton, Virginia. Add all the banks of forty rivers emptying into the bay and the twists of innumerable coves and creeks, and the bay's shoreline expands to cover 4,000 miles. The paddling possibilities are infinite, but here you'll find seventeen trips that are among the best.

They are mostly trips that longtime Chesapeake paddlers have enjoyed through the years, even though many more trips exist. No point on land is very far from water on the Chesapeake, and public launch ramps abound. Each trip offers something unique in the way of history, wildlife, scenery, crabbing, oystering, boats, exposure, and meeting the many people who earn a living from the bay.

You can paddle around a peninsula, out to one of the bay's 52 islands (only two are inhabited), wander around the marshes in the lower bay, circumnavigate a tidal island and wildlife refuge, go up and down a creek, or from one historic town to another. You can head up a river, cross it, and head back down the other side, visiting plantations or searching for fossils.

You can also cross the Chesapeake. The shortest crossing is at Annapolis (4 miles) and the longest is near the mouth of the Potomac River (30 miles). You cross the fossilized river bed of the Susquehanna River, which carved the bay, flooded with melted glacial water, and became a tidal estuary. That ancient bed marches down the middle of the bay, which measures 90 to 120 feet deep. This is where all the barges, destroyers, and naval aircraft follow the deep channel. The rest of the bay is fairly shallow, averaging 20 feet in depth. The modern Susquehanna, a mere shadow of its former size, empties into the top of the bay at Havre de Grace.

Chesapeake paddling can vary from ocean-like conditions to calmer trips such as an exploration of a cattail marsh near Mason Neck.

Another ambitious trip is out to Smith Island (7 miles). Many shoreline trips exist, though, and you never need be far from land, making this suitable kayak country for beginners. You just need to keep careful track of twists and turns in the marshes and creeks. It is possible to get lost here, so you have to be careful.

In all such excursions, the Chesapeake Bay reveals itself quietly. The bay's scenery is subtle rather than dramatic. But at the end of a long day trip, you are aware of the wealth you have seen and then the whole drama comes into focus in a mellow, quiet beauty.

"The Chesapeake does not impress those who know it best as the grandest or most of anything," says William Warner in *Beautiful Swimmers,* a Pulitzer-prize-winning book about the life cycle of the blue crab and the watermen who depend on it for a living (see Annotated Bibliography). While perhaps slow to form, one's impressions are unforgettable. Images linger long after the trip is past: at Point Lookout on the western shore where the Potomac meets the Chesapeake, a pair of oldsquaw barrel by our kayaks head to head. The thundering collapse of a bluff at Mason's Neck creates a ruckus of two dozen great blue herons sent screeching into flight. Kayaks scare up a thousand scaup, quiet except for the light rustling of their wings sounding like a waterfall. The long white porch of a Sotterly Plantation on the Patuxent River appears out of the early-morning mist.

Our impressions continue: Captain Laird throws our kayaks on top of his passenger ferry without any fuss so we can get to Smith Island before a blizzard hits. Frances Kitching, who owns the only motel on Smith, gingerly walks in my footsteps in the snow so her feet won't get wet. Two dozen tundra swans take off like thunder from a cove at Wye Island. The friendly waitress at Deal Island Seafood tucks the legs of soft-shelled crabs underneath their bellies for the squeamish diner. Snow geese lay out a restless white carpet at Blackwater National Wildlife Refuge on the Eastern Shore. The elegant—and fast disappearing—canvasback on the Patuxent appear in the midst of a raft of scaup. A wounded skipjack sits stuck up a creek at Deal Island. The impressions are unforgettable of this historic and wildlife-rich area.

The best times to paddle in the Chesapeake are fall and spring when the crowds have diminished, fewer powerboats zoom out from the marinas, the bugs (mosquitoes, greenheads, and no-see-ums) living in the marshes, and stinging jellyfish are absent. Vast migrations of birds along the Atlantic flyways are taking place, so you have a chance to witness nature in dramatic transition.

Charts

A good source of charts for paddling in the Chesapeake is the Alexandria Drafting Company's (ADC) waterproof *Chartbook of the Chesapeake Bay* (now in its fourth edition), available from most fishing shops and marinas or from ADC (see Appendix A). Detail of both the waterways and roads is excellent and can be used as a road map to reach public launch ramps, clearly marked by a trailered-boat symbol. The scale is 1:80,000, but the book has inserts of the larger scale 1:40,000 for, notably, Kent Narrows, Baltimore Harbor, Wye Island, Smith, and Tangier islands. It also includes river tributaries fairly high up, some on a scale of 1:40,000.

The chart book fits into a normal-size chart case so you can take the whole book along on your cruise. For navigating the vast, flat marshy creeks around Crisfield or areas south of Crisfield, a larger scale is advisable. Those you can obtain from NOAA at most local marine shops. A good map source is Fawcett's Boating Supply (410-267-8681) in Annapolis, Maryland. Regular NOAA charts are also available and appropriate numbers referenced below in trip data.

For land features (creeks, secondary roads, and land contours), use topographic-bathymetric (otherwise known as topo) maps published by the U.S. Geological Survey and the National Ocean Service. You can find them in most outdoor stores or write USGS, Reston, Virginia, 22092.

Maryland provides an excellent road map; Virginia's is less detailed, but you can find free county maps with more roads indicated at tourist information centers.

Access

In theory, wherever a road ends at waterside is a public launch spot. Native Americans and colonists in canoes used the bay and rivers as natural highways. In colonial times, tobacco farmers used their shallops and snows (two kinds of small open or half-decked vessels) to transport themselves around the bay. Few roads existed initially, and even when more appeared, transportation by water was still easier. Most plantation owners had a "rolling road," a grassy path smoothed by a roller, down to their private wharves. From here their ships would leave directly for England in the lucrative exchange of tobacco for British furniture and textiles. Towns also had roads down to a wharf. Today, any road that ends in a wharf is usually a watermen's way to the water and is theoretically public access. But finding these public ways is not easy without local knowledge. Private development has been intense. Marinas and condominiums have sprouted all over the bay's shores and overshadowed public ways to the water.

Since the Chesapeake has so many recreational fishermen, with ramps already built for them, many access spots do already exist. Much information is available because the Chesapeake has a strong sailboat and powerboat constituency as well as many recreational fishermen. "Sometimes you have to be a fisherman to be a kayaker," says Chris Conklin, who helped found the Chesapeake Paddlers Association. There's still a need for information for those carrying their boats to the water, however.

The best source for access is the *Chesapeake Bay and Susquehanna River Public Access Guide* published by several state agencies. Although out of print, it is still useful. Write to Department of Game and Inland Fisheries of Virginia for a free copy, as supplies last (see Appendix A).

Chris Conklin of the Chesapeake Paddlers Association maintains an updated list of launch spots with directions, which he makes available to the club's members. Joining this organization is worthwhile (see Appendix A).

DeLorme Mapping Company publishes road atlases for Maryland–Delaware and Virginia, in which public launch ramps are noted. The Maryland–Delaware atlas includes a special section on Chesapeake Bay, which indicates the habitats of oysters, clams, blue crabs, and bald eagles. The atlas costs $14.95 plus $4 shipping for the first atlas and 50 cents for the second. Call or write DeLorme Mapping Company (see Appendix A) or look for the atlas in most outdoor stores.

Try also *Guide to Cruising Maryland Waters* (around $18), published by the Maryland Department of Natural Resources Boating Administration, 560 Taylor Ave., Annapolis, Maryland 21401. *Virginia, a Saltwater Fishing Guide* lists public launch ramps by town. You can find the brochure at a tourist information centers.

The Chesapeake Trail

For the past several years, The Chesapeake Paddlers Association and its two hundred members have engaged in developing a sea-kayak trail spanning the entire 200-mile length of Chesapeake Bay. They plan to set up a trail on both the eastern and western shores by establishing overnight sites, preferably at 5-mile intervals. They want to create a "blue necklace" around the bay so kayakers can travel for days. For more information about the project, contact the Chesapeake Paddlers Association (Appendix A). For now, though, optimum kayaking is really day tripping because of the lack of public shoreside camping spots.

Although much of the land around the Chesapeake is in the public domain through state wildlife management areas, national wildlife refuges, or specially created preserves, the mix of recreation and wildlife management has not been really spelled out, so some work yet needs to be done on specifying site-specific camping spots for kayaking campers.

The Chesapeake has only fifty-two islands, and many are either privately owned, military areas (Bloodsworth), or long stretches of national wildlife refuge (Martin) of marshy ground.

The Chesapeake Bay Foundation (see Appendix A) has resources you may use as a member. It has dormitory accommodations in Tylerton on Smith Island and uses Port Isobel Island off Tangier Island as an environmental education center and sometimes allows kayakers to camp there.

The trail project is ambitious because the bay's shoreline is so long: in theory, trails could exist for the East Shore, West Shore, Atlantic Coast, and major river systems such as the Susquehanna, Potomac, and James—overall about 4,000 miles of shoreline.

Safety

Ron Casterline, who owns Annapolis Kayak Center on the South River in Annapolis, claims that boat traffic is the biggest safety factor in the Chesapeake, to the point where you must sometimes hang onto a buoy for a long time and wait for the boats to cross. That is why many people prefer to paddle off-season, when the recreational power boaters hibernate.

Recreational boat traffic emerging from the ever-growing marinas and bayside condominiums is plentiful. On nearly every creek is a marina, and in the warm months the marinas hatch swarms of power boaters. Power boaters don't necessarily see kayakers. They usually zoom along, many of them in the same area, creating confusing, kayak-tipping wakes.

One way to deal with the confusion of right-of-way is to put your paddle down on the boat and hold your elbows as if to say you're not going to do anything until the powerboater does, says Ron Casterline. (Always assume the other boat, power or sail, not to mention crabbing boats, barges, and military craft, has the right of way.)

Stay to the shallows where the larger boats don't go. Exercise caution when crossing a channel: If you are in a group, find the right time to sprint across (at the narrowest part of the channel) and keep your kayaks abreast. If the approaching boat does not slow down or alter course, make yourself as visible as possible by waving your paddle high in the air.

One way to avoid the powerboats is to choose your time accordingly. If you paddle weekend mornings, particularly Sunday morning, before noon, you will find less traffic. Also, paddling in winter on the bay can be very serene. You will need to wear a wetsuit or drysuit and it's a good idea to take the Annapolis Kayaking Center's cold-water paddling course in November (see Appendix A).

Also, large boat traffic belonging to the Navy and commercial shipping companies ply the waters and have absolutely no ability to stop to avoid running you over. Captains of large vessels have no line of sight on kayaks; radar will not pick up the kayak even if you have radar reflectors mounted on your boat; and besides, it takes a large tanker 5 miles to stop. To avoid them try to stay out of the deep-water channel altogether.

The good news is that the Chesapeake's waters tend to be gentle. The Chesapeake does not have large tides and water volume: the tidal range averages 1.5 feet. Very few hair-raising currents funnel through narrows, where wind-opposing tide could kick up a stir. Current flows at a maximum speed of 2 knots off Cape Henry in Virginia Beach, Virginia, at the bay's mouth. Current is strong under the Bay Bridge at Annapolis, but most current averages a little over 1 knot.

Furthermore, huge tidal marshes and meandering creeks, streams, coves, and sub-estuaries absorb any water overflow. The water has a lot of room to spread out and it does not get funnelled through inlets like some of the "gates," "narrows," or "holes" in New England or those inlets between the barrier beaches of Long Island and New Jersey.

Few cliffs exist that the sea can speed up and refract off. The bay is all sand and mud except for bulkheads. Fog is not much of a worry because Chesapeake waters are so warm.

That is not to say that the Chesapeake is devoid of hazards. Chesapeake Bay is one of the most benign areas in the country to paddle, which can build up a false sense of security: the dangers are not readily apparent.

In shallow water, waves get very confused, short and sharp, the kind that sailors slap against all the time. Violent summer storms from the heat buildup over the flat mainland come up swiftly and move fast. You can be caught out in the middle of the bay when a violent squall hits and should get off open water quickly. For open-water paddling, you should check the weather the night before. Plan to stay close to shore in the late afternoon. Also, talk to the the Coast Guard or the department of natural resources (see Appendix B) in the local area you are paddling for weather predictions and patterns.

Winds funnel down the riverbeds at tremendous speed. In a river valley such as the Rappahannock, 40- to 50-knot winds are not unheard of.

Prevailing winds (normal flow) are from the northwest. When you start out a trip in the morning, most likely the winds will be northwest. By afternoon in the summer, heat develops over the long, flat fields inland west of the bay, causing a rapid rise of air overland that draws the cooler air in off the water. This shifts the wind direction south to southeast, almost a 180-degree turn from the morning. It is wise to plan your trips around this wind shift.

Meanwhile, take heed close to shore. Although the Chesapeake does not have tremendous fetch where large, wind-driven swells can build up over the open ocean, at the edges, the sand shoals up, and you can be faced with waves at trip's end (though you'll have a soft landing). That may have been one factor in the death of a Chesapeake paddler in December of 1992. He was crossing the bay from Annapolis to St. Michael's (from the western to eastern shore), a distance of about 20 miles. Conditions were marginal—40 MPH winds, 46-degree water. It was the kind of weather where in a single stroke, you could broach and capsize. People speculate that he nearly made it to the other side but with fatigue and prolonged exposure was unable to stay upright in the growing fetch and steep waves in the shallows on the opposite shore.

The difference between water and air temperature can also be a problem. In October, November, March, and April, the air temperature is commonly 70 degrees. By contrast, the water temperature usually drops to the mid- to low 40s during these months. Immersion in 40-degree water while being dressed for 70-degree temperatures can be quite a shock.

Also, be aware of when hunting season is so your paddle isn't mistaken for a winged teal. In Maryland, the season generally runs September to January with different weeks designated for different waterfowl and upland bird species.

One last word on safety: Many areas are sometimes restricted to travel due to military practice all up and down the bay and rivers. Charts will show restricted areas. Lots of public notice of activity is available, but you must be aware of where to get the information. Call the Coast Guard (see Appendix B) to discuss such areas in your plans.

Despite all these warnings, it should be noted that sea kayaking is one of the best ways to get to know the Chesapeake and for the prepared paddler is nothing short of pure delight.

Ecology of Chesapeake Bay

Chesapeake Bay is the largest estuary in the United States. More than forty rivers empty into a semi-enclosed area with a mix of fresh and salt water. The result is a remarkably diverse ecosystem that supports a tremendous variety of wildlife and has produced some of the most important crab and oystering operations in the country. But some people worry that the Chesapeake, once one of the richest estuaries in North America, is now dead.

"In the past century more oysters have been harvested from the bay than any place else on earth. Yet takes have sagged to a few percent of historic harvests," wrote Tom Horton in an article, "Hanging in the Balance: Chesapeake Bay," that appeared in *National Geographic* in June 1993. Pollution is the major problem for this fragile ecosystem. Now, however, many private and public organizations are pulling together various funding sources to reverse the ill effects that have occurred over the past forty years. It is not an easy job. The insults come from many sources and locations.

Nutrient-rich runoff from farms as far away as central Pennsylvania causes growth of algae, which blocks sunlight from reaching the underwater plants on which ducks, geese, and swans feed and in which crabs hide to shed their shells. Meadows of underwater vegetation have disappeared over much of the bottom.

Also when the algae dies, it uses up oxygen needed by the bay's other plants and animals. Scientists have measured the deep channels and have found that during some summers, 15 percent of the bay's 15-trillion-gallon volume receives little or no oxygen.

Some farmers are trying to curtail the use of commercial fertilizer but it is on an individual basis, and for many, the far-reaching connections of their farms to the bay are remote. Pennsylvania legislators, however, passed a watershed bill in 1993 that reduces agricultural nutrient pollution from animal manure and fertilizers by requiring farmers to prepare nutrient management plans, which should help in reducing this runoff so destructive to the bay's wildlife.

Also, the bay's human population has nearly doubled, from eight million to fifteen million, in fifty years. Many natural areas are disappearing with the rise of homes and condominiums. Sewage pollutants from urban areas upstream also destroy water quality. The government has allocated millions of dollars to remove nitrogen from sewage discharge, which should help.

Years of disease, poor management, and pollution have devastated the bay's oyster colonies. Oysters are considered valuable filters because they remove algae and silt from the bay as they suck water through their systems. The oyster population used to be able to filter a volume of water equal to the entire bay every week or two. Now it takes the reduced oyster population almost a year to accomplish the same task.

Several volunteer organizations are working to restore the bay to health. One is the Chesapeake Bay Foundation (see Appendix A), with headquarters in Annapolis, Maryland. The foundation runs sea-kayak trips to Smith and Tangier Islands to educate people about the bay's environment. If you're interested in getting involved in saving the bay, this is a worthwhile organization to join.

The Beautiful Swimmers

What makes paddling on the Chespeake so special? Perhaps the major attraction is the working boats and the people who run them, a tradition as old as the Nanticoke and Powhatanic tribes who first lived here. You can see the watermen's deadrise workboats parked at every wharf with their crab pots stacked on the wharves and trotlines wrapped up. Crabbing runs from April to October, and it is a fine sight to see a workboat stacked high with crab pots going out for the first time in the spring.

The watermen's lifestyle determines a lot of the rhythm on the bay. They're up at 3:00 or 4:00 in the morning to go out in their boats for crabs while other family members stay on land picking, packing, and sorting. Dinner in watermen's communities is at 5:00 P.M.

It is said that the watermen from Tangier Island catch more crabs than anyone else in the bay—largely because they can join the Virginia dredging operation, banned in Maryland. Smith Islanders catch the next most. That is also because of the abundance of vegetation that still grows in Tangier Sound and allows the crabs a place to hide.

Eastern Bay and its tributaries such as the Wye are noted for the giant size of its "jimmies," male adult crabs. In fact they are so large—8 inches across—that some scientists have thought they may even be a sub-species, according to William Warner in *Beautiful Swimmers*. More realistically, scientists believe that the relative salinity of the Eastern Bay waters is conducive to fast crab growth and that the crabs have some food source as yet unidentified, according to Warner.

The Chesapeake is still the world's most intensive crab fishery. It has grown increasingly important to the watermen as the oyster industry has come to a standstill. Nearly half the national catch of blue crab comes from the bay. That has some worried that the blue crab, the tasty, beautiful swimmer, will be overfished. Maryland introduced a Crab Action Plan in 1993 to try to regulate commercial crabbing by the number of pots that can be used and licenses issued. The commercial crab catch in Chesapeake Bay dropped 40 percent from 1991 to 1992, according to the Chesapeake Bay Foundation. That's troubling in historic and cultural terms as well, for with the loss of Chesapeake's fisheries goes much of its uniqueness and heritage.

Meanwhile, it's easy to buy crabs fresh off the boat from the many shoreside operations and take them back to your campsite to cook. Here is a recipe for Maryland lady crab cakes:

Ingredients

> 1 pound crabmeat
>
> 1 cup Italian seasoned breadcrumbs
>
> 1 large egg
>
> 1/4 cup mayonnaise
>
> 1 teaspoon Worcestershire sauce
>
> 1 teaspoon dry mustard
>
> 1/2 teaspoon salt
>
> 1/4 teaspoon pepper
>
> Margarine or oil for frying

Remove all cartilage from the crabmeat. In a bowl, mix breadcrumbs, egg, mayonnaise, and seasonings. Add crabmeat and mix gently but thoroughly. If the mixture is too dry, add a little more mayonnaise or yogurt. Shape into six cakes. Cook cakes in a fry pan, in just enough hot oil to prevent sticking, until browned—about five minutes on each side. From the *Maryland Seafood Cookbook*. For a copy, send $1.50 to Maryland Cookbook, Seafood Marketing Authority, Annapolis, MD 21401.

Maryland's Eastern Shore

The Eastern Shore holds the most interest for paddlers, even though most of it is flat and low. Tidewater farms stretch down to the water in this important agricultural area. Watermen's boats line the wharves, and roadside signs abound for soft-shell crabs and peelers in family-run operations. Wildlife refuges preserve large tracts of open space between watermen's communities, farms, and historic towns.

From north to south, the first major area of interest is Elk Neck State Park, site of the annual Chesapeake Bay Sea Kayak Symposium in May. This is followed by Eastern Neck Wildlife Refuge, just north of the Bay Bridge from Annapolis to Kent Island. Farther south you run into the historic and genteel towns of St. Michaels, Oxford, and Cambridge, then access to islands such as Smith and Tangier from Crisfield. Just south of Pocomoke City, you cross into Virginia's narrow peninsula. Here are several trips on Maryland's Eastern Shore, which is part of the Delmarva (Delaware, Maryland, and Virginia) Peninsula.

Wye Island Circumnavigation: A Paddle into History

Charts: NOAA #12270 at 1:40,000

Trip Mileage: 12 nautical miles

Getting There: Wye Island is located just south of the Bay Bridge. Like many spots, it has several put-ins but the most convenient is Wye Landing. Take US 50 south to MD 213. Turn right and proceed 1 mile to Wye Mills. Turn left on MD 662 past the Wye Oak, then bear right again on Wye Landing Lane. Follow that lane 2.3 miles to Wye Landing. The launch ramp is paved and located just off the parking lot.

Camping: Camping is prohibited on Wye Island. The nearest state park is Martinak State Park (410-479-1619) at Denton, inland about 25 miles east.

Tidal Range: 1.2 feet at Kent Island Narrows

To get to Wye Island, turn off busy US 50, which descends the Delmarva Peninsula, onto MD 213. This takes you by the stately Wye Oak, a four-hundred-year-old tree held together by an intricate network of guy wires and said to be the largest white oak in the United States. You pass by cultivated fields, homes, and developments into one of the most historic areas on the Chesapeake. The grist mill in Wye has been in operation since 1671 and still grinds cornmeal by waterwheel. The nearby brick Episcopalian church dates to the 1600s when tobacco farmers eked out a living from a few acres of cultivated soil. The island itself is equally distinguished. Governor William Paca ran Wye Hall Farm on the eastern third of the island during the 1700s.

You are about to circumnavigate almost 15 miles around the wilderness, in the 2,500 acres of protected farmland and woodlots in the care of the Wye Island Preserve.

Wye Landing has several white crabbing sheds, a wharf, and a concrete launch ramp with corrugated surface. You launch into the Wye East River, which soon leads to a confluence of several waterways—Skipton Creek from the east, the Wye Narrows from the northwest, or a continuation of the Wye East River. Head south to circumnavigate clockwise—a good idea if you are expecting

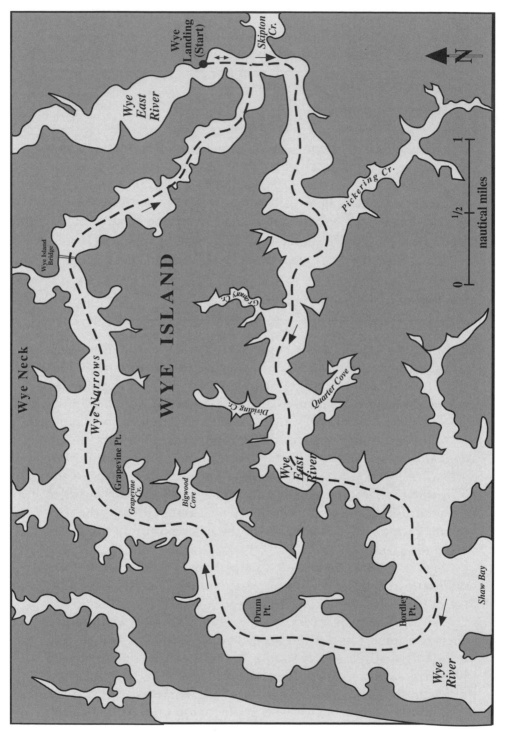

Wye Island

afternoon south winds. Choose your route depending on anticipated wind shifts of the day (listen to your weather radio). Overall, the trip is very protected, but the wind can be a factor as it funnels through channels or sweeps across broad reaches of the river. Going with the wind will make the trip more pleasant.

As you paddle, you may see huge flocks of ducks and geese. When we paddled there a workboat scared up at least 1,000 scaup (probably greater scaup because they are most commonly seen in large rafts on salt water when the lakes have frozen over) that darkened the sky. Just before Granary Creek, we disturbed hundreds of Canada geese out of a field, and nearly 30 tundra swans lumbered off the surface, launching into the wind. The slap of their wings against the water sounded like a large sail filling with wind on a jibe until these magnificent white frigates, necks stretched out straight, were at last airborne, graceful and honking.

Tundra swans (also called whistling swans) winter almost exclusively on Chesapeake Bay after spending summers in the Arctic tundra, adding a special note to winter paddling on the Chesapeake. Some come from breeding grounds as far away as Alaska

A discarded decoy found on Wye Island hitches a ride.

and northern Canada, nearly 4,000 miles, pausing briefly on the Great Lakes, then flying nonstop day and night to Atlantic winter headquarters on the Chesapeake and on down to North Carolina. Unlike their cousins the mute swans—introduced into this country from Great Britain as landscape decorations— the tundra swan is a wild native. You can tell the difference from afar by the neck stance: the tundra swan swims with its neck up straight, the mute swan in a curve. The tundra swan often shares the winter coves with the Canada geese, whose population in recent years has increased as they stay to feed in cornfields rather than migrating.

As we started off, we saw a bald eagle that soared down in front of us near the east end of Wye Island. It swooped down among the oak trees, then flew back into the fields ahead of us. The eagle allowed us to get fairly close as we paddled along in the calm water, then it took off again. You see many bald eagles in the Chesapeake. Together with the osprey, the eagle is making a great comeback with the elimination of DDT and with stricter penalties for people who harm them. Throughout the trip we also saw cardinals, turkey vultures, red-tailed hawks, buffleheads, seagulls, and great blue herons.

The day was overcast and threatening. Snow was in the forecast, but for the moment a gentle breeze blew at our backs, the water was calm, and we were just enjoying the peaceful scenery, the gray leafless trees, the clear fields of Wye Island, and the broad mainland fields to the south where large estates occasionally appeared.

It began to snow as we paddled along the south end of Wye Island, not more than a half-hour into our trip. We passed geese in the protected inlets of Wye before they got nervous and leaped up in a big gang, hooting and hollering; we felt bad until we realized that in this kind of stormy weather, ducks and geese tend to be unsettled and restless and change positions at the slightest provocation.

As we approached Bordley Point, the southernmost point of Wye Island, the waters opened up and the day became more overcast, and distant land seemed less distinct, hard to tell whether the point ahead was part of Wye Island or one of the mainland's long necks of the Eastern Shore. We knew we had to turn to the north, but it was hard to tell where.

Shaw Bay was to our left, and we turned around a point. It was clear that this was the end of the island. Across some houses were visible, indicators of the peninsula protecting Wye Island from Eastern Bay.

Suddenly, huge snowflakes began to fall, and our visibility became severely limited. We groped our way around the southwest end, unsure, except by intuition for the landscape, what was a cove or creek and what was an actual part of Wye Island. The shapes of the coves with names such as Grapevine didn't help. We knew we were in a civilized part of the world, but the island shore we kept securely to our right was preserved in wilderness, and the big estates to our left stood empty. No other boats were out and the wildfowl were far less abundant than on the island's other side. It was the season between crabbing and oystering and February is not a typical season for pleasure boating. Ironically, we felt completely isolated in this settled part of Maryland.

We continued to grope our way around, now in a driving wind and sleet. It was with relief that we spied Wye Island Bridge, and began to paddle toward it. It was only afterward we learned that in summer this bridge is swarming with "chicken neckers," the locals' term for tourists who fish for crabs using chicken necks. They line up on the bridge casting their lines over into the Wye.

We found our way back to Wye Landing by identifying the duck blind and pulled up to a still-deserted landing. The island is managed by the state (Maryland Department of Natural Resources), and you can make short hikes into the interior on nature trails from Ferry Point and Grapevine Cove. For more information on Wye's public use, call 410-827-7577.

Wye Island is the site of a paddling race sponsored by the Annapolis Rowing Club every September. Kayakers are welcome and the event is fun if you wish to make this circumnavigation against the clock and in the company of fellow paddlers.

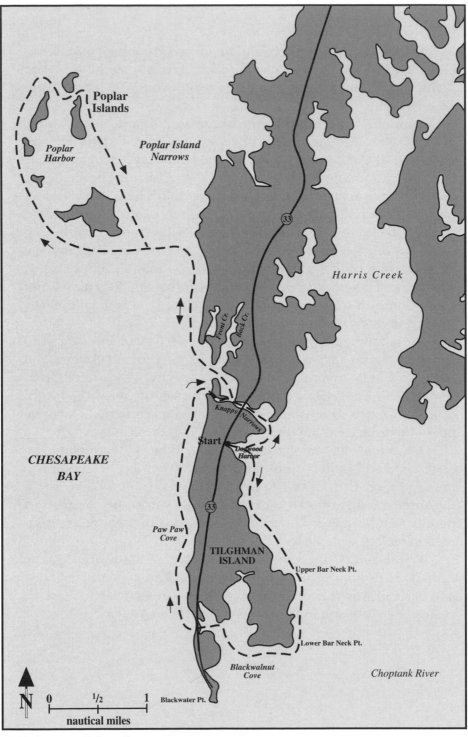

Poplar
Islands

*Poplar Island
Narrows*

*Poplar
Harbor*

33

Harris Creek

Front Cr.

Back Cr.

Knapps Narrows

Start

*Dogwood
Harbor*

**CHESAPEAKE
BAY**

33

*Paw Paw
Cove*

**TILGHMAN
ISLAND**

Upper Bar Neck Pt.

Lower Bar Neck Pt.

*Blackwalnut
Cove*

Choptank River

N

0   ¹/₂   1   Blackwater Pt.

nautical miles

Tilghman Island

Tilghman Island to Poplar Islands: The Last of the Skipjacks

Charts: NOAA #12266 at 1:40,000

Trip Mileage: 10 nautical miles

Getting There: From US 50 turn west onto MD 33 at Easton and follow that down, through St. Michaels, 22 miles to Knapp Narrows on Tilghman Island. One-half-mile past the Knapps Narrows Bridge on the left is the put-in at Dogwood Harbor, with marina and dock.

Camping: None, but Tilghman Island has several B & Bs. Wood Duck Inn (410) 886-2070 is located in Dogwood Harbor.

Tidal Range: 1.6 feet at Cambridge, Choptank River

The beauty of paddling around Tilghman Island and out to the Poplar Islands is seeing the working skipjacks (single-masted, beamy, shallow-draft boats used for dredging oysters) and workboats (long, wood, cabined motorboats used for crabbing) in action. The sight is particularly inspiring if you have stopped at the Chesapeake Bay Maritime Museum at Navy Point in St. Michaels and seen many of the working boats carefully preserved along the waterfront. A skipjack, bugeye (a two-masted, beamy, shallow-draft boat, larger than a skipjack), and buyboat (a large vessel used for buying oysters from boats working on the water), among others, may be moored at the docks; log canoes and duck hunting boats are stored in the sheds. Climb into the typical Chesapeake Bay screwpile lighthouse (a lighthouse in which piles are screwed into mud to prevent the piles from being heaved out by ice). Step into a miniature skipjack and sit at the tiller pretending you are sailing away for a day's dredge of oyster. (A small craft festival here in early October increasingly draws more kayakers who bring their home-built, wood-strip kayaks to display.)

So at Knapps Narrows it's a thrill to see the real working boats and be reminded that even though typical Chesapeake working craft are now preserved in a museum, a fishing industry still exists, if somewhat tenuously.

Because Tilghman Island provides immediate access to Chesapeake Bay to the west and the Choptank River to the east, it has for generations been a watermen's community. A fleet of workboats is based at Knapps Narrows, and a few sail-powered skipjacks and even a two-masted bugeye still operate from Dogwood Harbor, a half-mile south of the drawbridge. The toney yacht club recently built outside Dogwood Harbor flags a transition from oystering and crabbing to tourism and pleasure boating as mainstays of the island economy.

As you paddle out of Dogwood Harbor north toward Knapps Narrows, the broad Choptank opens up like an inland sea. You can just barely see the mainland to the east. Paddle north along Tilghman Island, and turn left at Knapps Narrows, marked by a lighted buoy. All along Knapps Narrows to your right and left are workboats lined up at the docks, their bows pointing out, interspersed with a few skipjacks, their "pushboats" suspended at the stern to allow them to dredge under power a few days a week.

The skipjack is an evolution of building style. The early colonists of the Eastern Shore took the natives' log canoe, literally a log burned out in the middle, to create a canoe, and developed it into a large boat by putting two, five, or even seven logs together for a hull. In the mid-nineteenth century crabbers and oystermen made further adaptations, adding two masts and a forward cabin. This boat was called a brogan. They built the larger bugeye to haul even more oysters as the seafood boom hit the Chesapeake after the Civil War. The skipjack appeared in the 1890s. According to the museum, it is the last commercial craft working under sails in the United States.

But the oyster industry is in trouble. In 1992, watermen found no oysters at all, according to the Kitchings on Smith Island, a family of watermen. They estimate that only about twenty skipjacks are left on the Bay and perhaps a dozen are still working craft. Every year, the state reseeds the oyster beds to keep the skipjacks going.

From the Narrows, we paddled north along the mainland toward the Poplar Islands. It was a mild February day, temperature in the low 60s, and was one of those days that makes winter paddling on the Chesapeake so appealing. We had the silty brown bay

The skipjack Virginia W. *sits ready to work at Knapps Narrows on Tilghman Island.*

entirely to ourselves. Gentle waves lapped under our hulls. The sun shone warmly. We were impressed with all the working craft, still alive and well. It was a good day to be on the Chesapeake.

The Poplar Islands are hard to spot. They are a group of quickly disappearing islands about a mile offshore. You will find no place to land here. Poplar used to be one big island but is now several pieces, according to Dr. Steve Leathermen, of the University of Maryland. Poplar was the Democratic Party's choice for their retreat during Franklin Delano Roosevelt's presidency. Congenial Democrats used to plan strategy here in their clubhouse with the help of two hundred bartenders. Truman was the last president to use Poplar. Because of the erosion, the Democrats moved the clubhouse to the Potomac River in the late 1940s.

If you want to stick to the mainland you can also circumnavigate Tilghman Island to the south of Knapps Narrows, a distance of about 6 nautical miles. Either way, at trip's end enjoy a dockside crab feast at the Crab Claw restaurant in St. Michael's, right next to the Maritime Museum.

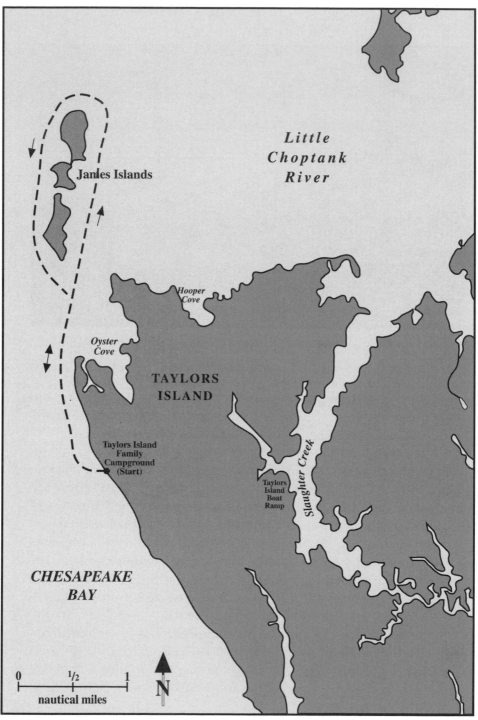

James Islands

James Islands: Eroding into Memory

Charts: NOAA #12264 at 1:40,000 or Small Craft Chart #12265

Trip Mileage: 8 nautical miles

Getting There: From US 50 at Cambridge, take MD 16 west through Church Creek. Stay on this road across Slaughter Creek. At the second Bay Shore Road sign, turn left. Make two more sharp left turns. Taylors Island Family Campground is on the right. You'll see the sign. Parking and launch fee is $2. The public launch spot is at Slaughter Creek, beyond the bridge on the right. (Note that some maps mistakenly place the spot elsewhere.)

Camping: No designated camping

Tidal Range: 1.2 feet at Taylors Island, Little Choptank River

The James Islands are three handsome islands a little more than a mile offshore to the north of Taylors Island. They are located at the mouth of the broad Little Choptank River, just to the south of the Choptank River. The area is where novelist James Michener based his novel *Chesapeake,* an historical account that covers the lives of the Choptank Indians, tobacco farmers, duck hunters, and watermen (see Annotated Bibliography).

Driving along MD16, you catch glimpses of extensive marshes, particularly behind Slaughter Creek. They resemble the Florida Everglades in their sweeping expanse of grass and sky.

The most direct access to the James Islands is from just south of Oyster Cove, from where it is about 1 nautical mile to the most southerly of the islands. The Taylors Island Family Campground will let you launch for a small fee in summer, even though you may have to wait your turn with the powerboaters, but it is a safe place to leave your car.

Slaughter Creek has an official launch spot (Taylors Island Boat Ramp) just past the bridge to Taylors Island on MD 16, but a launch there would extend your voyage considerably.

The James Islands used to be part of the mainland but erosion has separated them. You have only to paddle around these islands, where mud filters out about 10 feet or so, then paddle along the west side, where whole forests have crashed into the bay, to witness the banks' erosion.

The last of the James Islands are connected by a long sand spit, perfect for picnicking and camping.

Erosion, resulting from rising sea level and devastating higher storm tides, is a major problem in the bay. Some areas are eroding 10 to 15 feet a year. Some areas you paddle to during one year, but the next year you return, and there's no island left. Sadly, during the last century, people have had to abandon ten islands including Holland, which evacuated one hundred families. Homeowners try to stop erosion by building bulkheads and riprap (sustaining walls of stone jumbled together). Government agencies are trying to restore some of the islands: for example, the U.S. Fish and Wildlife Service is rebuilding Botken Island.

After launching from the campground, turn north and follow the shoreline, strewn with slender tree trunks lying every which-way like pick-up sticks, unloosened from the earth from the bay's rise in level. Aim for a nameless ledge just offshore and you might scare up several rafts of buffleheads. Then make the longer crossing to the southern James. The islands are totally deserted, covered by impenetrable loblolly pine forest. You may find a spot for a picnic on the edge of the forest in the sun and protected from the wind. The most northerly James has a long sand spit, the only break in the pattern of these islands, and a great place for a picnic.

On your way back, to extend your trip, you may want to explore Oyster Cove, where there is a cattle ranch and other sections of this northerly shoreline on the Little Choptank.

Hooper Islands: Remote Peninsula

Charts: NOAA Chart #12261 or Small Craft Chart #12230

Trip Mileage: 7 nautical miles

Getting There: From U.S. 50 at Cambridge, take MD 16 west through Church Creek, then bear left on MD 335. Pass Blackwater National Wildlife Refuge. At the T intersection with MD 336, turn right to stay on MD 335 southbound, which turns into Hooper Island Road. Continue south, cross the bridge to Upper Hooper Island at Honga. Cross another bridge at Fishing Creek to Middle Hooper Island. Follow the road until it ends at Hoopersville. The launch is on the left in Muddy Hook Cove by the crab restaurants.

Camping: None

Tidal Range: 1.2 feet at Taylors Island, Little Choptank River

The southern tip of the Hooper Island chain is about as remote as it gets near the mainland. Maryland State Road 35 takes you three-fourth of the way down Middle Hooper Island. The state government built the Narrows Ferry Bridge between Upper Hooper and Middle Hooper in 1980, and you can feel how less settled Middle Hooper is than Upper Hooper. The Muddy Hook Cove Boat Ramp is located at Hooperville. From here you can do a circumnavigation of Lower Hooper Island, reachable only by boat across the Thorofare. The relief is flat, and the views across the Honga River (previously called the Hungry River, derived from kayhunge, the Powhatan word for river) are beautiful.

Set out from Muddy Hook Cove and head straight across the cove to Dicks Point then to Thorofare Point. Depending on what the current (which can run very swiftly) is doing through the Thorofare, either paddle through the Thorofare now or continue on around Lower Hooper Island. Opposing wind and tide can create some good waves through this narrow passage. If you go through now, you reach Thorofare Cove, a lovely protected cove that opens onto the broad bay. Paddle around Fishing Point, admiring the wide views across the bay, then make your way around Nancy's Point, Creek Point (where a creek empties), Billy's Point, Ware

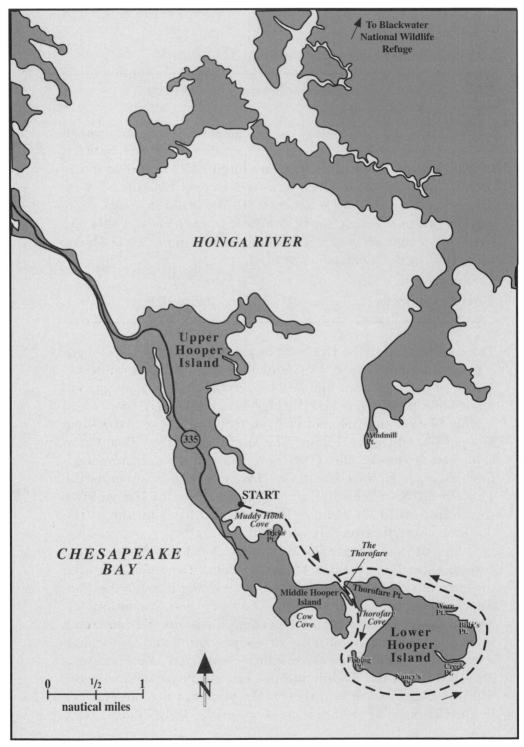

Hopper Islands

Point, and so back to Thorofare Point. Here you have a wide view across the Honga River to Windmill Point. Note that the southern end of Hooper can get fairly exposed to wind and waves.

Because Lower Hooper is virtually uninhabited, you will see much wildlife including ospreys, oyster catchers, kingfishers, old-squaw, scoters, and loons. The summer brings good fishing for perch, spot, flounder, and trout around the southern point of the island. This is a good day's paddle in terms of stamina and not recommended as a casual outing, particularly since Lower Hooper is so deserted.

This trip is not for everyone because of its remoteness and flatness, but seeing this part of the world is a truly unique experience. Be on the lookout for the Hooper Island Drake, a workboat built here, whose curved stern design imitates the torpedo boats that steamed up and down the bay before World War II.

Blackwater National Wildlife Refuge, located just to the north, is one of the biggest overwintering areas for geese and ducks on the Atlantic Coast so you will be sure to see lots of wildfowl when paddling around Hooper. The refuge is an immense area that covers more than 16,000 acres, consisting of marsh, magnificent loblolly pine forest, open water, and farms. Watch for large eagle

Hooper Island watermen burn the fields to allow new plant growth and to find muskrat holes.

nests atop the pines and the birds themselves—Blackwater is a favorite breeding area for the bald eagle. In March and April waterfowl migrate northward including snow geese.

Sadly, Blackwater is collapsing and has lost nearly one third of its marsh, or about 5,000 acres, according to a refuge official. The solid, stable marsh has been converted to shallow water on top of muck within the last 50 to 100 years. That is because the sea-level rise (possibly due to global warming) has drowned the marsh and killed the marsh grass. Meanwhile, the land surface is dropping, possibly due to too much ground water withdrawal. The two separate phenomena have twice the impact on Blackwater's loss of marsh. As ever, these seemingly secure wildlife areas on the Chesapeake are very fragile. Meanwhile, other parts of the refuge continue to be a major stopover for snow geese and home to nearly a dozen breeding pair of eagles.

At Fishing Creek, try Old Salty's Restaurant for family-style seafood.

Deal Island: Forgotten Fishing Villages

Charts: NOAA Chart #12231 or Small Craft Chart #12230

Trip Mileage: 4 nautical miles

Getting There: At Salisbury, turn off US 50 to US 13 southbound. At Princess Anne, turn right (west) onto MD 363. Follow MD 363 through Monie, Dames Quarter, Chance, Deal Island, all the way to Wenona, where the road ends near the launch ramp in Wenona Harbor. *Alternate launches:* Deal Island Harbor and the next peninsula down at Rumbley on Goose Creek off MD 361.

Camping: Janes Island State Park in Crisfield is the nearest camping, about 35 miles distance. See Smith Island, below.

Tidal Range: 2.0 feet at Crisfield, Little Annemessex River

Drive the 3-mile length of Deal Island along MD 363 to the end, and you will reach Wenona, which has a small, snug harbor with several skipjacks. The public ramp is at the north end of the parking lot. If you arrive on a Sunday morning you may find many watermen playing pool inside Arby's General Store across the street from the launch ramp. Go into the store to check on the day's weather and general lore.

From the launch, you can circumnavigate Little Deal, a low-lying, marshy uninhabited island, where the Manokin River meets Tangier Sound. A counterclockwise circumnavigation gives you the strong northwest wind pushing you down Tangier Sound and surfing you into the island, then a slog up the other side. Beware of the southern fork of the island. You may inadvertently turn into the cove between the two prongs instead of the waterway. Turn left (north) at the second prong for the circumnavigation back to Wenona. An alternate, more ambitious itinerary is a 4-nautical-mile crossing to South Marsh Island. The island is a splendid wildlife area run by the Maryland Department of Natural Resources. Unlike its north and south neighbor islands, Smith Island, which is inhabited, and Bloodsworth, which is a government bombing range, South Marsh is undisturbed. It has large colonies of herons and egrets and is a treasure for wildlife watching.

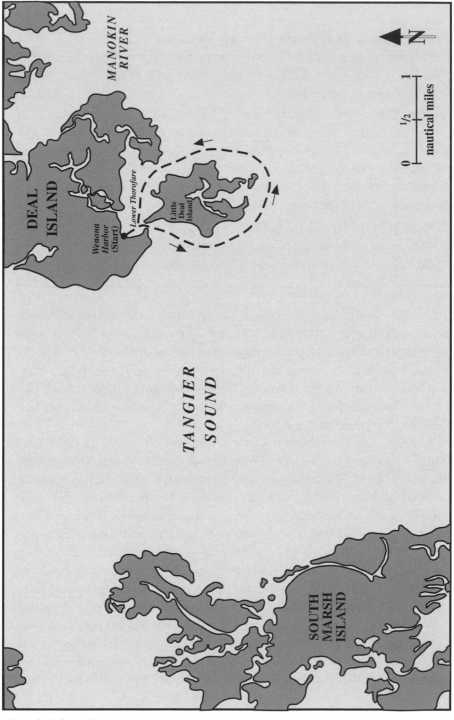

Deal Island

A skipjack sits abandoned in Wenona Harbor.

Upon return, we admired the workboats and skipjacks anchored in the harbor. Sadly, an abandoned skipjack sat up a creek in disrepair. These single-masted vessels still dredge for oysters in winter. State law allows them to use their "yawl boats" for power only on Monday and Tuesday. From 1,000 skipjacks at the turn of the century, just more than 20 remain and only about a dozen still work today. The rest are at the bottom of the bay or pulled up to rot like this one.

You can also paddle out of Deal Island Harbor, on the southwest side of the Deal Island Bridge. Here, Island Seafood Deli is a friendly place and a good spot to eat softshell crabs or crab cakes and lounge on the dock, watching the watermen unload their day's catch, observe a soft crab shedding operation, see how an oyster hatchery works, or watch crab pickers. Wenona and Deal Island crabs are shipped all over the world, and several family-run operations are located in the area.

The Skipjack Races take place here every Labor Day when the bay's last remaining skipjacks from Deal Island, Chance, Wenona,

Mount Vernon, and Tilghman compete with one another for the $1,000 first-place prize.

As you drive down the island, you will see the chapel (watch for historic-marker sign) of the "Parson of the Islands," the Reverend Joshua Thomas, a waterman who conducted much of his ministry from the site of his chapel. His followers from Smith and Tangier islands and Saxis in Virginia would arrive in sailing vessels by the hundreds to listen to him preach, using parables with symbols from fishing and oystering.

For an interesting post-paddle side trip at Dames Quarter (formerly called Dam Quarter—nobody knows the reason for the name change, but speculation has it that the local Methodists and Episcopalians changed it because they didn't want to live in a place with that name any longer), take Riley Roberts Road, across from Arby's Cash & Carry, south out to the water impoundment into the Deal Island Wildlife Management Area. You may see wigeon, swans, great blue herons, Canada geese, black ducks, pintails, and shovelers. From here, you can look back across to Deal Island, a long, flat, black stretch of cordgrass to a few stands of trees and the condominiums that stand out so distinctly at Wenona. You can understand why the early colonists called Deal Island Devil's Island because they thought only the devil could possibly live here. A Methodist minister changed the name to Deal so his flock wouldn't think that the devil had some rights to live on the island.

Circumnavigation of Smith Island: Communities of Hardy Watermen

Charts: NOAA Chart #12231 or Small Craft Chart #12230

Trip Mileage: 6.5 nautical miles

Getting There: Follow US 50 to Salisbury. At Salisbury, take US 13 south through Princess Anne (stay on the main route; don't take the business route). Just before Westover, take MD 413 south. MD 413 goes straight down to the ferry dock, down the main street in Crisfield. It's a forty-five-minute ferry trip from Crisfield to Ewell on Smith Island.

Getting to Smith—and Tangier Island, farther south—is an adventure in itself. All the boats—mailboats, ferries—take off at 12:30 P.M, leaving like a parade to points of Smith and Tangier. From Smith, the mailboat has an afternoon run at 3:30 or 5:00 (in summer). In winter, this run takes place if there is someone on the mainland who needs to be picked up.

Captains Terry and Larry Laird (410-425-5931) are very accommodating to kayakers and will load your kayak onto the Captain Jason I or II to take you to Smith or back. Fees are $10 per person and $10 per boat roundtrip.

Camping: In Crisfield, Janes Island (not to be confused with James Island farther north) State Park has pleasant camping and is a good base camp from which to paddle numerous areas on the lower Eastern Shore. You launch directly into the Annemessex Canal. Contact Janes Island Campground, 26280 Alfred Lawson Drive, Crisfield, MD 21817; (410) 968-1565. Open April 1 to October 31. Cabins open year-round ($63 for a six-person cabin), two-night minimum.

Directions to Janes Island State Park: Follow Main Street (MD 413) away from County Dock for 1.3 miles, then turn left on MD 358. Follow the twisty road for 1.1 miles, then turn left at the large sign for Janes Island State Park. After passing the park office, go less than 0.1 mile, then turn left for Camping Area A and the boat launch ramp.

Tidal Range: 2.0 feet at Crisfield, Little Annemessex River

Caution Areas: Crossing from Crisfield to Smith can present hazards as wind and current rises. This 12-mile trip should only be made by

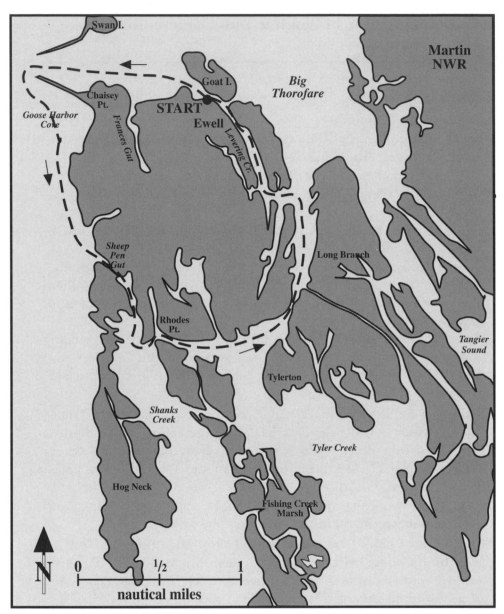

Smith Island

the most prepared and experienced sea kayaker. Check in at the Coast Guard station (located at the south side of the harbor at Crisfield) before making this crossing.

Around Smith Island, it's easy to feel edgy when paddling a kayak. Here you've paddled or taken the forty-five-minute ferry 12 miles across Tangier Sound from Crisfield on the mainland, and you find marshy thorofares and creeks, easy places to get lost without your trusty charts. Smith's three towns—Ewell and Rhodes Point, connected by a 2-mile road, and Tylerton on its own island—barely rise high enough off their hammocks to give you a sense of security. As ever in the Chesapeake, the visual interest is in the watermen and their crabbing and oystering operation, and the wildlife, both of which there are plenty on Smith.

The island looks like a substantial piece of land, but the definition between land and bay is nebulous. In fact, Smith Island is an archipelago of several islands, nine miles north to south and four miles east to west, marked by creeks, thorofares, points, ditches, swashes, marshes, islands, guts, and coves.

Your best bet is to follow the numbers of the day markers in the Big Thorofare, the main channel through which working boats and mailboats travel to and from Smith Island. Your visual reference will be the three towns, which you can see from wherever you are. More than anything, the three towns resemble medieval villages rising up at the edge of the fields; the only element missing to make this image complete is the towering spire of a Gothic cathedral. However, Tylerton and Smith oblige with high towers of their Methodist churches (you can also see their water towers from well off shore).

Smith is still very much a watermen's community. It has amber light, wind, ducks, shades on the windows. Boats in the harbor have an assured sameness to them. You won't find any marinas. You see the 40-foot-long workboats lined up along the waterfronts and crabbing paraphernalia strewn around the docks: piles of wire-mesh crab traps stacked up, an errant crab scrape (a series of metal poles with twine-bag dragged behind a boat), all testimony to Smith's hardy watermen's specialty—trapping and

Workboats hibernate under snow at Ewell, the main town on Smith Island.

sending softshell crabs to market in a timely manner. Tangier Sound has a great deal of eelgrass which supports the crab industry (grass beds provide important hiding areas for young crabs).

You'll hear the elongated drawl of the natives—Elizabethan, they say, from the coast of Cornwall, England. Among the natives you'll find endurance, calm in the face of an unpredictable life of making a living from the sea. Each town has fig trees, pear trees, mimosas, and pomegranates, which makes spring a particularly fragrant time to visit here. The graves in the cemeteries are built above ground so they won't be awash in the spring tides. The high-school students commute daily to Crisfield for their education. Towns have wooden shanties along the harbors that house family-owned soft crab shedding operations (crabs are kept until they shed their hard shells and then are marketed as soft-shell crabs). Most residents ride bikes and keep their cars on the mainland where they need them. The only road is a 1-mile stretch from Ewell to Rhodes Point.

A circumnavigation stopping at Smith's three towns is a good way to get a feel for the island. You can launch from the public

Kayaker Forrest Dillon straps the kayaks on deck for the crossing from Crisfield to Smith Island.

ramp in Ewell, in the workboat basin just to the west of Ruke's Store. The circumnavigation trip length is 6.5 nautical miles.

Paddle out of the workboat basin to the left (west) along the the narrow waterway between Ewell and Goat Island where all the workboats are parked. Just over your right shoulder (north) is Goat Island, so called because of the herd of about twenty goats who live there. Islanders are said to predict rain or snow when the goats visit the water's edge for salt from the marsh grasses. Paddle past Frances Gut and Chaisey Point. The broad waterway behind you (east) marked by several daymarkers is the Big Thorofare. Ahead out the jetties is the west channel. Both these channels, with about 4 to 6 feet of draft, are the way big boats reach Ewell.

Just to the north of Ewell is the Martin National Wildlife Refuge, more than 4,000 acres of marsh, broken by shallow channels. In spring and summer, it is haven to such species as great blue heron, black-crowned night heron, little blue heron, and Louisiana (tricolor) heron, that nest in large preserved rookeries in the hammocks. Other species are the glossy ibis, snowy egret, osprey, otter, and mink. The refuge, managed by the U.S. Fish and Wildlife Service, has a visitor center in Ewell. Located in the Tyler House, the center is open daily April through December. Contact Blackwater Refuge (410-228-2677) for more information.

Winter waterfowl around Smith include oldsquaw, bufflehead, and black duck. Kayakers are allowed to land on Swan Island, which has a sandy beach. It is very easy to get lost in all these creeks and inlets—as shallow as 8 inches in some places—and these should be navigated with extreme caution. Kedges Lighthouse marks the refuge's northern boundary.

Paddle west through the inlet, out the stone jetties and into the bay. Here you can often find a heavy chop from opposing wind and tide. Head down the west side of Smith Island, which can be very exposed in a west or northwest wind. Press on. You'll be in the lee coming back. Pass Goose Harbor Cove, then through Sheep Pen Gut to Rhodes Point. Pass by the Marsh family's boatyard, which has the only dry dock on Smith for boat repair. You may see several kinds of sandpiper on low-tide flats.

Formerly called Rogues Point due to the presence of pirates, the islanders changed the name to the more respectable Rhodes Point. Paddle through the channel just to the south of Rhodes Point toward the white houses of Tylerton and the lighted buoy. Then head for marker "Green 1." [Tylerton, originally named Drum Point, has the most ornate architecture of any of the towns. Here you can visit the Chesapeake Bay Foundation House. This is an environmental-education center frequented by students and adults from the Bay watershed area who participate in the Foundation's three-day seminar program. Contact the Chesapeake Bay Foundation (see Appendix A).]

Other landmarks include the Methodist church, the one-room Tylerton school, the store located by the county dock, and the Tylerton library, built from a converted bookmobile. Once back on the water, you can follow the Big Thorofare back to Ewell, following the green markers. Just before Green 5 and right after the lighted buoy, turn left into Levering Creek and so back to Ewell.

No official camping is permitted on the island (and one colleague who did camp nearby said his camp was visited by several rats). We would recommend Frances Kitching's Smith Island Motel, Ewell, MD 21824; 410-425-4441 or 424-3321, open year-round. It's the only motel on the island (eight rooms), identifiable by the satellite dish out front. Frances allows you to leave your kayaks on the front lawn. Security is not a problem. Smith has no police but there does not seem to be a need for them.

Born on Smith Island, Kitching was one of the first to start letting guests into her home and is very involved in hospitality to visitors and helping out islanders alike. She's trying to bring a museum to the old Skipjack Restaurant, and you can buy autographed copies of Mrs. Kitching's "Smith Island Cookbook," across the street at the author's home.

For dinner at nonwatermen's hours (watermen eat at 5:00 P.M.), Ruke's, right at the ferry wharf, is a rustic country store with a flea market and small restaurant that serves pizza, subs, and hamburgers and is the local Saturday night hangout. No alcohol is sold on the island. You can get most supplies at Charlie's grocery store, which doubles as the pool hall on winter Saturday afternoons.

Smith's residents are very friendly despite the hordes of day tourists who descend on the island in summer to eat a meal at one of the crab restaurants and take a quick tour of the island before getting back on the 4:00 P.M. boat. Anyone in a car waves to a pedestrian. If you're sensitive to the ways of the island, you'll be treated hospitably. For example, don't disturb crabbers when they're in boats or shed, unloading, sorting, and packing.

Don't miss the workshop of Edward Jones, who carves beautiful model skipjacks as well as buyboats and workboats. He used to run a 40-foot boat, a photo of which hangs in his workshop, but reports he hasn't missed it a bit since selling it. "Had to put it up twice a year, in spring and fall, to scrape and paint it." Four years ago, he started building model boats and finds that more agreeable to his lifestyle.

Smith-Tangier Triangle

Another trip possible from Smith Island is paddling the Smith-Tangier triangle. That is, you paddle out to Smith (aim for the gut), then paddle the 7 miles down to Tangier, marsh-island hopping along the way, then paddle or take the mailboat back depending on conditions. That would also apply to your crossing to Smith.

These crossings, however, are long—from Smith, it's 7 miles from Crisfield to landfall on Smith. From Tangier Island, it's 8 miles to landfall at Cedar Island south of Crisfield. You must be absolutely prepared for an open-water crossing. You can expect current and waves out in the middle as you hit deeper water in the channel. Tangier Sound has a strong current within a channel three to five miles wide. The trip is more suitable for an experienced paddler in summer-type conditions, but circular trips are a good idea because you're not bound to go straight out and straight back.

To paddle from Smith to Tangier, paddle down Smith between Cheeseman Island and South Point Marsh. You'll only have about 6 inches of water so you may need to go outside Cheeseman. Follow Shanks to Goose Island to Tangier. Note that these islands are marshes as opposed to real islands. For camping: a group of Chesapeake Paddlers has camped in Cod Harbor within the sandy spit; or you might try to obtain camping permission from the Chesapeake Bay Foundation, which owns and uses Port Isobel Island for environmental educational purposes (see Appendix A).

In the 1870s and 1880s, Crisfield was the major oyster-processing center on the Eastern Shore. The town expanded into the marsh and creek on the south end by oyster shells, so much processing was going on. Crisfield, like many other towns, has now turned its attention to crabs and is a major crab exporting center.

A pre-paddle and post-paddle dining spot in Crisfield is Watermen's Inn, located on 9th and Main Street, not far from the ferry dock. It is run by Brian and Kathy Julian, a young couple from Rhode Island. The crab cakes and breaded oysters are outstanding. The menu has several reasonably priced items both for breakfast and dinner. To dine with the ferry captains and their helpers, head down to the Dockside Restaurant.

Pocomoke River: Intimate Woodlands Near the Bay

Charts: Small Craft Chart #12230

Trip Mileage: 12 nautical miles roundtrip from Shad Landing State Park to second bridge, located at Porter's Crossing Road, Wesley; 5 nautical miles roundtrip to Snow Hill

Getting There: From US 50, east of Salisbury take US 13 south to MD 12 toward Snow Hill. Take MD 12 southbound 15 miles to Snow Hill. At Snow Hill, take US 113 south to Shad Landing State Park. Entrance is on the right.

Camping: The Shad Landing Area of the Pocomoke River State Park is managed by the Maryland Department of Natural Resources. Campsites throughout the forest near the river. $10 a night. Short drive to launch area. Ample parking. Call (410) 632-2566.

Tidal Range: Not available

The Pocomoke is southern Maryland's largest river and perhaps its most beautiful. A deep channel of 30 to 40 feet runs through it, making it historically important—in colonial times boats carried freight up to Pocomoke City and Snow Hill. Pocomoke City's importance as a trading port was eclipsed by Baltimore in the nineteenth century, but today some fuel oil barges still make it up to Snow Hill.

The river starts 12 miles out of Ocean City, Maryland, and empties about 50 miles later into Pocomoke Sound at Chesapeake Bay just below Crisfield.

The Pocomoke is a good alternative when the wind is kicking up on the bay or the Atlantic (you can often find a lee side on the river) and is also an indicator of the great contrasts that Chesapeake Bay and its environs provide. The river has an extensive bald-cypress swamp (the northernmost stand of this southern tree) and is one of Maryland's richest wildlife locales, with a tremendous variety of both woodland and water birds.

Launch at the Shad Landing Area on the east side of the river, just south of Snow Hill. Shad Landing includes a large marina on Croakers Creek (a short paddle brings you to the river itself), a

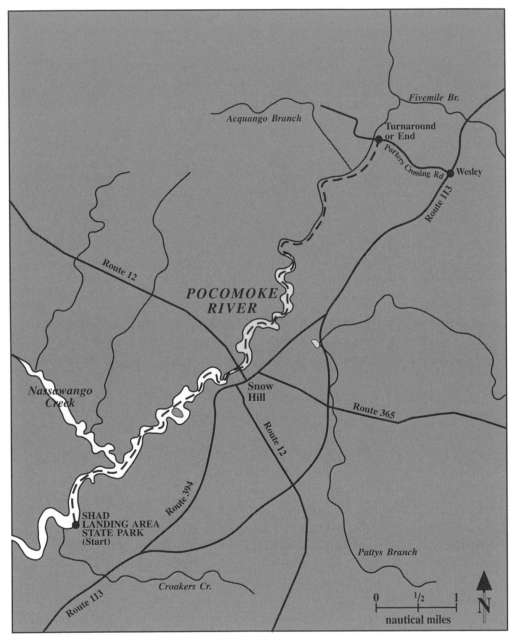

Pocomoke River

Pocomoke River's bald cypress swamp is the northernmost stand of this southern tree.

paved ramp suitable for kayaks, and a snack bar. The campground is large and campsites numerous—in all, a good base for a trip up the Pocomoke.

Head upriver. The first 3 nautical miles to Snow Hill are through a slow peaceful wilderness with only two farms (one abandoned), several channel markers, and lots of birds, including the pileated woodpecker, turkey vultures, and mallards. Woodland birds such as chickadees, nuthatches, and golden-crowned kinglets flit through the trees. A great blue heron sails across Nassawango Creek (much of it preserved by The Nature Conservancy), one of the only navigable feeder creeks. A well-marked nature trail lets you stretch your legs. In Snow Hill, a peacock struts along the shore.

Nassawango Creek was the site of an important early iron-making operation, Nassawango Iron Furnace, in the 1830s and 1840s. Furnace Town workers made the iron through the use of iron ore (bog iron in the creek), charcoal fuel (from the surrounding forests), and calcium carbonate (from oyster and clam shells dredged from Chincoteague Bay or used from the shell heaps left from the Native Americans). The company, however, was barely profitable and went out of business in 1847. You can visit the restored Furnace Town, which once housed fifteen families, to see the remnants of a working iron village.

From Shad Landing to the bridge at Snow Hill, you paddle alongside a thick forest of pine, swamp hardwoods, walnut, maple, and black gum trees with an understory of holly, mistletoe, and laurel. From the Snow Hill Bridge to the Porter's Crossing Bridge at Wesley (the river is tidal to Porters Crossing), you will penetrate deeper into the northernmost bald cypress swamp in the United States as you paddle through a huge number of little cypress islands.

From Porter's Crossing above, the Boy Scouts have created the Pocomoke Canoe Trail. A wood sign near the bridge (the best launch is on the southwest side) gives distances from one bridge to another north of here. Up to Whiton the cypress trunks get very large, providing a different atmosphere.

Of course, you can forget all the long itineraries and just poke along Croakers Creek (turn left at Shad Landing and bear right at the first fork—numbered markers will lead you along) for some relaxed bird watching. The trip is about 1.5 miles, but what you lose in distance you more than make up in an incredibly rich display of wildlife.

Although it is a wide river in places, the Pocomoke has an intimate feel to it, heavily wooded as it is on either side. Below Snow Hill, the river doesn't have much current. The best time time to paddle here is in early spring when the dogwood and pink laurel bloom, and you may be lucky to catch a glimpse of the rare prothonotary warbler.

Maryland's Atlantic Shore

Assateague National Seashore: Wild Beach and Protected Bay

Charts: Small Craft Chart #12211

Trip Mileage: 7 nautical miles to Jim's Gut, 17 nautical miles to Pope Bay

Getting There: To get to Maryland access point at Sinepuxent, take US 50 east to Berlin. At Berlin, go east on MD 376. It's 9 miles to Assateague Island. Launch from Ferry Point on the island (more appropriate for day tripping), or the state launch facility on the northwest side of the Sinepuxent Bridge.

Camping: There are backcountry campsites at Tingles, Pine Tree, Jim's Gut, and Pope Bay. Car camping also available at the Assateague National Seashore (campground office 410-641-3030) and Assateague State Park (410) 641-2120.

Tidal Range: 2.5 feet at Harbor of Refuge, Chincoteague Bay

Assateague is a magnificent, 35-mile barrier beach, stretching over two states, Maryland (21 miles) and Virginia (14 miles). Perhaps best known for its wild ponies memorialized in Marguerite Henry's children's book *Misty of Chincoteague,* Assateague Island lies east and north of Chincoteague Island. The beach is protected by Assateague Island National Seashore and Chincoteague National Wildlife Refuge.

At Assateague Island National Seashore, Chincoteague Bay on the inside of the barrier beach is accessible to kayakers by four "canoe camping" sites situated under the pines at the edge of the bay: Tingles Island, Pine Tree, Jim's Gut, and Pope Bay.

You have only to drive a few miles north from the visitor's center to Ocean City—the Miami Beach of Maryland, with mile upon mile of high-rise hotels and condominiums—to appreciate the wildness of this magnificent barrier beach. Assateague became a national park in 1965 in part to protect it from development already started. In the 1950s and 1960s, developers planned to sell nearly six thousand housing lots in an area 130 blocks long. They even started

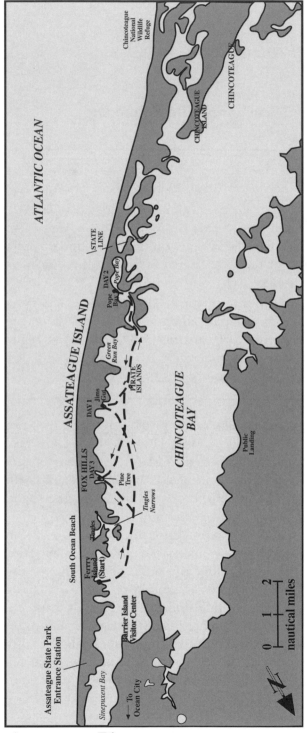

Assateague River

On Assateague Island, wild ponies wander right by your campsite.

paving the access road, Baltimore Boulevard, which got as far as the state line. The remains can be seen near the ranger station.

Drive through the park gates ($4 entrance fee, good for seven days) over the Verrazano Bridge and through Assateague State Park. The bridge is named after the same Giovanni da Verrazano who discovered Manhattan. He was the first recorded European explorer in the Chesapeake in 1524 and once anchored near Assateague Island for an expedition. Two miles down, you'll reach the Campground Registration Office at the National Seashore Entrance Station (not to be confused with the Barrier Island Visitor Center on the other side of Verrazano Bridge). Here, you obtain your free backcountry permit at the ranger station, open 9:00 A.M. to 5:00 P.M. The season is February 1 to October 1 for the backcountry permits (advanced reservations for backcountry sites are not accepted). Overnight vehicle permits may be obtained at this office. A water station is located across the street from the ranger station.

You launch from the Old Ferry Landing. If you're paddling to Pope Bay (13 miles), you need to get to the ranger station by noon or the rangers won't issue you a permit. They also don't issue permits when a small-craft advisory is in effect.

You put into the broad Chincoteague Bay and paddle by many of the small, unnamed, low-lying green marsh islands. To the left, you can see the dunes of Assateague and an occasional pony brows-ing by a pool of water near water's edge. To the right you see the low relief of the mainland. Often it is windy, and you many find yourself clawing your way to the first campsite at Tingles then zooming back effortlessly with the wind. Because the bay is so shal-low, you often run aground on sandbars at low tide, and you pretty much have the bay to yourself except for other canoeists or kayak-ers you might meet along the way.

The campsites are identifiable from the water by canoe trail signs. Pope Bay is the most difficult to find. For the others, you can pretty much follow the shore until you see the signs. To find the Pope Bay campsite, look for the channel that separates Assateague Island from three offshore islands, make your second left (east), then continue to follow the shoreline until you reach a small chan-nel right before Pope Bay opens up. Turn left (east) and follow that channel into the campsite.

Camping is in a loblolly pine forest on high ground on a mix-ture of sand and pine needles, except at Pope Bay, where shade is limited. The camping areas have about four or five sites, lantern hook, chemical toilets, picnic tables, fire grills (with lots of dead wood around). Fires are restricted to the grills because of fire hazard.

You are a short walk to your kayak and about a 0.25-mile-walk to oceanside beach on a well-marked path. You cross marshland where you are sure to see a few of the ponies munching away or drinking fresh water from the top of the salt-water ponds. The ponies are not domesticated. They bite and kick and are unpre-dictable so it's best not to disturb them.

April is probably the best month to visit here. The weather is warm, but the bugs have not yet arrived. Some years the bugs don't become really thick until July, according to the ranger. But if the weather stays consistently warm beginning in March, bugs will be plentiful in May. "You'll die," she pointed out. Ironically, May is probably also the busiest month for the backcountry sites.

The paddling can often be windy here, and the bay can kick up in the chop. Often it feels easier just to get out of your kayak and walk it. The trade-off, of course, is that the windier it is, the fewer bugs there are.

The National Park Service boundary goes out .5 mile into the bay. For the Maryland side, you will need four maps, available at $2.50 each from the National Park Service Visitor Center at the entrance to the park.

The area has several owners whose varying rules you need to follow and fees you need to pay. The northern 2 miles are owned by the state of Maryland and the rest by the National Park Service. The southern end is owned by the U.S. Fish and Wildlife Service, which has designated its part of Assateague and Chincoteague Islands as the Chincoteague National Wildlife Refuge.

As for the famous ponies, the National Park Service manages the herd on the northern end of Assateague. The northern herd numbers about 150 to 160 and stays fairly stable. The ponies are hardy creatures, drinking salt water when they do not find enough fresh water in the ponds. At Chincoteague the Chincoteague Volunteer Fire Company owns the herd. Each year the firemen round up the ponies on Assateague and herd them across the channel to Chincoteague for the annual July auction. The pony swim is a popular tourist attraction. Foals not sold return to Assateague.

Like the bears of Yellowstone National Park, the ponies have gotten used to people. If a car slows down, nearby ponies may shuffle over for a handout. The ranger warns that they might bite if they don't get what they want when they stick their noses in your car. "They're moody," she said.

Other access to Assateague includes the mainland town of Public Landing, which will put you in the bay directly across from Jim's Gut campground. It's a little more than 5 miles across Chincoteague Bay. You can get a backcountry permit for Assateague National Seashore the day before your trip. Motor boat traffic is minimal because Chincoteague Bay is very shallow, with only one channel down the middle.

Besides the ponies, Assateague is well known for tremendous migrations of birds in spring and fall, including tree swallows. It is also a major monarch butterfly flyway. You may spy a fox or a Sitka fawn. Introduced to the island in the 1930s by the Boy Scouts, this Asian species of deer now outnumbers the whitetailed deer four to one, and annual hunts are allowed on the refuge to manage the herd.

For information on Assateague Island National Seashore, call the Barrier Island Visitor Center at 410-641-1441.

Virginia's Eastern Shore

For about five months of the year, spring and fall, kayaking on Virginia's Eastern Shore is wonderful. The waters off both the sea side and the bay side are inviting, the marsh-covered shores and white sand beaches are deserted. The creeks are long, winding, and beautiful. Not many powerboats venture out into the large expanses of shallow water. Tides and currents are relatively gentle and storms, although often sudden and fierce, forecast their arrival with black thunderheads.

The Eastern Shore has long been an isolated spot, a 10-mile-wide peninsula that is basically an extension of Maryland but which has had neither close ties to that state nor to the rest of Virginia across the bay. The Bay-Bridge Tunnel has helped improve communication, but most residents don't like to pay the $20 toll too often and leave the crossing to tourists and business people. The peninsula's inhabitants consist mostly of farmers tilling the very rich soil here and fishermen crabbing, oystering, and fishing. Place names are a mix of Accomack Indian names such as Nassawadox, Wachapreague, and Onancock and English names like Cape Charles and Exmore.

The 70-mile strip of barrier beaches, salt marsh, and shallow bays on the Atlantic side of Virginia's Eastern Shore represents one of the last wild places on the mid-Atlantic coast. The Nature Conservancy owns most of the barrier islands from Metompkin Island south to Smith Island; interspersed are private and public lands. TNC began buying up the islands from developers in 1969 after a major housing project failed due to environmentalists' pressure and a recession. Currently, the Conservancy owns 40,000 acres of islands, marshes, and upland, creating what is known as the thirteen-island Virginia Coast Reserve.

If you stop into TNC headquarters in Brownsville, the director may inform you of some challenges to kayaking in the Reserve: no place to camp, unpredictable winds funnelling through the creeks and across shallow bays impeding your progress, winding creeks in which you can get lost, few other boats around for assistance, mos-

138

quitos and greenheads when the wind dies, and most importantly nesting colonies of birds, some whose species hang on a thread of survival. Virginia Coast Reserve Director John Hall says TNC wants to encourage recreational use in the preserve but it doesn't feel equipped to handle such use—which is not its job anyway—and is looking for input on how kayaking and canoeing might work in the preserve. Still, TNC allows day use on ten of the islands. Their visitor's guide states "Unless you are experienced in navigating the bays and creeks which provide access to the islands, your best advice would be to sign up for one of the Reserve's natural history field trips, which are led by staff naturalists. If you go on your own, take the appropriate navigational charts for the area that you'll be visiting. The islands have no sanitary facilities or fresh drinking water. During the summer, sun screen and insect repellent are recommended. Parramore, Revel's, and Ship Shoal are currently closed because of contract stipulations at the time of purchase."

The fact is that kayaks, with their low windage, shallow draft, and the use of a rudder can handle these conditions quite well. The area is nothing short of intriguing for its wildness on a very settled mid-Atlantic coast. With sensitivity to the environment, judgment, and paddling with the tides, several enjoyable trips can be made in this remote wilderness. Be sure to bring navigational charts for the area and plenty of bug repellent, sunscreen, and drinking water. For more information on visiting the islands contact TNC in Brownsville (see Appendix A).

Kayaking Virginia's entire chain of barrier islands from Assateague to Fisherman, about 70 miles, is possible. You follow an undredged section of the Intracoastal Waterway, which is well marked by navigational buoys. You will probably have the waterway to yourself too, because larger boats now stay to the Atlantic or use Chesapeake Bay. However, you need to plan an itinerary carefully because of the lack of designated camp sites.

Public camping spots are limited to the newly established Kiptopeke State Park bay side not far from Cape Charles and Assateague Island National Seashore Atlantic side. You can also avail yourself of many private camping areas, motels, and historic B & Bs. Contact the Eastern Shore Chamber of Commerce, Mercantile Building, Accomac, VA 23301; 804-787-2460.

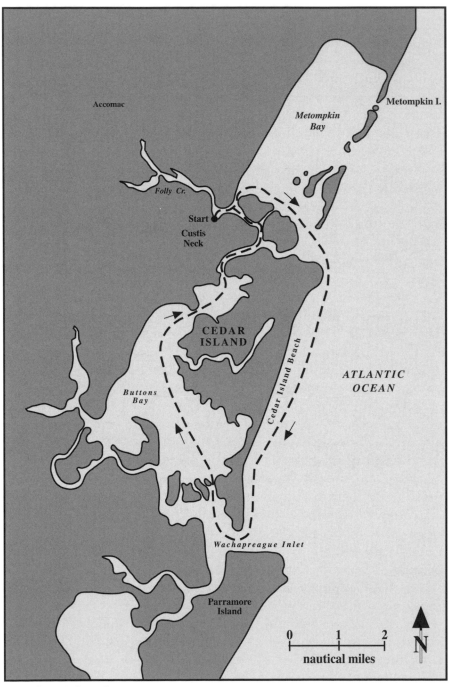

Accomac

Metompkin I.

Metompkin Bay

Folly Cr.

Start

Custis
Neck

CEDAR
ISLAND

Cedar Island Beach

*ATLANTIC
OCEAN*

*Buttons
Bay*

Wachapreague Inlet

Parramore
Island

0   1   2

nautical miles

N

Cedar Island

Circumnavigation of Cedar Island: Last of the Wild Places

Note: this description contributed by William Pettijohn.

Charts: Small Craft Chart #12210; ADC's Map of Virginia Barrier Islands; General Highway Map, Accomack County, prepared by Virginia Department of Transportation

Trip Mileage: 13 nautical miles

Getting There: From US 13 south, take Front Street (Business 13) 2 miles to Drummondtown Road (VA 605). Turn left on Drummondtown and go 2.2 miles to Custis Neck Road; turn left and go 1.4 miles to Folly Creek Road, where you'll reach the Accomac Town Landing launch point. **Alternate:** Continue on Drummondtown Road 1.7 miles to Burton Shore, go left on Burton Shore Road for 1.4 miles, and turn left on the short gravel road to Burton's Landing.

Camping: No established sites

Tide Range: 3.6 feet at Metompkin Inlet.

Caution Areas: There are often breakers in the inlet between Cedar Island and Metompkin Island. Incoming and outgoing currents in both Metompkin and Wachapreague inlets can reach as much as 3 knots and standing waves are often present in opposing winds.

This is a good trip in which to experience the Virginia Coast Reserve because Metompkin and Cedar islands are fairly close to the mainland so you don't have large windy, shallow bays to cross. You will experience unspoiled beach and marshland, you'll see what the barrier islands looked like before the mid-Atlantic Coast became paved over in development. Opportunities for bird watching are exceptional.

The approaches to Cedar Island through the tidal marshes and creeks are typical of those behind the barrier islands of Virginia. Small pine hummocks and a few hunting blinds are the only landmarks rising above the marsh grasses. Metompkin and Cedar islands are low and sandy; Metompkin now has only a few bushes after the storms of recent years. Until recently, Cedar Island had 30- to 40-foot-high dunes with rank growths of cedar trees. Now it is only a few feet above the water and the cedar groves have mostly been washed away.

A picturesque old Coast Guard station now used as a private club on the north end of Cedar is currently in danger from erosion. Several large beach houses that in 1989 were located on the dunes have been moved to the south end of the island; their cut-off pilings can still be seen in the surf. Many sea and barrier island birds abound on both Cedar and Metompkin and the only no-trespassing signs you see are those of the U.S. Fish and Wildlife Service protecting the nesting habitat of the piping plover. Surf fishing for a variety of species including blues, sea trout, and drum is sometimes good (a license is not required). Plenty of driftwood is available on the beach for campfires.

Launching at Accomac town landing is from paved and bulkheaded ramps, and there is always sufficient water depth. Except on the most popular holidays, there is ample parking, and even then when the spaces around the ramp are taken, it is only a short walk to alternative spots. The launch is also regarded as a safe place to park (parking at the alternate launch site at Burton's Landing is not as safe; vehicles left for several days have been vandalized).

To reach Metompkin Inlet from Accomac town landing, paddle east on Folly Creek .5 mile, turn left for .25 mile to the inland waterway navigation marker. Turn right for .5 mile to another marker, then turn right again and paddle another .5 mile to a red navigation buoy. By this time, the old Coast Guard station can be seen to the left. After passing it, turn to the north to find the inlet between Cedar and Metompkin islands. The inlet has no navigation markers and if the waves are high or there is fog, you will have to feel your way out. After you turn east into the inlet, it is about 200 yards to open water where you turn to the south and paddle parallel to the Cedar Island beach.

Cedar Island is about 7 miles long. On the ocean side, a wide, coarse sand beach is mixed with piles of shells. Depending on the wind, the surf can range from almost none to very high and difficult. In the summer, hoardes of black and greenhead flies make life unpleasant except in a strong offshore breeze. Wachapreague Inlet flows between Cedar's south end and Parramore Island. Channel buoys mark the inlet, and there is a good deal of fishing-boat traffic.

Metompkin Inlet is calm on a quiet day. The old Coast Guard Station is in the background./Photo by William Pettijohn.

After coming through the inlet, it is about 5 miles northwest across the tidal flats to where Inland Waterway markers will again guide you back past the old lifeboat station and to Folly Creek.

The alternate launch site is on the shore of Floyds Bay and is never crowded. It has a sandy beach and old launch ramp but sadly enough, although there are trash containers, visitors here seldom seem to use them. Also, for about an hour each side of low tide, the water is too shallow for a kayak to get out to the Intracoastal Waterway, so due attention has to be paid both coming and going. It is, however, a pleasant spot and cuts a mile or two from the trip.

Although Cedar Island has many houses, long stretches of the beach are deserted. The north end, except for the old lifeboat station, is now also devastated. The ocean has reclaimed much of the north end, and homeowners have been forced to cut their houses off the pilings and move them to the island's center. Except for not intruding on the piping plover and small tracts of private property around houses and cabins, there are no prohibitions against daytime use. Overnight camping on Metompkin, which is owned by the Nature Conservancy, and the unmarked sections of Cedar, also owned by TNC, is prohibited. Much of Cedar Island is privately owned and campers without permission have been known to be asked to leave. Bottom line: get permission.

The marine stores at Wachapreague sell the Barrier Island map ($2.95) referenced above, as well as official charts. Also, for 75 cents a photocopy of the Cedar Island area chart is available. The Accomack County Highway map is available free from the Highway Department District office and US 13 and Court House Road in Accomac. It does not show the location and numbers of navigation aids.

Back Creek and Hacks Neck: Catch Enough Fish for Dinner

(Note: this description was contributed by William Pettijohn.)

Charts: NOAA Chart #12226, ADC's Chart of the Southern Chesapeake Bay, or Virginia Department of Transportation General Highway Map of Accomack County

Trip Mileage: Variable from 4.5 nautical miles minimum

Getting There: From US 13 south and Painter, Virginia, turn right on 1st Street and go 2.1 miles to Pungoteague Road. Turn right for 1.1 mile and jog left in Pungoteague to Harbortown Road. Take Harborton Road 2 miles where it runs into Hacks Neck Road and continue on Hacks Neck 3 miles to launch point.

Camping: No established sites

Tidal Range: 1.5 to 2 feet

Caution Areas: The primary danger in summers are the violent line squalls that often sweep across the Chesapeake Bay. Strong winds, lightning, seas to 6 feet, and heavy rain can arrive within a few minutes of the first warning of heavy black clouds in the southwest. Local marine patrols and the Coast Guard often travel the shore warning boaters off the water when thunderstorm warnings are issued. However, it is recommended that kayakers carry radios tuned to the NOAA weather station that broadcasts from Eastville, VA, and keep a sharp lookout on hot summer afternoons.

The Chesapeake Bay shore is readily accessible to kayakers throughout Accomack County. Thus, this trip is merely one of dozens that are available. It is described because of the extraordinary beauty of this section of the bay, excellent access, pleasant and safe paddling, and two possibilities: catching enough fish for supper and primitive camping on deserted sand bars and beaches.

The launch point at Back Creek is adjacent to the Nandua Creek crab processing plant. Here, as they have for many years, a group of women "pick" (take the meat from) crabs, which is then packed for shipping throughout the area. A small dock on Back Creek is where the crabbing boats deliver their catch, which is then

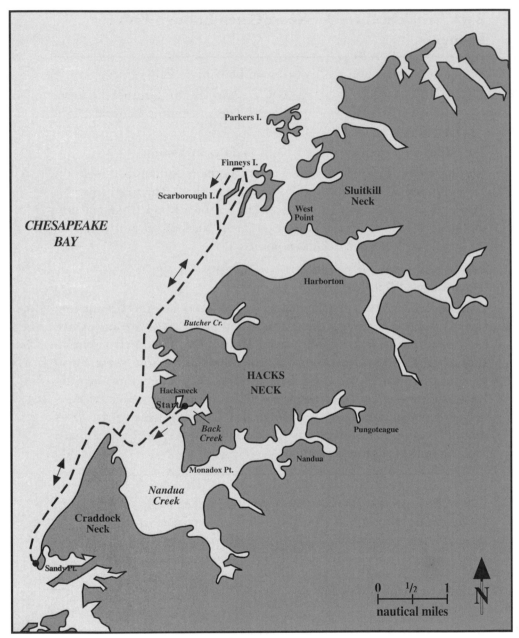

Back Creek and Hack's Neck

steamed in large pots for the pickers, and if you don't feel like fishing for supper, you can buy about the best backfin crab in the
world and make your own crab cakes out on the sandbars.

While the crab facility is sometimes a little smelly, usually the
wind blows inshore away from the launch point. The launch point
itself is an old, seldom-used ramp, and an adjacent clean grassy
area allows for unloading and loading. In fact, the entire area
around the docks and the launch point is usually immaculate. The
parking is ample and safe. The activities around the crab facility
and docks discourage vandalism and pilferage.

To get to the open bay, paddle out Back Creek into Nandua
Creek and then follow the channel markers. At high- or half-tide
turn right (west) immediately after exiting Back Creek. This illus-
trates one of the characteristics of this area: large, shoaly stretches
that can have 2 or 3 inches of water at low tide and 2 feet or so at
high. While these areas are a bane to power boaters, they can provide kayakers with broad highways free from the dangers of power
boats.

The first sandbars are about 2 miles from the launch point
and extend intermittently southward down the bay for several
miles. You will follow them by turning left (south) into Chesapeake
Bay and paddling down to Sandy Point and back. Some of the
sandbars are high enough above the water for camping in good
weather, but since they come and go, it is difficult to say exactly
where they may be located at any particular time. Wood is scarce
on them so it may have to be collected along the shore and taken
out or bottle gas used for cooking. It is best to locate a primitive
camping spot at high tide. Then the possibility of being driven off
during the night by a sudden storm can best be avoided by finding
a spot 3 feet or so above high water.

Five or six miles to the north an area containing many small
uninhabited islands with sandy beaches begins and stretches
almost to the border with Maryland. A good itinerary to follow is
up past Butcher Creek to Finneys Island, paddling around Scarbor-
ough Island and back. There once were houses and cottages on
most of these uninhabited islands, and now, though still privately
owned, many are seldom visited.

But there is also a downside; from mid-June to early September, there are not only the flies similar to those on the Barrier Islands, but the waters are also infested with jellyfish (sea nettles) that make swimming and other watersports very uncomfortable and potentially dangerous. This is somewhat compensated for by the usual abundance of small pan fish, hardheads, or what are locally called croakers, which range from 7 to 12 inches in length; spot, a 1/2- to 3/4-pound fish distinguished by a large black spot close to the dorsal fin (a most delicious small fish); the odd sea trout; keeper-sized flounder (14 inches long); whiting; puppy drum; and others. Almost always enough can be caught for supper. A Virginia Bay fishing license is required unless you are under sixteen years of age or over sixty-four. You can bottom fish from kayaks next to the deep water of the boat channels along this entire shore.

As noted, the paddling is relatively easy. No strong currents exist, and it is usually not necessary to paddle long distances from a friendly shore. Offshore a mile or so, the waves can pick up to a foot and a half or so in the usual breeze and make for more challenging paddling. Of course, in a strong (15–20 knots) northwest wind, which is not too uncommon, the wave action can be greater and paddling conditions range from challenging to downright unpleasant.

ADC charts of the Lower Chesapeake Bay are available at the boating store in Wachapreague, Virginia. The Accomack County map referenced above is available at the District Highway office located at the intersection of US 13 and Courthouse Road during office hours (8:00 A.M. to 5:00 P.M.) weekdays, except holidays.

Kiptopeke to Fishermans Island: Southern Terminus of the Delmarva

Charts: NOAA Chart #12224 or Small Craft Chart #12221

Trip Mileage: 13 nautical miles

Getting There: From US 13, the main highway down Virginia's Eastern Shore, look for signs to Kiptopeke State Park just past Cape Charles (if heading south) and just over the Chesapeake Bay Bridge-Tunnel (if heading north). Kiptopeke is nearly at the southern tip of the peninsula.

Camping: Kiptopeke State Park has campsites just a short drive from the launch area. The campground opens the first week in April. The fee is $8.50 a night plus tax. Call (804) 331-2267.

Tidal Range: 2.4 feet at Cape Charles Harbor

Caution Areas: A good rip moves in and out of the Intracoastal Waterway channel at Cape Charles.

Kiptopeke is a newly created state park in Virginia, several miles south of the town of Cape Charles. Cape Charles was established in 1886 when the New York, Philadelphia, and Norfolk Railroad extended its line southward down the Delmarva Peninsula. Kiptopeke itself was the old bayside ferry landing to Norfolk before the 17.6-mile-long Chesapeake Bay Bridge-Tunnel was built in 1964 at the southern tip of Virginia's Eastern Shore peninsula, linking Cape Charles to Norfolk, Virginia. The bridge eliminated the need for the many car ferries serving the Eastern Shore. Before the bridge was built, this was one of the wildest places on the east coast, right off the end of nowhere.

Drive down to the launch ramp. Several World War II-era Liberty ships form a breakwall. This area has long stretches of beach, with beautiful shells, both to the north and to the south, much of it backed by steep bluffs. Except for the bridge, you see no human trace. Some serious surf pounds off the shoals in the bay, from which you should stay well away. Beware, there is a good rip coming in and out of the Intracoastal Waterway channel down at Cape Charles.

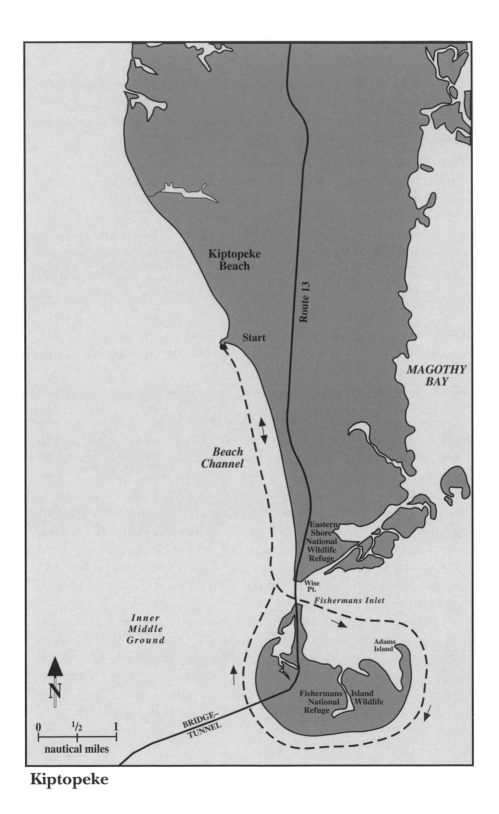

Kiptopeke

From Kiptopeke, paddle down to Fishermans Island, a National Wildlife Refuge run by the U.S. Fish and Wildlife Service. The refuge is a 1,000-acre barrier island consisting of brackish marsh, beach, and upland plants. The Bridge-Tunnel road passes right over the island. The refuge supports a wide variety of migrating and nesting bird life including waterfowl, shorebirds, raptors, and songbirds, as well as the endangered brown pelican (Fishermans Island is this pelican's northernmost habitat).

Incidentally, Kiptopeke is the name of the brother of the Nussawattocks Indian Chief Debedeavon, Indians of the Eastern Shore with whom Captain John Smith, the early English explorer, established friendly relations when he arrived here in the 1600s.

The Western Shore

When you cross the Chesapeake Bay Bridge-Tunnel the world changes drastically. The Western Shore of the Chesapeake, encompassing both Virginia and Maryland, is less hospitable to paddlers than the Eastern Shore. Hampton Roads, at the mouth of the bay, has one of the world's largest naval bases. Newport News, Norfolk, and Virginia Beach are all connected to the military in some way. When paddling in this area, you will need to watch for aircraft carriers, nuclear submarines, and the like.

The Western Shore is a lot more populated with the major cities of Baltimore, Annapolis, and (up the Potomac) Washington, D.C. From north to south are the off-limits Aberdeen Proving Grounds, heavily settled Annapolis, cliffs, followed by the Potomac River (wide to cross), Rappahannock River, Mobjack Bay, and Norfolk.

Still, some extremely beautiful and interesting trips notable for their wildlife and history can be had. If you head down the peninsulas to places like Gwynn's Island, Deltaville, Windmill Point, or Reedville, you will encounter quaint towns and churches, watermen who can trace their ancestors back to the Cornwall coast in England, old fishing vessels, spontaneous hospitality, and extraordinary bird life.

Some of the Chesapeake Bay's major rivers enter into the bay here and many provide scenic journeys in and of themselves. From north to south, the rivers are the Susquehanna, Patuxent, Potomac, Rappahannock, York, and the James.

A final word: if you have visions of paddling around the Tidal Basin at the Jefferson Memorial in Washington, D.C. during cherry-blossom season, don't. The Tidal Basin is not open to privately owned boats, but you can rent a two-person push-pedal boat.

Circumnavigation of Jamestown Island: History on the James River

Charts: NOAA Chart #12248

Trip Mileage: 9 nautical miles

Getting There: From I-64, take VA 199 west to the Colonial Parkway. Follow Parkway to VA 31 and Jamestown Festival Park. Launch from the Jamestown Yacht Basin (804-229-8309) off VA 31 across from the Jamestown Festival Park.

Camping: None

Tidal Range: 2 feet at Jamestown Island

The James River is broad, wide, silty, and one of the most historic rivers on the East Coast. Jamestown is not very accessible to kayaks. No public launch ramp exists. The Jamestown National Historic Park strictly prohibits launching from its grounds and landing on Jamestown Island is also not allowed. Signs throughout remind you of that. Still, the trip is a rewarding circumnavigation of one of the most historically significant islands in the United States.

You can launch from the Jamestown Yacht Basin (500 feet up from the first bridge in the park), which is mostly geared to power boats so you may want to come here in the off-season. The Basin requests a $3 launch fee. From the Jamestown Yacht Basin, you paddle south out Powhatan Creek. At the confluence of Powhatan Creek and the Back River, go straight ahead on Powhatan Creek, go under the causeway bridge of the Colonial National Parkway. Turn right (northwest) upriver. Pass Glass House Point, after which you reach the historic ships that mark the riverside portion of Jamestown plantation. The journey's highlight is paddling up to and around the replicas of the three ships that brought the first colonists across the Atlantic from England. The *Goodspeed, Susan Constant,* and especially the *Discovery* seem much too small to have crossed the Atlantic safely. Just beyond is the terminal for the Jamestown-Scotland Neck Ferry off Rte. 31. The ferry is one of three crossings that provided transportation across the James River in the early 1700s.

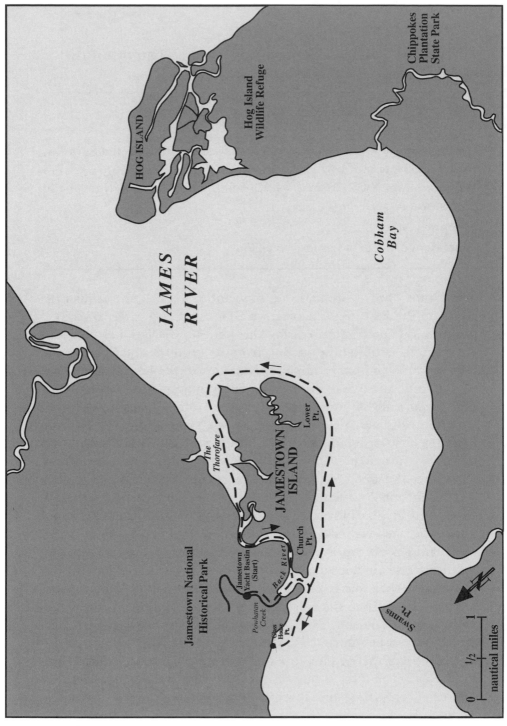

James River

One of the highlights of a James River trip is paddling under the Susan Constant, *a replica of one of the very small boats that brought the first settlers to Jamestown.*

The first settlers arrived in 1607, making Jamestown the first permanent English colony in America. Conceived as a profit enterprise, the Virginia Company sent out its first colonists in 1606 under the command of Captain Christopher Newport. It took them four months to cross the Atlantic Ocean with a short stay on the island of Dominica in the West Indies. They entered Chesapeake Bay and landed in the James River at a point they called Archers Hope. They named their fort James Towne after James I, then King of England.

Dissent broke out among the new settlers, but a strong leader emerged, Captain John Smith, who took matters in hand and forced the dissenters to work to maintain the settlement. In 1609, however, he was injured and returned to England. While he was away, the "starving time" took place when almost 500 settlers died of starvation, disease, and confrontations with the Native Americans. Only about 60 colonists survived. By 1619, many more settlers had arrived in Jamestown and in communities up and down the James River, and the colony was thriving. Tobacco growing and exporting fueled the economy and encouraged other English immigrants to start their own settlements.

As you paddle along, you'll probably wonder why the Jamestown settlers chose this spot. Possibly it was because the

James River was close to the mouth of the Chesapeake and they felt more secure on a sandy isthmus which they could defend. Today there are large, mature stands of pine and oak, marshes (the settlers used the marsh grass for roof thatch), and creeks. Many redwing blackbirds occupy the marsh in Powhatan Creek. You may also see great blue herons, bald eagles, cormorants, cardinals, scaups, and canvasbacks.

After looking at the ships, head east on the river. As you paddle up the broad river, the current is not particularly strong even though the river becomes tidal at Jamestown. You can see across to Hog Island and a power plant. You pass several small, sandy beaches. Watch out for submerged pilings and snags.

Paddle past Church Point. You pass excavated foundations of early homes and building sites, monuments, and a statue of Captain John Smith, Virginia's first governor. A sculpture of Pocahantas, his compatriot who is believed to have prevented her father, Chief Powhatan, from killing Smith by offering her own life instead, is also here but is located inland on a wooded trail so you can't see it from the water. You also pass the Anglican brick church tower erected in 1649.

You round Lower Point, then head northeast along the eastern end of Jamestown Island. Now you have left behind any signs of the historical settlement. As you round the point into the Thorofare, you pass a lovely pine forest. These mature pine forests with tall trees and pine needle floors continue along the north side of Jamestown Island as you make your way down this broad passage. The mainland side, meanwhile, is covered with holly bushes.

The Thorofare narrows, and you begin to wind through the more intimate Back River. Just before you turn back toward your starting point at the Jamestown Yacht Basin, you will pass a lovely broad marsh full of reeds and hosting many redwing blackbirds. Turn right (north) into Powhatan Creek and so back to your start.

Jamestown fell into disuse when the colonists moved the capital to Williamsburg, a few miles away, in 1699. Paddling around here is like passing through a historical mystery novel with the mystery still unsolved. Archaeologists have excavated only about one-third of the 60 acres that make up James City, and many answers still lie in the ground. Save an extra day for actually visiting the historic site on foot.

Point Lookout: Oldsquaw at the Mouth of the Potomac

Charts: NOAA Chart #12286 or Small Craft Chart #12285

Trip Mileage: 8.5 nautical miles

Getting There: From US 301, take MD 5 south. MD 5 turns into MD 235 about 6 miles out of Charlotte Hall. Follow MD 235 south all the way south, where it becomes MD 5 again. Follow that route down to Point Lookout, the end of the peninsula and the end of the road.

Camping: Point Lookout State Park (301) 872-5688 has several camp-sites and a public launch ramp not far from the campground.

Tidal Range: 0.8 feet at Sunnybank, Little Wicomico River

Point Lookout is an extraordinary place. Most notable is the width of the Potomac River, whose mouth is like an inland sea stretching 12 miles from Point Lookout south to Smith Point. As you paddle out of the launch spot, you can look across to the southern shore of the river, where lie the birthplaces of George Washington (Wakefield), James Monroe (Monrovia), and Robert E. Lee (Stratford Hall). They grew up on the rich farmlands of the southern shore of the Potomac on the plantations of the Virginia tidal coast.

The suggested trip is around the lighthouse, up north to Tanner Creek, then out into the bay for about a half-mile and back to the launch site. You can add distance by traveling around Lake Conoy and enjoying the multitude of wildlife that comes alive at dusk.

We were there the second day of March. Light northwest winds were expected to move around to the southeast. The air temperature was above 50 degrees—the first time in more than a week that only a long-sleeved shirt was needed. We set out from the boat launch at Point Lookout State Park. The ranger was going out in his boat for the first time that season to test its motor. It coughed and wouldn't start. We slipped our kayaks easily into the water and took off with the ease of a motorless craft. We paddled out the channel between two substantial rock jetties, out of Lake Conoy. Just beyond the jetties, a boat was setting stakes for menhaden nets. The air was quiet, the waters still as we looked across to the other side of the

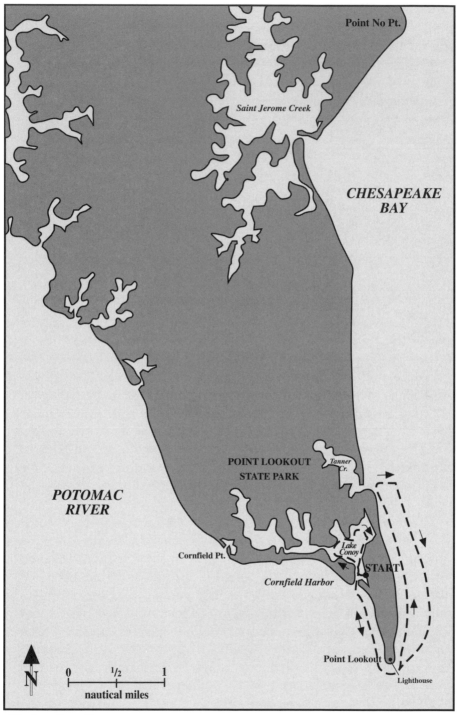

Point No Pt.

Saint Jerome Creek

CHESAPEAKE BAY

POINT LOOKOUT STATE PARK

Tanner Cr.

POTOMAC RIVER

Lake Conoy

Cornfield Pt.

START

Cornfield Harbor

Point Lookout

Lighthouse

N

0   ½   1

nautical miles

Point Lookout

Potomac. Fog rolled off the end at Smith Point. Just a few hundred yards offshore, we spied ten ducks—oldsquaw, mostly males, but we heard them first. The males had gathered and were talking noisily in courtship calls—ow-owalett is the call of this most talkative sea duck. Their white heads and pointed tails were distinctive against the backdrop of still water and a low shore across the Potomac.

These were the first oldsquaw we had seen in such great numbers and the first since we saw the pairs out on Smith Island. The oldsquaw is a tundra bird. Its habitat runs from northern Alaska eastward along the arctic coast of Canada and the islands to Greenland, south to southern Hudson Bay and northern British Columbia. It winters along the coast south to the Carolinas so we were seeing it near its southern boundary. Other birdlife we noted included loon, heron, bufflehead, kingfisher, and other sea ducks.

We pulled out of the lake and headed south around the point, past the Coast Guard Station and lighthouse. We were struck by the aqua-green, silt-free quality of the water. We paddled up north along the shore in search of a channel through Deep Creek, but it had silted over. A cut through the beach from the bay into the marsh shown clearly on the chart had been closed up by the shift-

*Point Lookout Lighthouse guards the wide mouth of the Potomac River where it meets Chesapeake Bay./*Photo by Forrest Dillon.

ing sands. We walked across the beach and found the drowned channel. It led across phragmites into a marshy pond, now choked off from the tidal floods of the bay.

As we turned back (with more time, you can paddle up to Tanner Creek), we chose a route about .5 mile off the beach, far enough to be paddling in a nice little chop in a southeast breeze. The low-lying land of Lookout Point State Park was to our right and we could see dimly Maryland's Eastern Shore partially obscured by haze on the horizon to our left. From this perspective, our trip took on a different flavor and we felt invigorated as we pushed into the opposing wind and waves surrounded by circling oldsquaw. At one point, a pair came flying right at us over our left shoulders.

A naval jet kept flying around, possibly an FA-18. Seeing jets and helicopters around the Chesapeake is like seeing Canada geese. You finally just ignore them.

The state park is a great place to spend a few days with tent camping, beaches on Lake Conoy and bayside, much birdwatching, and a fish-cleaning station at the launch ramp for your catch of the day, which you can cook over the open grill at your campsite.

Cape Lookout has a sadder, more desolate history as explained by the numerous signs around the park. Originally, it was a popular resort spot with a hotel and many beach cottages. During the Civil War, the government turned the hotel into a hospital and eventually, after the Battle of Gettysburg, a prisoner-of-war camp for Confederate soldiers. Camp Hoffman, as it was called, became the largest POW camp of the war. The POWs suffered from freezing temperatures, disease, and starvation. More than three thousand Southerners died here. The government built a monument in the 1900s to them, visible along MD 5 on the way to the launch ramp. One of the survivors was poet Sidney Lanier, who wrote about his and others' woeful experiences at Camp Hoffman.

For local knowledge, stop at Blue Wind, a kayak specialty store in California, Maryland, not far from Point Lookout (see Appendix A).

Patuxent River: Clarks Landing to Sotterly Plantation

Charts: NOAA Chart #12261

Trip Mileage: 8 nautical miles to the plantation and back along the southern shore; 8.5 nautical miles from the plantation to Broomes Island along north shore back to put in.

Getting There: From MD 235 at California, MD, just to the north of Lexington Park, look for green sign to Clarks Mill Road. From the south, turn right (east) and continue about a mile (pass another sign for Clarks Mill Road), then turn right at Moose Patuxent Lodge at a corner. Continue down the road, which dead ends after 3 miles onto the ramp. Park on either side of the ramp. *Alternate:* The boat launch just beyond this public access ramp is located next to Clarks Landing Bar, which charges $3 to launch.

Camping: None

Tidal Range: 1.2 feet at Solomons Island, Patuxent River

Caution Areas: The waters south of Clarks Landing have restricted access due to a naval installation.

Upon paddling from Clarks Landing, out Cuckold Creek, around Half Pone Point into the Patuxent River, you may run into a raft of hundreds of scaup. The pintails may be noisily singing their mating call over and over again. But the most special treat will be spotting canvasback ducks, increasingly rare in the Chesapeake.

The canvasback's scarcity is not due to its reputation for being one of the best-tasting ducks—the result of their diet of wild celery—but more to the loss of breeding habitat by the draining of large marshes. Each fall, large numbers migrate from breeding grounds in the west eastward to winter on the Great Lakes and along the Atlantic Coast. So it is always a treat to see this increasingly rare duck. The canvasback is a prince among its scaup cousins. It is a powerful duck with stark white body, long elegant reddish head, and long, sloping bill, which makes its profile distinctive.

You work your way north up the fairly developed southern shore of the Patuxent. Much of the shore is bulwarked with many

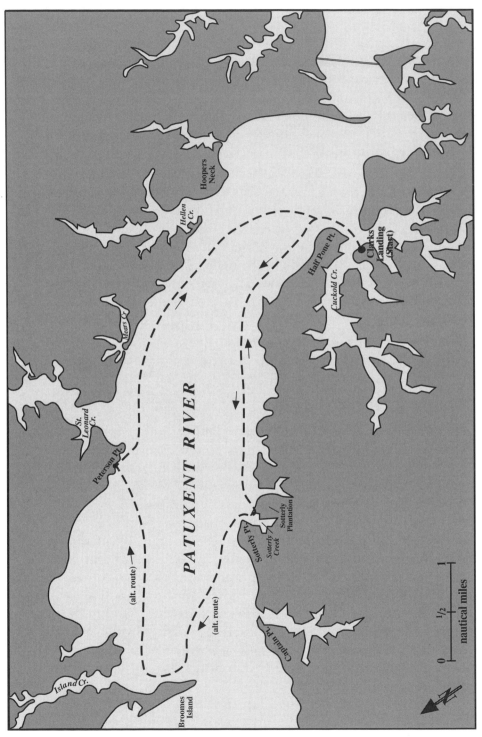

Patuxent River

private homes so landing is not really possible. It is a relief to reach the unspoiled open fields of Sotterly Plantation, a good place to stop for a picnic.

The landing for the plantation is just next to Sotterly Point, which sticks out into the river. A small, white house, wharf, and long, gentle sandy beaches backed by reeds mark the spot. You can paddle into Sotterly Creek and land near a few picnic benches, then make the short hike up the gentle slope to the plantation house beside a cultivated field along Rolling Road. An eagle nests nearby. The fields and pastures spread out toward the Patuxent, the creek rimmed by tall oak trees. Here you can sense the early days of tidewater Maryland, when all that lined the Patuxent were plantations such as these: long fields, genteel homes with long porches, and neighbors visiting each other by boat. The trading boats came right into Sotterly Creek. The Rolling Road, created by

The Rolling Road will take you from the wharf to Sotterly Plantation.

Sotterly Plantation's porch designs may have inspired George Washington's plans for Mount Vernon.

a barrel rolled to make a path, led from each plantation down to its wharf and creek.

Sotterly Plantation is open to the public. The managers, a private Maryland corporation charged by the Ingalls, the former owners, to manage the plantation, request that you call them from the dock by the telephone located there. An entry fee to visit the grounds ($1) or house and grounds ($5) provides you with an historic river plantation experience that is well worth the price of admission. Sotterly is open daily from June 1 to October 31 (closed Mondays), 11:00 A.M. to 4:00 P.M. or by appointment April, May, and November, (301-373-2280). The grounds, including the Rolling Road, gardens, and farm exhibit, are open year round. You can visit for free on Patuxent River Discovery Day, the first Saturday in May.

James Bowles, son of a London merchant and an influential Maryland officeholder, was the first to build a house here, about 1717. In 1729 his widow married George Plater. The Platers named the plantation after their family home in Suffolk, England, and occupied this spot for almost one hundred years. They expanded the house into a distinctive mansion with a 100-foot portico porch and so drew the attention of George Washington, who may have used Sotterly as a model for Mount Vernon.

The Platers exported tobacco to Europe and imported manufactured goods. Mabel Satterlee Ingalls, who traced her roots to Sotterly Hall in England, inherited the plantation in 1947 and gave it to the Sotterly Mansion Foundation to oversee in 1961. It remains a working farm and claims to be the oldest continuously operating plantation in the country.

The best view of the plantation is from about .5 mile from shore out on the Patuxent. Here you can see the entrance to the creek, a thin green triangle of crops, and the house half-hidden in the trees sitting perched above the sloping fields, its red roof and long white portico visible from a distance. The view provides an overall sense of gracious living in an earlier time.

To extend your trip, you can cross the Patuxent to Broomes Island, then turn east to Peterson Point, which has some nice sand beach. Often the usual helicopter or plane on training mission from the U.S. Naval Testing Center will be overhead. The water quality is quite good, green and clear.

The Calvert Cliffs, just to the north (not shown on map), are an alternate paddling site near here. This site has deposits of more than six hundred species of fossils dating to the Miocene Period (ten to thirteen million years ago), and some fossil collecting is allowed. Fossils that wash ashore may be kept, but digging or climbing in the cliffs is not allowed. Also, the Calvert Marine Museum at Solomons Island is well worth a visit. A major tourist town, Solomons Island has many restaurants.

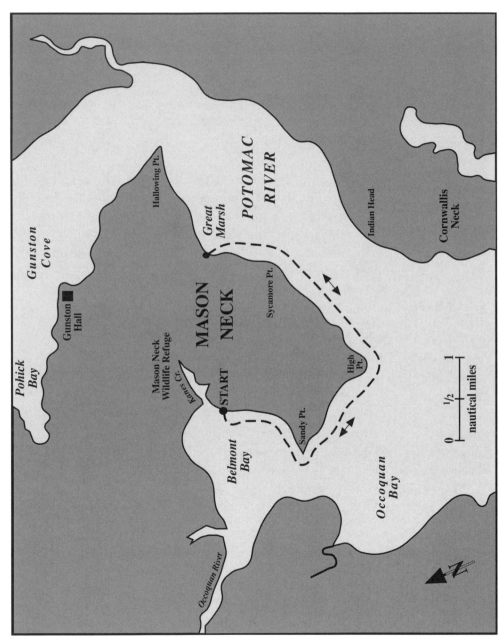

Mason Neck

Mason Neck: Bluffs and Eagles

Charts: NOAA #12289 or Small Craft Chart #12285

Trip Mileage: 11 nautical miles roundtrip

Getting There: From the Beltway part of I-95, take I-95 south into Virginia to exit 163 (VA 642-Lorton Road). Watch for Gunston Hall's brown and white sign. Go east one mile to US 1. Take a right (south) and go 1 mile to stoplight and turn left (east) to VA 642 (Gunston Road). Watch for brown and white sign for Gunston Hall on left. Just beyond the sign is a Y intersection. Bear right at Mason Neck State Park sign and continue past the National Wildlife Refuge parking area. The road winds down through lovely woods to the visitors center. The launch ramp is located to the left of the visitors center.

Camping: Pohick Bay Regional Park. Follow directions above, but when you turn onto VA 642 (Gunston Road), go 3.5 miles and watch for park entrance on left (north).

Tidal Range: Not available

Caution Areas: Just offshore from Sandy Bay is a boat channel leading out of Occoquan town, which is filled with power boaters in summer.

It is truly extraordinary that a preserved wilderness such as Mason Neck exists so close to Washington, D.C. But through a strong coalition of land preservation organizations, a very large, special piece of land has been set aside. Mason Neck is a distinct peninsula that juts eastward into the Potomac about 20 miles south of Washington. Due to a recent, massive cleanup effort the Potomac downstream of Washington, D.C. can again be used for recreation. Never an industrial area, the Potomac has remained fairly pristine. It is surprisingly scenic and also undervisited. However, by comparison to Point Lookout at the mouth of the Potomac, about 80 miles downriver, the water here is quite silty, and various logs float around.

To view this from the kayaker's point of view, head down the road to Mason Neck all the way to the end. Mason Neck National Wildlife Refuge occupies the south end of the neck, but you put in at the state park into Belmont Bay. You launch down the bluff at a sandy beach, next to the visitors center. Drive your car down, then park in the visitors center parking lot.

Paddle southwest about 1 mile to Sandy Point, then around Sandy Point about 1.25 nautical miles to High Point. Here you reach the open Potomac. You pass several dykes enclosing ponds, with all sorts of sounds emitting from wildlife that you can hear but can't see.

Mason Neck has one of the largest great blue heron colonies in Virginia. At High Point, you may see dozens of great blue heron in a heron rookery, all squawking and every once in awhile taking to lumbering flight from precarious perches.

Mason Neck's tall cliffs are one of the largest protected eagle nesting sites on the East Coast.

Next, head along the northeastern shore, past high bluffs, tall trees, and many eagles either sitting in branches or soaring from one tree top to another. This is the refuge's eagle nesting area. (Officials specifically established the refuge to preserve nesting, feeding, and roosting habitat of the bald eagle.) Head up to Sycamore Point, then around the corner into Great Marsh. Poke into the northerly creek and find the deck overlooking a fork in the creek, an excellent picnic spot at the Great Marsh trail head. Here you can observe beaver slapping tails and working on their houses, and also wood duck.

Beyond lies the settled shore of Hallowing Point, and if you continue you will reach Gunston Hall and Pohick Bay State Park, site of a camping area and another launch spot. Two cars will allow you to paddle around the entire Mason Neck peninsula.

While in the area you may consider a paddle on the Potomac at Washington, D.C. You can launch near Watergate right along the Potomac from Thompson's Boat Center (2900 Virginia Avenue, N.W. on Rock Creek Parkway at Virginia Avenue, next to the C&O Canal; 202-333-4861), open March through November. Launch from the floating pier for $2 (season passes available for $30). A parking area is located right above the launch. You can drive your car down to unload. The parking area gets fairly crowded and has a two-hour limit.

From Thompson's you can paddle upriver to Fletchers Landing fighting a mild but increasing current and paddle by the C&O Canal National Park that parallels the Potomac. You can also paddle across from Thompson's and explore Teddy Roosevelt Island. The Potomac River is tidal all the way to Washington, D.C., hence the name of the Tidal Basin at the Jefferson Memorial.

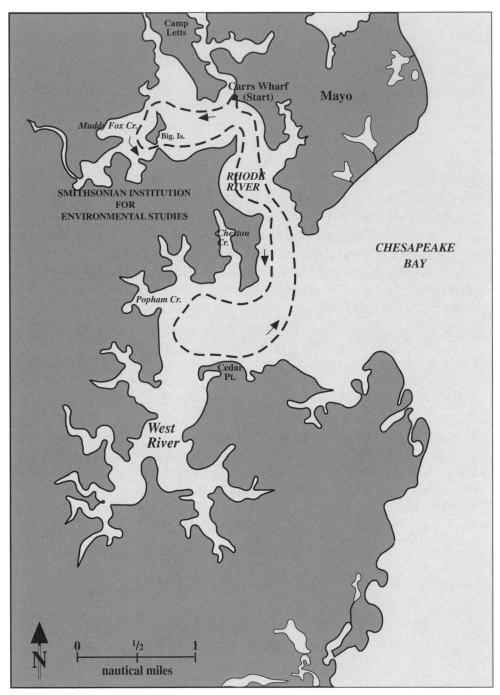

Carrs Wharf

Carrs Wharf: Open Space Near Annapolis

Charts: NOAA #12270 or Small Craft Chart #12263

Trip Mileage: 8 nautical miles

Getting There: Take MD 214 east into Mayo, take a right at the Mayo Post Office onto Carrs Wharf Road. The landing is straight ahead. It is a sand launch with a small parking area and picnic tables and puts you right into the Rhode River.

Camping: None

Tidal Range: .09 feet at Annapolis, Severn River

Caution Areas: Beware of many power boaters crossing the Rhode River.

Carrs Wharf is located just to the south of populous Annapolis, which sends more yachts into the Chesapeake than any other town or city along the bay. Carrs Wharf is located in Arundel County, which surprisingly has more coastline than any other county in Maryland. Carrs Wharf puts you into the meeting place of two rivers, the Rhode and the West. This is a good spot to paddle near Annapolis because it gets less boat traffic than the Severn, the river upon which Annapolis is located. You can poke up into little creeks and paddle past a blend of suburbia and unspoiled countryside.

Paddle past Camp Letts YMCA building toward Conte's Wharf. Above on the hill, you can see the tall chimneys of a three-story structure from an old plantation. Three islands are out in the bay. High Island has lost half of itself within the last year due to erosion, according to local paddlers.

Paddle past the land preserved by the Smithsonian Institution for Environmental Studies. Beyond Conte's Wharf you can see the Institution's testing post for water salinity, pollution, temperature etc. The institution buys homes as they become available for sale in a unique effort to turn this area back to wilderness.

Cheston Creek is around the end, where you may see a bald eagle and many scaup. Erosion of islands and cliffs around here is swift and powerful. Cross over the Rhode River to the church camp on the Mayo side, then follow the shore back to the launch.

You can extend your trip by paddling into the mouth of the West River, past Popham Creek and over to Cedar Point and so on back to the point at Mayo.

Ron Casterline and Cindy Cole paddle by one of the deserted islands in the West River near the Smithsonian's Institution for Environmental Studies.

You can see across the bay to Tilghman Island. Local paddler Ron Casterline has done this crossing on a fairly calm day, something he calls "not a big deal," provided, that is, you pick your day. It's 7 miles over and 7 miles back. You choose a far-out point from which to cross and expect to encounter waves and current in the middle in the deeper section (130 feet or so) of the old Susquehanna River bed. Watch for large boats coming and get out of their way before you cross paths.

If you wish to brave the more populous Severn River and get a taste of downtown Annapolis, launch from Tuxant City Park on the south side of Spa Creek. Then paddle up Spa Creek to City Dock. Pass the resident skipjack and fireboat at the very end of Ego Alley, the part of the harbor deepest into the city itself. Ego Alley ends in a park setting of brick steps and seats. The wall is lowest to the water here, and ladders and tie-up hooks are available for anyone to dock. You can walk around the charming downtown area of Annapolis not far from the Naval Academy, admire the capital a couple of blocks away, and get some crab cakes at Buddy's Crabs & Ribs.

You won't see too many working boats down this way. The state-owned wharf for watermen provides the real workers of the harbor the only place left to moor without paying the astronomical fees of Annapolis marinas. Without such a haven, all working boats would have left the harbor years ago.

Baltimore Harbor: Stars and Stripes at Fort McHenry

Charts: NOAA #12281 or Small Craft Chart #12273

Trip Mileage: 9.5 nautical miles

Getting There: From Washington D.C. Beltway, take I-95 north to Baltimore. Just before the tunnel toll plaza, take MD 2 south. Cross over the bridge and take the next left (east). Broening Park's parking area and ramp are just to the north of Harbor Hospital.

Camping: None

Tidal Range: 1.2 feet

Caution Areas: Beware always of the movements of large ships, particularly at berth. They could be in the process of leaving.

Why kayak the inner city when so much accessible wilderness lies around the major metropolitan areas of the Chesapeake? Because Baltimore's south side is one of the more interesting city areas to explore. You can paddle up to the National Aquarium past the *Pride of Baltimore II* (a topsail schooner completed in 1988), under the deck of the restored *Constellation* (launched from Fell's Point in 1797 and one of the world's oldest wooden ships still afloat), haul your boat up right next to this old frigate, and walk into the food arcade for a huge selection of international food—stuffed grape leaves, tacos, pizza, ice cream, yogurt, oysters, hamburgers, or croissants.

Launch from Broening Park just to the east of the US 395 bridge and next to the hospital. Sometimes the Balto Rowing Club—the large building just upriver—will let you use its changing rooms. Some local sea kayakers store their boats at the club.

From Broening Park, cross the middle branch of the Patapsco River to Ferry Bar. Paddle past several large piers with container ships. This is the first place you will have to worry about channels. The piers have access to the Ferry Bar Channel (east section). Scoot by these piers after making sure none of the container ships is moving. Stay close to shore to Fort McHenry, identifiable by the earth ramparts, low-lying brick buildings which were the original barracks, and most prominently the fifteen-striped, fifteen-starred American flag. This large flag flapping in the breeze over the two wide converg-

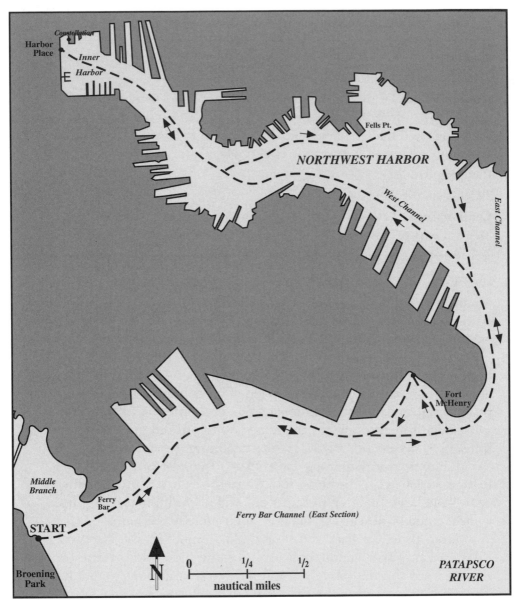

Baltimore Harbor

The restored Constellation, *one of the country's oldest wooden warships, sits moored Baltimore's Inner Harbor.*

ing channels of the Patapsco River is a replica of the flag after which our national anthem, "The Star Spangled Banner," was written. The British attacked Fort McHenry in 1814 (during the War of 1812), and throughout the smoke and fire, the famous flag flew.

You can land on a small beach (probably awash in harbor debris—by all means avoid a landing capsize or you will be picking debris out of your cockpit) on the southwest side of the park to visit Fort McHenry. This is your only landing spot. From here, you can walk up to the grassy knoll and join the throngs of tourists climbing on ramparts, measuring cannons, and wandering through historic displays in the barracks.

From Fort McHenry, paddle around to the Northwest Harbor along piers here belonging to the Navy, Procter and Gamble, and Domino sugar—you can smell the cinnamon when it is being unloaded. You remain close to the West Channel along the piers

A Sunday morning paddle through Baltimore Harbor leads to the city's South Side.

here so extra caution should be used. Then find the gravel spit. A channel to the left will lead you to the Inner Harbor (watch out for water shuttles) and follow the triangular shaped building of the aquarium and masts of the *Constellation*. Paddle to the northwest corner of this square-shaped basin. Here you can haul yourself up onto the sidewalk, pull your boat behind you, and visit Harbor Place, a collection of ethnic food stalls.

Make your way back along the north side of the Northwest Harbor. Here you pass old storage buildings converted into condos with elaborate marinas; past Fells Point, a national historic district with cobblestone streets; and beyond past more piers as industrial Baltimore reasserts itself. Look beyond to the bridge and cranes in the distance at the Francis Scott Key Bridge and the mouth of the Patapsco River that leads to the Chesapeake to get an overall sense of this commercial gateway to the bay.

In all, this is a very entertaining trip. The only down beat is the brown, dried ooze that has to be washed from the kayaks back home. Baltimore Harbor has come a long way in terms of cleanup from the steel mills but still has a long way to go. Still, that should not deter anyone from paddling around here on a quiet Sunday morning.

Postscript

PADDLING IN THE MID-ATLANTIC AREA constitutes exploration in one of the most settled areas of the Atlantic coast. As I hope this book has demonstrated, however, many wild and hidden spots can be found for the paddler with a yen to meander or investigate.

Also, the wilderness you encounter may be one of your own making by wandering down a creek in the Chesapeake in the early spring, by paddling a mile offshore, by kayaking early in the morning on a weekend, or by paddling in winter when you have no neighbor to wave to. These are some of the conditions that contribute to my definition of a "wilderness" experience, even in this densely settled region.

We are always looking for ways to make these journeys more rewarding. If you paddle these routes and have suggestions for other itineraries or put-ins or if a destination has radically changed due to erosion, marina construction, or change in ownership, we would like to hear about it. If new opportunities open up for access or camping, we would also like to know. Please send your comments to Appalachian Mountain Club Books, 5 Joy Street, Boston, MA 02108.

Meanwhile, if you find some special hideaway, cove, or creek while diverging from the routes described in this book, it's okay—keep it to yourself.

Appendix A
Useful Addresses

Land Owners and Managers

New York

Fire Island National Seashore Headquarters
120 Laurel Street
Patchogue, NY 11772
(Smith Point: 516-289-4810)

Fire Island AMC Camp at Atlantique
11 West Mill Drive, #14-C
Great Neck, NY 11020
516-466-5628

Gateway National Recreation Area
Floyd Bennett Field
Brooklyn, NY 11234
718-338-3828

The Nature Conservancy
Long Island Chapter
Cold Spring Harbor, NY 11724
516-367-3225

New York City Department of Parks & Recreation
The Arsenal at Central Park
New York, NY 10021
212-360-8133

Oyster Bay National Wildlife Refuge
c/o Wertheim National Wildlife Refuge
P.O. Box 21
Shirley, NY 11967
516-286-0485

New Jersey

Cape May Observatory
707 East Lake Drive
Cape May Point, NJ 08212
609-884-2736

Edwin B. Forsythe National Wildlife Refuge
Brigantine and Barnegat Divisions
P.O. Box 72, Great Creek Road
Oceanville, NJ 08231
609-652-1665

Gateway National Recreation Area
Sandy Hook, Box 530
Fort Hancock, NJ 07732
908-872-0115

Island Beach State Park
Shore Road, Rt. 35 Southern Terminus
Seaside Park, NJ 08752
908-793-0506

Liberty State Park
Morris Pesin Drive
Jersey City, NJ 07305
201-915-3400

Ocean County Department of Parks and Recreation
1198 Dandon Road
Tom's River, NH 08573
908-506-9090 or 609-971-3085

Delaware

Prime Hook National Wildlife Refuge
RD #3, Box 195
Milton, DE 19968
302-684-8419

Cape Henlopen State Park
42 Cape Henlopen Drive
Lewes, DE 19958
302-645-8983

Maryland

Assateague Island National Seashore
Route 2, Box 294
Berlin, MD 21811
410-641-1441

Assateague State Park
Route 2, Box 293
Berlin, MD 21811
410-641-2120

Blackwater National Wildlife Refuge
Route 1, Box 121
Cambridge, MD 21613
410-228-2677

Eastern Neck National Wildlife Refuge
Route 2, Box 225
Rock Hall, MD 21661
301-639-7056

Martin National Wildlife Refuge (see Blackwater NWR)

Maryland Department of Natural Resources
Tidewater Administration, Tawes State Office Building
Annapolis, MD 21501
800-688-FINS

Smithsonian Environmental Research Center
PO Box 28
Edgewater, MD 21037
301-261-4190

Virginia

Chincoteague National Wildlife Refuge
Box 62
Chincoteague, VA 23336
804-336-6122

Department of Conservation and Recreation
203 Governor Street, Suite 302
Richmond, VA 23219
804-786-1712

Department of Game and Inland Fisheries
4010 W. Broad Street
Richmond, VA 23230
804-367-1000

Fisherman Island National Wildlife Refuge
c/o Eastern Shore of Virginia NWR
RFD #1, Box 122B
Cape Charles, VA 23310
804-331-2760

Mason Neck National Wildlife Refuge
14416 Jeff Davis Highway, Suite 20A
Woodbridge, VA 22191
703-690-1297

Mason Neck State Park
7301 High Point Road
Mason Neck, VA 22079
703-339-7265

Virginia Coast Reserve
The Nature Conservancy
Brownsville Farm
Nassawadox, VA 23413
804-442-3049

Virginia State Parks
203 Governor Street, Suite 302
Richmond, VA 23219
804-786-1712

Outdoor and Instructional Organizations
American Canoe Association (ACA)
7432 Alban Station Boulevard, Suite B-226
Springfield, VA 22150-2311
703-451-0141

ACA Committee for Disabled Paddlers
RFD #2, Box 246
Dunbarton, NH 03301
603-528-8721

Appalachian Mountain Club
5 Joy Street
Boston, MA 02108
617-523-0636

Hudson River Waterway Association
P.O. Box 173
Nyack, NY 10960
201-333-5857

Trade Association of Sea Kayaking (TASK)
P.O. Box 84144
Seattle, WA 98124
206-621-1018

Publications
Atlantic Coastal Kayaker
P.O. Box 520
Ipswich, MA 01938

Folding Kayaker
P.O. Box 0754
New York, NY 10024-0539

Sea Kayaker
6327 Seaview Ave. N.W.
Seattle, WA 98107

Sea Kayak Clubs and Associations

Appalachian Mountain Canoe Club
64 Lupine Way
Stirling, NJ 07980

Association of North Atlantic Kayakers (ANorAK)
34 East Queens Way
Hampton, VA 23669

Chesapeake Paddlers Association
P.O. Box 3873
Fairfax, VA 22038

MAK (Mad American Kayaker)
P.O. Box 3276, Church Street Station
New York, NY 10008-3276

MASK (Metropolitan Association of Sea Kayakers)
195 Prince Street (Basement)
New York, NY 10012

MCKC (Metropolitan Canoe and Kayak Club)
P.O. Box 021868
Brooklyn, NY 11202-0040

Monaco Canoe Club
Box 244
Island Heights, NJ 08732

Paumanok Paddlers
18 Stuart Court
Hampton Bays, NY 11946

Sebago Canoe Club
Paerdegat Basin & Avenue N
Brooklyn, NY 11236

Tantallon International Sea Kayaking Association
12308 Loch Carron Circle
Ft. Washington, MD 20744

Sea-Kayak Symposiums

East Coast Sea Kayak Symposium (*mid-April*)
861 Riverland Drive
Charleston, SC 29412
803-762-2172

Chesapeake Bay Sea Kayak Symposium (*mid-May*)
P.O. Box 1184
Beltsville, MD 20704-1184
301-595-2867

Advanced Coastal Kayaking Workshop (*mid July*)
University of New England
Biddeford, Maine
L.L. Bean, Inc.
Freeport, ME 04033
800-341-4341, ext. 7800

Atlantic Coast Sea Kayaking Symposium (*mid-July*)
Castine, Maine
L.L. Bean, Inc.
Freeport, ME 04033
800-341-4341, ext. 7800

Jersey Shore Sea Kayaking and Canoe Show (*mid-September*)
Berkely Island County Park
Bayville, NJ
609-971-3085

West Coast Sea Kayaking Symposium (*mid-September*)
TASK
P.O. Box 969
Mukileto, WA 98275
206-348-4912

Sea Kayak Equipment Stores

New York

The Boat House
2855 Aqueduct Road
Schenectady, NY 12309
518-393-5711

Carman's River Canoe Inc.
2979 Montauk Highway
Brookhaven, NY 11719
516-286-1966

Cold Brook Canoes
Route 28, Box 43
Boiceville, NY 12412
914-657-2189

Eastern Mountain Sports (EMS)
25 W. 60th Street
New York, NY 10023
212-397-4860

Jones Outfitters
37 Main Street
Lake Placid, NY 12946
518-523-3468

Main Beach Surf & Sport
PO Box 1359, Montauk Highway
Wainscott, NY 11975
516-537-2716

Mountain Sports
RR #1, Box 219, Route 12N
Barneveld, NY 13304
315-896-4421

Outdoor Traders
85 Westchester Avenue
Pound Ridge, NY 10576
914-764-0100

Peconic Paddler
89 Peconic Avenue
Riverhead, NY 11901
516-727-9895

New Jersey
Campmor
810 Route 17 North
Paramus, NJ 07653
800-526-4784

The Jersey Paddler
1756 Route 88
Brick, NJ 08724
908-458-5777

Klepper Folding Kayaks
168 Kinderkamack Road
Park Ridge, NJ 07656
908-476-0700

Ocean Paddler Inc.
303 Overlook Drive
Neptune, NJ 07753
908-988-3211

Wee Boat Shop
2007 Greenwood Lake Turnpike
Hewitt, NJ 07421
201-728-0535

Delaware
Millpond Paddler
Route 26
Millville, DE 19970
302-539-2339

Maryland
Annapolis Kayaking Center
Pier 7 Marina
49 S. South River Road
Edgewater, MD 21037
410-956-5031

Blue Wind
9001 Three Notch Road
California, MD 20619
800-442-5834

REI
9801 Rhode Island Avenue
College Park, MD 20740
301-982-9681

River & Sea Watersports, Inc.
Beltsville Plaza 1
11000 Baltimore Avenue #104
Beltsville, MD 20705
301-595-2867

Springriver Corporation
311 Third Street
Annapolis, MD 21403
410-263-2303

Springriver Corporation
5606 Randolph Road
Rockville, MD 20852
301-881-5694

Virginia

Chesapeake Light Craft
34 S. Pershing Drive
Arlington, VA 22204
703-271-8787

Recreational Equipment, Inc. (REI)
3509 Carlin Springs Road
Bailey's Crossroads, VA 22041
703-379-9400

Seven League Sea Kayaks
34 E. Queens Way
Hampton, VA 23669
804-722-5711

Springriver Corporation
2757 Summerfield Road
Falls Church, VA 22042
703-241-2818

Conservation Organizations

Chesapeake Bay Foundation
162 Prince George Street
Annapolis, MD 21401
410-268-8816

Committee to Preserve Assateague Island
616 Piccadilly Road
Towson, MD 21204
301-828-4520

The Hudson River Sloop Clearwater
112 Market Street
Poughkeepsie, NY 12601
914-454-7673

Save the Peconic Bays
P.O. Box 449
Mattituck, NY 11952

Scenic Hudson
9 Vassar Street
Poughkeepsie, NY 12601
(914) 473-4440

Hudson River Foundation
40 West 20th Street, Ninth Floor
New York, NY 10011
(212) 924-8290

Ferries

To Long Island
Cross Sound Ferry
2 Ferry Street
P.O. Box 33
New London, CT 06320
203-443-5281
516-323-2525

To Lewes
Cape May-Lewes Ferry
P.O. Box 827
North Cape May, NJ 08204
609-886-9699
800-64-FERRY

To Smith Island from Crisfield, MD
Island Princess, Island Belle II
Captain Otis Ray Tyler
P.O. Box 28
Ewell, MD 21824
410-968-3206

The Captain Tyler II
Captain Alan Tyler
Somers Cove Marina
Crisfield, MD 21817
410-425-2771
(also leaves from Pt. Lookout, MD)

The Captain Jason I & II
Captains Terry and Larry Laird
General Delivery
Ewell, MD 21824
410-425-5931, 425-4471

To Smith Island from Reedville, VA
Spirit of Chesapeake
Captain Gordon Evans
Route 1, Box 1910
Reedville, VA 22539
804-453-3430

To Tangier Island, from Crisfield
Tangier Island Cruises
Captain Rudy Thomas
10th and Main Street
Crisfield, MD 21817
301-968-2338

To Tangier Island from Reedville, VA
Tangier and Chesapeake Cruises, Inc.
Warsaw, VA 22572
804-333-4656

To Tangier Island from Onancook, VA
Hopkins & Bros. Store
2 Market Street
Onancock, VA 23417
804-787-8220

Map Sources
ADC Maps
6440 General Green Way
Alexandria, VA 22312
800-ADC-MAPS or 703-750-0510

Better Boating Association
Box 407
Needham, MA 02192
800-242-7854

DeLorme Publishing Company
P.O. Box 298
Freeport, ME 04032
800-227-1656

Faucett's Boating Supply
110 Compromise Street
Annaplis, MD 21401
410-267-8681

Maryland Nautical Sales
1400 East Clement Street
Baltimore, MD 21230
410-752-4268

South Street Seaport Book Store and Museum
207 Front Street
New York, NY 10038
212-669-9400

New York Nautical Instruments
140 West Broadway
New York, NY 10013
212-962-4522

United States Geological Survey
Reston, VA 22092
703-648-6892

Department of Game and Inland Fisheries
4010 W. Broad Street
Richmond, VA 23230
804-367-1000

W.T. Brownley Company
118 W. Plume Street
Norfolk, VA 23510
804-622-7589

Appendix B
Emergency Contacts

THE COAST GUARD serves as search-and-rescue coordinator for all maritime emergencies and is the appropriate point of contact whenever you are concerned for your someone else's safety. The following is a list of cities and towns with Coast Guard Stations:

New York: New York, Eatons Neck, Fort Totten, Rockaway, Short Beach, Shinnecock, Montauk

New Jersey: Sandy Hook, Shark River, Manasquan Inlet, Beach Haven, Atlantic City, Great Egg Harbor, Townsend Inlet, Cape May

Delaware: Indian River Inlet, Roosevelt

Maryland: Ocean City, Taylors Island, Crisfield, Annapolis, Baltimore, Still Pond

Virginia: Chincoteague, Little Creek in Norfolk, Parramore Beach, Hampton Roads, Milford Haven, Potomac River at Dalgren

In a distress situation, use flares or any other distress signalling device to catch the attention of another boater who can assist or call the Coast Guard for you. If you're carrying a VHF radio, call the Coast Guard on Channel 16 VHF/FM, 2182 kHz or 156.8 mHz, which is a dedicated distress and calling frequency. The Coast Guard monitors Channel 16 at all times. Once connected to the Coast Guard, follow its directions for switching to another frequency, if necessary.

What to tell the Coast Guard:
- Who you are
- Your location or position
- What is wrong
- Kind of assistance desired
- Number of people in your party
- Description of your boat
- Safety equipment on board
- Any special problems

EPIRBS (Emergency Position Indicating Radio Beacons) have a built-in frequency of 121.5 and 243 mHz and are monitored by transoceanic aircraft which relay the distress message to the Coast Guard.

Float Plan

Name and phone numbers of kayaker(s):	(1) _____
	(2) _____
	(3) _____
	(4) _____

Description of Kayaks Deck color, hull color, length, etc.	(1) _____
	(2) _____
	(3) _____
	(4) _____

Colors of expected paddling clothes	(1) _____
	(2) _____
	(3) _____
	(4) _____

Trip Expectations

Put In Location _____

Take Out Location _____

Approximate Route _____

Latest Expected Return Date _____

If Overdue or In Case of Emergency, Contact _____   _____

Radio: AM/FM receiver_____   Shortwave receiver_____
Aircraft frequency transmitter _____
Marine band transmitter_____   ELT or EPIRB_____

Survival Equipment: Tent style and color_____
❏ First-Aid Kit   ❏ Spare Paddle   ❏ Flares   ❏ Smoke
❏ Panels   ❏ Weapons_____

Auto Description/License No. _____
Where parked _____

Other Information _____

This kayaking float plan is compliments of Blue Water Paddler, *the Alaska Ocean Kayaking Digest, Box 105032, Anchorage AK 99510.*

BEAUFORT WIND SCALE

Beaufort Number	Seaman's description of wind	Velocity m.p.h.	Estimating velocities on land	Estimating velocities on sea	Probable mean height of waves in feet	Description of Sea
0	Calm	Less than 1	Smoke rises vertically	Sea like a mirror		Calm (glassy)
1	Light Air	1–3	Smoke drifts; wind vanes unmoved.	Ripples with the appearance of scales are formed but without foam crests.	1/2	Rippled
2	Light breeze	4–7	Wind felt on face; leaves rustle; ordinary vane moved by wind	Small wavelets, still short but more pronounced; crests have a glassy appearance. Perhaps scattered white caps.	1	Smooth
3	Gentle breeze	8–12	Leaves and twigs in constant motion; wind extends light flag.	Large wavelets. Crests begin to break. Foam of glassy appearance. Perhaps scattered whitecaps.	2-1/2	
4	Moderate breeze	13–18	Raises dust and loose paper; small branches are moved.	Small waves, becoming longer, fairly frequent white caps.	5	Slight
5	Fresh breeze	19–24	Small trees in leaf begin to sway; crested wavelets form on inland water.	Moderate waves, taking a more pronounced long form; many white caps are formed. (Chance of some spray.)	10	Moderate
6	Strong breeze	25–31	Large branches in motion; whistling heard in telegraph wires; umbrellas used with difficulty.	Large waves begin to form; the white foam crests are more extensive everywhere. (Probably some spray.)	15	Rough
7	Moderate gale	32–38	Whole trees in motion; inconvenience felt in walking against wind.	Sea heaps up and white foam from breaking waves begins to be blown in streaks.	20	Very Rough
8	Fresh gale	39–46	Breaks twigs off trees; generally impedes progress.	Moderately high waves of greater length; edges of crests break into spindrift. The foam is blown in well-marked streaks along the direction of the wind.	25	High
9	Strong gale	47–54	Slight structural damage occurs.	High waves. Dense streaks of foam along the direction of the wind. Sea begins to roll. Spray may affect visibility.	30	
10	Whole gale	55–63	Trees uprooted; considerable structural damage occurs.	Very high waves with long, overhanging crests. The surface of the sea takes a white appearance.	35	Very high
11	Storm	64–73		The sea is completely covered with long white patches of foam lying along the direction of the wind. Everywhere edges of the wave crests are blown into froth. Visibility affected.	40	
12	Hurricane	74–82		The air is filled with foam and spray. Sea completely white with driving spray; visibility very seriously affected.	45 or more	Phenomenal

Source: United States Coast Guard Auxiliary

Glossary Of Terms

beam sea A sea in which waves are hitting your boat from the side, often over the gunwale.

baidarka Originally a boat designed by the Aleuts of Alaska, with two seats and great storage capacity for long, exposed voyages; adapted with a third cockpit by Russian fur traders.

beach rips Otherwise known as riptides, countercurrents that take excess water back to sea after waves have broken on the beach.

bore A steep-fronted wave caused by tide entering a shallow channel.

broach The turning of a boat parallel to the waves, subjecting it to possible capsize.

bulkheads Air-sealed compartments built into the bow and stern sections of the kayak to provide structural support, buoyancy, and dry stowage with access through hatches.

chine The intersection of the bottom and sides of a flat or V-bottomed boat.

clapotis Waves caused by colliding walls of water, bearing resemblance to a mountain peak.

coaming Ridge around the cockpit edge to which the sprayskirt is attached.

dead reckoning Position on the water that is deduced from the distance and direction paddled away from a known location.

draw stroke Maneuver to move the kayak sideways in which you pull the driving face of the paddle blade toward you in a vertical position.

drogue Device dragged astern to check the boat's speed or to keep the stern up to the waves in a following sea.

drysuit A one- or two-piece nylon-coated, waterproof suit with latex seals at neck, wrists, and ankles to keep water out; usually worn in winter conditions.

ebb tide A receding tide.

eddy A current of water running contrary to the main current; in its larger form, a whirlpool.

Eskimo bow rescue Assisted rescue in which a capsized victim grabs onto bow of another boat and raises him- or herself to the surface.

Eskimo roll Self-rescue in which the capsized victim rights him or herself without leaving the boat by sweeping and pushing down the paddle blade using hip thrust. Many variations exist.

estuary A passage where the tide meets river current.

fair tide When the tide and boater are traveling in the same direction.

feathered paddle Blades positioned at right angles to each other to reduce windage when paddling into the wind.

fetch Distance over which wind raises the waves.

ferrying Paddling a course upstream of your destination that will result in a straight tack across the current.

fiord Narrow inlet of sea between high banks or rocks.

flood tide A rising tide.

folding boat A boat with a canvas or nylon hull that can be collapsed into one or more carrying bags.

following sea A sea with waves that come from behind the boat.

foul tide Going against the direction of the tide.

groins Sea walls.

head sea A sea in which waves come directly in front of the boat.

Kevlar Carbon-fiber material used in rigid kayaks for lightness and strength.

knot A measure of speed equal to 1 nautical mile, about 6,080 feet, per hour.

lee shore Shore toward which the wind is blowing.

nautical mile About 6,080 feet or $1/7$ longer than the statute mile of 5,280 feet.

overfall Area where current streams collide and often a wave is formed when one current falls over the other.

paddle brace Technique that allows a paddler to remain upright in a breaking wave on the beam by leaning the boat and paddling into the wave.

paddle float A portable flotation device, most commonly a double-walled, inflatable plastic bag, attached to the end of the paddle that acts as an outrigger in a self-rescue.

paddle leash A piece of cord that attaches the paddle to the wrist of the paddler to ensure that the paddle doesn't get lost.

PFD Personal flotation device, otherwise known as a life-jacket.

pitchpole Action in which the boat is thrown end over end in very rough seas or breaking surf.

pogies Tubular mits attached to the paddle by Velcro tabs to protect the hands from cold and spray yet maintain direct hand contact with the paddle shaft.

reflection Water cast back from a surface.

refraction Water changing direction and speed.

reversing fall Inland-water tidal current that reverses flow at the same location during flood and ebb current.

rotomolded Kayak molded by melted plastic, generally stronger and less expensive but heavier than fiberglass models.

rudder A vertical metal plate attached to stern used to steer the boat, operated by cables running forward to foot controls.

sculling A paddle stroke in which you draw the paddle back and forth in small arcs or a Z-formation, used to move a kayak sideways or for support when boat is leaning sideways on the water.

sea anchor Any device used to reduce a boat's drift before the wind.

shoal Shallow area in the sea, often sand bank or rock ledge.

skeg Blade to provide tracking, usually placed just behind the seat in a recessed box that can be lowered from the keel.

slack water Slow flowing or still water that occurs for a brief time between ebb and flood current.

spray skirt A skirt made of neoprene or nylon designed to be worn by the paddler and attached to the coaming to prevent water from entering the cockpit.

sweep stroke Paddle is swept way out away from boat to maneuver boat to the left or right, usually accompanied with the boat leaning in intended direction.

tidal rip An area of fast, turbulent water with steep waves that occurs when a strong current is abruptly altered, occurring on shoals, at points of land along the shoreline, and in opposing currents.

West Greenland kayak Originally a swift, single-seat kayak designed by the natives of Northern Canada and Greenland for hunting and travel.

wetsuit A tight-fitting, two-piece suit made of $1/8$-inch thick neoprene foam which serves to trap a thin layer of water warmed by the body while providing a protective barrier from cold ocean water.

windward shore Land from which the wind is blowing.

Annotated Bibliography

THE FOLLOWING is a list of recently published sea-kayak books, other boating manuals, guides, personal accounts, and videos of interest to the mid-Atlantic paddler.

Sea Kayaking Manuals

Association of North Atlantic Kayakers (ANorAK), *Northeastern Coastal Paddling Guide.* Wenham, MA: *Messing About in Boats* magazine, 1984.

A forty-page collection of reprints from ANorAK newsletters and *Messing About in Boats* magazine, this guide provides details on seventeen coastal areas from Maine to New Jersey and includes useful data on launch sites, sea and shore conditions, chart references, maps, and campsites.

Burch, David, *Fundamentals of Kayak Navigation.* Chester, CT: Globe Pequot Press, 1987.

Director of the Starpath School of Navigation in Seattle, David Burch covers very thoroughly the topics of chart reading, "close inshore" navigation, navigation aids, compass use, dead reckoning, piloting, tides and currents, trip planning, and navigation at night, in the fog, and in traffic. Included are many useful charts and diagrams to illustrate the points taken, but examples are based on locations on the West Coast.

Daniel, Linda, *Kayak Cookery.* Chester, CT: Globe Pequot Press, 1986.

Linda Daniel draws easily on the direct connection of the sea-kayaking environment with its cooking, including opportunities for crabbing, trolling, clamming, and foraging for intertidal foods. The book covers packing, natural and foreign-food shopping, long-trip provisioning, traveling with sourdough, fishing and foraging, and menu planning. The second half is dedicated to recipes including a section on fresh seafood and directions for a Native American-style salmon bake.

Dowd, John, *Sea Kayaking: A Manual for Long Distance Touring,* 2nd ed. Seattle, WA: University of Washington Press, 1988.

John Dowd, founder of *Sea Kayaker,* has revised his 1981 edition. He draws on twenty-five years of paddling experience for a serious instruction manual on equipment, technique, seamanship and rescues, navigation, weather, reading the sea, hazards, storm procedures, first aid, survival, and planning an expedition. The underlying message is preparation for long voyages, based on his trips in the tropics, Pacific Northwest, New Zealand, and South America, although he keeps the expert and beginner equally in mind.

Hutchinson, Derek, *Guide to Sea Kayaking*. Chester, CT: Globe Pequot Press, 1985.

Derek Hutchinson, a coach for the British Canoe Union, covers the kayak, equipment, paddling strokes, rescues, special problems afloat, handling double kayaks, navigation, hazardous wildlife, emergency aid, survival strategy, and planning a trip. He also addresses some of the more survival-oriented aspects of sea kayaking such as scaling cliffs, glacier climbing, snow-shelter construction, and bear-country precautions. The illustrations—especially the one on harbor hazards—are excellent.

Hutchinson, Derek, *Eskimo Rolling*. Camden, ME: International Marine Publishing, 1988.

The book covers a wide variety of rolling techniques and is a must for anyone who has spent hours in the pool staring at the bottom. It covers instruction, confidence-building practice, detailed guidance for instructors, step-by-step student exercises, and draws on personal anecdotes of several paddlers.

Nordby, Will, editor, *Seekers of the Horizon*. Chester, CT: Globe Pequot Press, 1989.

Personal accounts of distinctly unusual trips, gathered by sea-kayak writer Will Nordby, make for great armchair adventure reading. Most of the trips are long expeditions testing stamina and judgment, ranging from Hans Lindemann's hair-raising account of his 1956 solo trans-Atlantic voyage (his second) in a double-sailing Klepper to a voyage down the inland waterway in a paper canoe by Chris Cunningham. Frank Goodman has relevant words on macho paddling off the Scottish coast. Other trips include Greg Blanchette's 1985 circumnavigation of Hawaii, Chris Duff's 8,000 mile solo, Paul Kaufmann's one-day paddle on San Francisco Bay.

Seidman, David. *The Essential Sea Kayaker: A Complete Course for the Open Water Paddler*. Camden, ME: Ragged Mountain Press, 1992.

This book takes you through sea-kayaking skills step by step. Author David Seidman poses as a beginner seeking answers to typical questions a novice paddler would have. He relies on his instructor Andy Singer, a longtime kayaker, to illuminate the way. The text is clear and comprehensive but not exhaustive; it is accompanied by excellent sequential illustrations drawn by Singer.

Washburne, Randel, *The Coastal Kayaker's Manual: A Complete Guide to Skills, Gear, and Sea Sense.* Chester, CT: Globe Pequot Press, 1989.
  In twenty-one comprehensive chapters, Washburne takes you through the basics of sea kayaking, including sea kayak types, gear and accessories, basic paddling skills, emergency procedures, trip planning, tides, hypothermia, and so forth. Washburne is an experienced sea kayaker and nicely combines personal anecdotes with sound advice.

Washburne, Randel, *The Coastal Kayaker: Kayak Camping on the Alaska and B.C. Coast.* Chester, CT: Globe Pequot Press, 1983.
  The book is part instruction manual and part trip guide, emphasizing trips from Alaska's Glacier Bay to British Columbia's Vancouver Island, coastal zones of mild climate and protected bays and inlets. It also includes chapters on hull design, kayak features, navigation, kayak loading, rescues, and camping. Washburne gives specifics on how to get to the North Coast by land, sea, and air and comments on wilderness beauty and Native American culture.

Videos

What Now? Sea Kayak Rescue Techniques. Rockport, ME: Maine Sport Outdoor School, 1993.
  Maine Sport Outdoor School guides Shelley Johnson and Vaughan Smith provide a clear and informative on-water illustration of various rescues in this eighteen-minute color video: paddle float self-rescue, the paddle float and sling self-rescue, the T-X aided rescue, the T-shakeout aided rescue, the bow-to-bow aided rescue and the bow-to-bow with sling aided rescue.

Boating Manuals

ADC's Chartbook of the Chesapeake Bay, 4th edition. Alexandria, VA: Alexandria Drafting Company, 1993.
  This is a waterproof, tearproof 101-page collection of charts covering the Chesapeake Bay in Loran coordinates including all tributaries and enlargements of major ports. The maps indicate headings, local navigational aids and names of waterways, boating ramp locations, fishing areas, wrecks, and artificial ramps.

Boating Almanac for New Jersey, Delaware Bay, Hudson River, Erie Canal, Lake Champlain, Vol. 3 1993. Severn Park, MD: Boating Almanac Co., 1993.

Of main use to kayakers is the Almanac's provision of a launching ramp index, including public ramps, which are positioned on charts. Charts and tide tables are also provided. Volume 2 covers Long Island and Volume 4 Chesapeake Bay, Delaware, Maryland, Washington, DC, and Virginia.

Chesapeake Bay and Susquehanna River Public Access Guide. Richmond, VA: Virginia Department of Conservation and Historic Resource, Maryland Department of Natural Resources, DC Department of Recreation, and Pennsylvania Fish Commission, 1989.

This excellent resource provides detailed maps of various sections of the Chesapeake in Virginia, Maryland, and Pennsylvania (Susquehanna River) and gives data related to the public access to the shore to be found in the region in table form keyed to the maps. Within that table are public launch facilities. The softbound pamphlet also includes write-ups on what makes each area so special in terms of wildlife, geography, or history.

The Delaware Estuary Public Access Guide. Philadelphia, PA: The Delaware Estuary Program, 1993.

This pamphlet consists of ten maps that cover the Delaware Bay and Delaware River shoreline from the Falls are Trenton, NJ, to Cape May, New Jersey and Cape Henlopen in Delaware. Each map indicates the location of public access sites for boats as well as recreational facilities and historic and cultural places of interest in the Delaware estuary.

Eldridge, Robert, *Eldridge Tide and Pilot Book.* Boston: Robert Eldridge-White, 1994.

A definitive guide to tides and currents from Boston Harbor to Chesapeake Bay, this book published annually is indispensable to any boater. It includes US Department of Commerce Tidal Current Charts that detail the set and speed of currents at several points throughout the tidal cycle, particularly useful for New York City.

Guide to Cruising Maryland Waters. Annapolis, MD: Maryland Department of Natural Resources Boating Administration, 1994.

Published every two years, this chart book includes twenty charts covering Chesapeake Bay, Atlantic Ocean, and rivers from the C & D Canal, MD, to Chincoteague, VA. The scale is 1:80,000 with fifty insets of major harbors and rivers on a scale of 1:20,000 to 1:80,000. The book also includes tidal current charts, information on how to use charts, and weather information.

The NYNEX Boaters Directory, New York and Connecticut, New Jersey editions. Wakefield, MA: NYNEX Telephone Company, 1989.

Produced by the NYNEX telephone company that serves New England and New York, these directories are about two-thirds marine business yellow pages with the first third covering useful descriptions of local harbors accompanied by charts, public boat launches, Coast Guard stations, tide tables, and boating rules. Unfortunately these books are scheduled to go out of print. They can be ordered as supplies last from NYNEX Information Resources Co., 83 Pine Street, West Peabody, MA 01960.

River Guides

Gertler, Edward. *Garden State Canoeing: A Paddler's Guide to New Jersey.* Silver Spring, MD: The Seneca Press, 1992.

Ed Gertler has covered nearly every type of waterway in New Jersey, including creeks, whitewater runs, and tidal estuaries. He presents the waterways according to their geographic distribution in the state and includes a table of vital statistics for each: gradient, difficulty, distance, time, scenery, and map number.

Gertler, Edward. *Maryland and Delaware Canoe Trails.* Silver Spring, MD: The Seneca Press, 1979.

This is an enormously useful and well-mapped guide to rivers and creeks in Maryland and Delaware, written by the same author who covered canoeing in New Jersey.

Giddy, Ian. *The Hudson River Waterway Guide. A Trail Guidebook for Small Boaters.* Nyack, NY: The Hudson River Waterway Association, 1994.

This guide is a mile-by-mile identification and short description of sights, launch ramps, camp sites, train stations, hotels, and B & Bs along 140 miles of the Hudson River (the tidal Hudson) from Troy, New York, to Liberty State Park, New Jersey. The identifications follow nautical charts of the river, which makes this very useful as an on-water guide. Other elements include a short history, tips, references and sources, tide chart, flora and fauna to be found along the way, and geology. The guide is available through HRWA membership.

Williams, John Page. *Exploring the Chesapeake in Small Boats.* Centreville, MD: Tidewater Publishers, 1992.

Written by a canoeist, this guide covers eight major areas on both the Eastern and Western shores, all of them rivers and creeks. Williams does not venture out into the bay. Part One covers an overview of the bay, an analysis of boats for the purpose—both motored and self-propelled—and provides a compendium of natural history gear to appreciate the marine flora and fauna. He describes the salt marshes and tidal estuaries through the seasons with wildlife to be seen. Part Two details eight tripping areas: the upper, middle, and lower Eastern Shore; the upper and lower Western Shore; the Potomac and Rappahannock Rivers; and the James River and Hampton Roads. Here Williams evokes the spirit of the places and includes specifics on put-ins and shoreside facilities with telephone listings, local history comments, and so forth.

Related Reading

Bowen, John. *Adventuring in the Chesapeake Bay Area, The Sierra Club Travel Guide to the Tidewater Country of Maryland, Virginia, and Washington, D.C., from Baltimore to the Virginia Capes.* San Francisco, CA: Sierra Club Books, 1990.

Although this guide covers a wide spectrum of outdoor activities—beachcombing, birdwatching, bicycling, camping, and fishing—it is a useful landward guide for the boater. It describes national and state parks, national wildlife refuges, some boat launches, includes a section on exploring Smith and Tangier islands, and gives driving directions and hours of operation.

Dunwell, Frances F. *The Hudson River Highlands.* New York: Columbia University Press, 1991.

This environmental lawyer provides an engaging history of the Hudson River Highlands using many colored illustrations. Dunwell emphasizes the powerful symbol the Highlands has played for Dutch folklorists, sailors, West Point's military establishment, Hudson River painters and writers, spa seekers, millionaire estate builders, and environmentalists who fought successfully to keep a major utility from blasting Storm King Mountain for a hydropower project.

Fisher, Alan. *Day Trips in Delmarva.* Baltimore, MD: Rambler Books, 1992.

This is a guide to southern Delaware and the eastern shores of Maryland and Virginia. (Delmarva incorporates the names of those three states.) The book provides useful landside information regarding road directions, boat schedules, and historical background to many of this peninsula's most interesting places, which are also appealing sea kayaking areas.

Michener, James. *Chesapeake.* New York: Random House, 1978.
   This prolific writer of historic novels covers the drama of the found-ing families of the Eastern Shore of Maryland where the Choptank River flows into Chesapeake Bay. Michener starts the saga in 1583 when Pen-taquod becomes chief of the Choptank Indians and continues to 1978 when descendants of the early settlers, the Paxmores, witness the ero-sion of their native island. He describes all types of Chesapeake Bay dwellers—watermen, hunters, farmers, craftsmen, servants, merchants, officials, and their families.

Murphy, Robert Cushman. *Fish-Shape Paumanok, Nature and Man on Long Island.* Great Falls, VA: Waterline Books, 1991.
   A description of the geology, climate, natural environment, and people of Long Island through history, this collection of the author's essays is said to be a milestone in the history of conservation because it was the first publication to deal with Long Island as an environmentally and historically distinct region. During his life (1887–1973), Dr. Mur-phy, bird curator at the American Museum of Natural History, watched Long Island change rapidly as the natural areas he had loved and stud-ied became paved over with housing developments, shopping centers, and roads.

Warner, William. *Beautiful Swimmers.* Boston: Little, Brown and Company, 1976.
   Winner of the 1977 Pulitzer Prize for nonfiction for this book, Warner manages to convey the biology of the Atlantic blue crab, how it is caught, picked and packed, and sent out from the crab houses to the restaurants. He gives several vignettes of how Chesapeake watermen make a living from the blue crab and gives you a taste for Deal, Kent Island, Crisfield, Smith, and Tangier Islands through the seasons. He covers boats such as the skipjacks, scrapers, draketails, and log-sailing canoes. He even manages to convince you that *Callinectus sapidus* (beau-tiful tasty swimmer) is a beautiful creature.

About the Author

TAMSIN VENN is a longtime outdoor writer based in Ipswich, Massachusetts. She is founder of the magazine *Atlantic Coastal Kayaker* for which she has reported on areas from Florida's Everglades to Newfoundland's bays. She is author of *Sea Kayaking along the New England Coast* (Boston: Appalachian Mountain Club Books, 1991). She has written for the *Boston Globe, Boston* magazine, *Skiing* magazine, *Paddler, New England Living,* and *Physicians Lifestyle* magazine.

As travel editor for *Skiing* magazine, she wrote more than one hundred articles on ski resorts throughout the world and compiled its annual guide to ski resorts in the United States, Canada, and Europe. As an editor for *North Shore Weeklies,* she won an award for the best newspaper of the year from the New England Press Association. Ms. Venn has also co-authored *The Faunal Remains from Arroyo Hondo Pueblo* (Santa Fe, New Mexico: School of American Research Press, 1984).

She is an AMC member and a licensed Maine Guide.

About the AMC

THE APPALACHIAN MOUNTAIN CLUB pursues a vigorous conservation agenda while encouraging responsible recreation, based on the philosophy that succcessful, long-term conservation depends upon first-hand experience of the natural environment. Sixty thousand members have joined the AMC to pursue their interests in kayaking, canoeing, hiking, skiing, walking, rock climbing, bicycling, camping, and backpacking, and—at the same time—to help safeguard the environment in which these activities are possible.

Since it was founded in 1876, the Club has been at the forefront of the environmental protection movement. By cofounding several of New England's leading environmental organizations, and working in coalition with these and many more groups, the AMC has positively influenced legislation and public opinion.

Volunteers in each chapter lead hundreds of outdoor activities and excursions and offer introductory instruction in waterborne and back-country sports. The AMC education department offers members and the public a wide range of workshops, from introductory camping to the intensive Mountain Leadership School taught on the trails of the White Mountains.

The most recent efforts in the AMC conservation program include river protection, Northern Forest Lands policy, Sterling Forest (NY) preservation, and support for the Clean Air Act.

The AMC's research department focuses on the forces affecting the ecosystem, including ozone levels, acid rain and fog, climate change, rare flora and habitat protection, and air quality and visibility.

At the AMC headquarters in Boston and at Pinkham Notch Visitor Center in New Hampshire, the bookstore and information center stock the entire line of AMC publications, as well as other trail and river guides, maps, reference materials, and the latest articles on conservation issues. Guidebooks and other AMC gifts are available by mail order (AMC, P.O. Box 298, Gorham NH 03581), or call toll-free 800-262-4455. Also available from the bookstore or by subscription is APPALACHIA, the country's oldest mountaineering and conservation journal.